Fighting Like a Community

Fighting Like a Community

Andean Civil Society in an Era
of Indian Uprisings

RUDI COLLOREDO-MANSFELD

THE UNIVERSITY OF CHICAGO PRESS   CHICAGO AND LONDON

RUDI COLLOREDO-MANSFELD is associate professor of anthropology at the University of North Carolina, Chapel Hill.

The University of Chicago Press, Chicago 60637
The University of Chicago Press, Ltd., London
© 2009 by The University of Chicago
All rights reserved. Published 2009
Printed in the United States of America

18 17 16 15 14 13 12 11 10 09   1 2 3 4 5

ISBN-13: 978-0-226-11402-6 (cloth)
ISBN-13: 978-0-226-11403-3 (paper)
ISBN-10: 0-226-11402-3 (cloth)
ISBN-10: 0-226-11403-1 (paper)

Library of Congress Cataloging-in-Publication Data
Colloredo-Mansfeld, Rudolf Josef, 1965–
   Fighting like a community : Andean civil society in an era of Indian uprisings / Rudi Colloredo-Mansfeld.
      p. cm.
   Includes bibliographical references and index.
   ISBN-13: 978-0-226-11402-6 (cloth : alk. paper)
   ISBN-13: 978-0-226-11403-3 (pbk. : alk. paper)
   ISBN-10: 0-226-11402-3 (cloth : alk. paper)
   ISBN-10: 0-226-11403-1 (pbk. : alk. paper)   1. Indians of South America—Ecuador—Politics and government. 2. Indians of South America—Ecuador—Government relations. 3. Indians of South America—Ecuador—Social conditions. 4. Community organization—Ecuador. 5. Community development—Ecuador. 6. Indian activists—Ecuador. 7. Political activists—Ecuador. 8. Political participation—Ecuador. 9. Ecuador—Politics and government. 10. Ecuador—Race relations.   I. Title.
   F3721.3.P74C65 2008
   305.898'0866—dc22

                                                            2008034265

TO MY FATHER,
FERDINAND COLLOREDO-MANSFELD,
WHO TAUGHT ME WHY SUCH FIGHTS NEED TO BE ENGAGED
AND TO MY MOTHER,
SUSANNA COLLOREDO-MANSFELD,
WHO SHOWED ME HOW

Contents

Illustrations

Figures

Tables

Maps

Preface

Economic anthropologists win small facts the hard way. When designing my doctoral research in 1994, I wanted to find out how much farming people did in the rural areas of the Otavalo township. I decided to examine production by means of a time-allocation study, and so once I arrived in the community of Ariasucu, I surveyed residents, constructed a stratified sample, and obtained permission from sixty households to drop by for spot observations. Over the next eleven months, I would set off at times and on days that were selected at random by a program on my laptop. I walked up and down the mountainside, greeting people, noting their work, doubling back to recheck empty houses, and calming the bony dogs that rushed at me as I moved along the trails. The dogs, in fact, were a nightmare. In the course of gathering some 5,000 observations, I was bitten three times, and I had to undergo one series of rabies shots.

For my pains, I discovered that "direct, in-the-field agricultural tasks take up less than 7 percent of the time for women and 5 percent for men" (Colloredo-Mansfeld 1999, 19). The results of my household objects inventories were equally "matter of fact." I found, for example, that 94 percent of the thirty-two households that cooperated with my inventory project had a *tulpa* (K. open hearth). This last number had disappointed me. When working on these inventories, all the houses that I first visited had tulpas. More than that, a tulpa was the *only* item they had in common on the forty-object checklist that I was using. Certain that every compound had a hearth somewhere, I was prepared to trumpet a cooking fire as a deep sign of cultural continuity. Then, as I was perfunctorily asking the owner of the last house in my sample about her tulpa, my respondent delighted in telling me that she had none. She did all of her cooking on gas stoves. In the end, the two months of inventories wound up as a table in the book and a brief discussion of the contrast between the real and ideal home life (Colloredo-Mansfeld 1999, 109–11).

In relaying these trials, I am not claiming that these kinds of economic studies are harder than other anthropological research. Rather, they illustrate something of the price paid in the name of fairness. As I tried to document the economy in 1994, I had my intuition about the importance of farming or the setup of a normal Andean kitchen. The point of my methods, though, was to keep intuition at bay. I had to plod along. If I were to do this part of the job right, I would have to visit empty houses or record the same piecework weaver at the same loom day in and day out. As far as my study went, all goods belonged; all actions (and inaction) counted.

In this book, I have shifted my concern from economics to politics. Even so, the arguments offered here have been profoundly shaped by both the dull repetitions and the unpredictable exceptions that turned up in Ariasucu. To begin with, the results taught me how deceiving all those cornfields around Otavalo were. The rural economy was not an agrarian one. While still culturally and economically important, farming accounted for a small portion of people's workaday concerns. Most were more likely to be selling goods to tourists than cultivating crops; houses had a greater chance of having radios than yokes. Over three different research trips in two provinces, I came to know indigenous communities as extraordinarily diverse economies and rural households as unpredictable spaces, some furnished with the barest essentials of subsistence production and others equipped with the latest in consumer electronics. Thus, when I later read the growing literature on Ecuador's indigenous movement, I became increasingly dismayed at the portraits of indigenous work. At best, authors described the new, post–land reform livelihoods without linking any political creativity to urban careers. At worst, authors simply accepted that Indians lived from their fields, taking the pro-peasant agenda of the movement as a statement of economic reality.

Perhaps more important than my findings, though, was the experience of trying to be so evenhanded in such formal terms. Committed to record like cases (residents of one specific sector) in a like fashion (a coded entry for type of work or thing), I could not rule out objects and activities because they struck me as uncharacteristic of the community. Rather, I began to take for granted that Kichwa peoples go about basic tasks in deeply different ways. Over time, these differences set up a crucial issue for me when it came to contemporary Indian politics: indigenous political power has grown in the Ecuadorian Andes just as it is becoming clear that there is no longer a shared way of being Kichwa. Highland native peoples divide along class lines, profess different values, migrate for long periods of time, and are at ease in other cultural settings.

This book argues that this internal pluralism—not the sharing of core values—has driven the politics, uprisings, and electoral victories of Latin America's most comprehensive indigenous movement. In part 1, I trace the personal careers of an artist, a capitalist, and an artisan-activist to reveal how individuals build lives that are indigenous and yet irreconcilable with values that other indigenous people hold. Part 2 presents episodes in which these value conflicts are worked out: a collective work party to build a bridge, a violent act of community justice, and a small community's "trial" of thieves from a powerful neighboring sector. Each of these chapters in turn illustrates the workings of a fundamental building block of community organization: lists, jurisdictions, and councils. In part 3, I detail how the techniques of community politics have set up people to take on the state and defend indigenous self-determination. Here the cases include a migrant group's negotiations with Quito officials to save their marketplace, a family's efforts to have one of their own released from prison, and a mass mobilization of communities to protest a free trade agreement between Ecuador and the United States.

These events reveal an energized indigenous world shaped by the successes of the national uprisings, the drive to establish urban communities, the importance of native places, and the costs of the political boundaries indigenous people erect within them. Challenging current scholarly arguments about the political importance of shared identity, I make the case for "vernacular statecraft" or the mechanisms of community politics—list making, elected councils, territorial jurisdictions—that have been appropriated from the state to manage internal differences and set the foundation for national political action.

Acknowledgments

If the material for my first book drew from intense and often formal studies compressed into a year of work, the information presented here is quite different. It stems from a fifteen-year engagement with families, leaders, trade groups, and the changing settings of Tigua and Otavalo, Ecuador. Duration has often been the key for understanding how community politics played out, and I am deeply grateful to those who have made such continuity possible.

My field research in Ecuador began in 1991 in Tigua. Since that first summer, I have returned again and again and visited with José Vega and Mercedes Cuyo. In 1996 and 1999, Juan Luis Cuyo and Puri Cuyo were supportive hosts to me in Quito. Their son Fabian guided me through the many neighborhoods of Quito to introduce me to the painters who made the city their home in 1999. Julio Toaquiza was very generous with his time the day I finally caught up with him in Tigua Chimbacucho. I have also valued the conversations I have had with Alfredo Toaquiza, and his willingness to share his opinions of and vision for contemporary Tigua art. Francisco Cuyo has also been very direct and insightful in the appraisals that he shared during our interviews about Tigua artists' associations. Finally, Jean Colvin's commitment to Tigua development and her knowledge of the realities of Guangaje parish continually impress me. I strongly recommend her book on Tigua painting to those who seek a more comprehensive overview of the art form than the one offered here (Colvin 2005).

In Ariasucu, Elena Chiza and Antonio Castaneda have claimed me as their wandering son, Chesca as their new daughter, and our children Sky, Mia, and Zoe as among their grandchildren. I only hope that we can live up to their generosity and example. Traveling from Cuenca or Bogotá to be with us, their children and daughter- and sons-in-law have helped us

meet the obligations of fiestas and face the uncertainties of strikes. We cannot imagine life in Ecuador without Lucita, José, and Alex; Esthela, Rafael, and Jhon; Jaime, Blanca, and Andy; and Humberto. For similar reasons, I thank Alejandro Teran and Maria Juana Maldonado as they have supported us in our new residence in Peguche.

The Union of Indigenous Artisans of the Plaza Centenario of Otavalo has offered crucial logistical support for my research in Otavalo since 2001. I thank especially Segundo Maldonado, Rocio Lema, Humberto Lema, and José Antonio Lema. While we met during his tenure as vice president of the union, Licenciado José Manuel Quimbo has now been a confederate in scholarly activities in the United States and a valued counselor in various projects in Imbabura province. Myriam Campo, Blanca Arellana, Toa Maldonado, and Adriana Muenela have between them provided years of creative and conscientious assistance with research into the workings of the Otavalo economy.

In Quito, my colleagues and students at FLACSO have opened my eyes to new currents in Ecuadorian politics and indigenous issues. Fernando Garcia has a knack for both bringing me up to speed on the movement and clueing me in to what needs to happen next. Carlos de la Torre has helped me find ways to connect with students at FLACSO and find outlets for my work in Quito. I continue to find his work on politics, the press, populism, and education to be among the most helpful analyses of contemporary Ecuador. Luciano Martinez and Liisa North's work in Tungurahua has provided crucial insights into the workings of the highlands' rural economy.

I undertook the bulk of this work while I was with the Department of Anthropology at the University of Iowa. Much of this material has benefitted from engagement with my colleagues there: Laurie Graham set up the American Ethnological Society panel where I first presented my analysis of community justice; Virginia Dominguez read drafts of the journal piece in which I filled out the argument. Mike Chibnik has been a thoughtful co-observer of the similarities and differences between artisan worlds in Oaxaca and in Ecuador. I also greatly value the comments of the Anthropology Department's "book group." My erstwhile colleague from the Department of History, Mark Peterson, kept me on my toes through our extended collaboration on material culture, and if our projects did not wind up directly on these pages, at least some of the intellectual energy of our efforts did. In practical terms, the University of Iowa generously supported this work with a Career Development Award and a Faculty Scholar Award. A Fulbright Lecturing Research Award made possible my course at FLACSO, as well as a six-month stay for my family in Peguche in 2006.

I continue to benefit from my relationship with the University of Chicago Press and am grateful for the support that David Brent has shown throughout this project and especially for the constructive reviewers he found for the manuscript. Patricia Conrad in Iowa City, Iowa, did a tremendous job updating John Steinberg's original maps so that they could be used to tell the story of the anti-TLC strike.

During our 2006 extended stay in Peguche, my family and I were lucky to have a number of relatives, friends, and neighbors come and visit us. Along with the morale boost that came with their stay, Daniel Deikema, Janet Andrews, and their son Scott showed inspirational good humor during the trials of the anti-TLC strike.

And although our son Sky has reminded me in the past that it is *my* work and not his work that takes us all down to Ecuador, I cannot help but be impressed with and grateful for the way he and his sisters Mia and Zoe have made parts of life in Otavalo their own. Mia's grace in her effort to make a go of third grade at the elementary school was remarkable, as was her perseverance as the only girl in her group at the escuela de futbal. Sky rebounded from the struggle to adapt to a new school to become an indispensable midfielder on the Atahualpitas soccer team. It is not just that the Atahualpitas won the first prize pig at the parish soccer tournament, but that Sky got some of his teammates to learn recess games from Lincoln Elementary. Zoe, who learned to crawl on a cement patio in Ariasucu, became a productive contributor to weaving and farming chores that took place on the patio in Peguche.

Finally, if this is my work, it is only possible because of the way Chesca has supported our household through this work's research and subsequent writing. In the pages below, I talk about how the indigenous art of Tigua, Ecuador, emerged through a way of working that was *kusawarmi*, or husband-wife. My name on this book, just like the painter's signature on the canvas, has merely made me the most visible half of a paired effort that made the scope of this project possible.

* * *

Chapters 3, 4, 6, 7, and 8 contain material that has been previously published and I gratefully acknowledge permission granted by the following publications:

Chapter 3: "Tigua Migrant Communities and the Possibilities for Autonomy among Urban Indígenas." In *Millennial Ecuador*, edited by N. Whitten, 275–95. Iowa City, IA: University of Iowa Press, 2003.

Chapter 4: "The Power of Ecuador's Indigenous Communities in an Era of Cultural Pluralism." In "Indigenous Peoples, Civil Society, and the State in Latin America," edited by Edward Fischer. Special issue, *Social Analysis* 51, no. 2 (2007): 86–106. © 2007 Berghahn Books.

Chapters 6 and 7: " 'Don't Be Lazy, Don't Lie, Don't Steal': Community Justice in the Neoliberal Andes." *American Ethnologist* 29, no. 3 (2002): 637–62. © the American Anthropological Association.

Chapter 8: "Autonomy and Interdependence in Native Movements: Towards a Pragmatic Politics in the Ecuadorian Andes." *Identities: Global Studies in Culture and Power* 9 (2002): 173–95.

FIGURE I Ecuadorian president Naboa (in white shirt), Otavalo mayor Mario Conejo (waving to crowd), and other politicians attending the installation of Luis Maldonado as first indigenous Minister of Social Welfare, Peguche, 2001

Communities and Movements

If they call us Indians, we will rebel as Indians.—Blanca Chancozo, Federation of Indigenous
People and Peasants of Imbabura

Community Politics, Episode 1

In early 2001, nineteen years after the power company unrolled the first
trunk lines in the highland community of Ariasucu, the final fifteen or
so houses received electricity. The council, and especially its vice president, had worked for years to bring light to all residents. At last, they got
$9,000 for materials and the power company authorized an engineer to
oversee the installation.

The work then proceeded through the following sequence of acts:
(a) an unelected "electrification committee" stepped in, struck a deal with
the neighboring community of La Compañía to tap its power lines, and
convinced the engineer to configure Ariasucu's grid accordingly; (b) the
vice president's allies from upper Ariasucu attacked the new committee's
work party, threw rocks at the leadership, and refused access to La Compañía's electricity; (c) the engineer quit; (d) some present and past council members met with the community of Agato, worked out access to its
power grid, and resecured the materials allocation; (e) volunteer work
parties cleared paths for the power lines, utility poles went up, households

purchased meters, and the lines were strung; (f) the vice president refused to stand for reelection; (g) all of Ariasucu had electricity.

I heard this account in June 2001. Even though I had been recording the sector's rivalries for a decade, this one still surprised me. Of course, I could have predicted some of these fights. The factions broke along an economic fault line, with poorer, upper-community residents feeling betrayed by the deal making of better-off households. Also, once residents turned to the neighboring communities, they revisited a regional political-cultural divide. In the local imagination, La Compañía stood for a hardened, native politics that prized self-determination and celebrated the rowdiness of the old ways. Central Agato stood for steady economic growth and an entrepreneurial ethic. That is, Ariasucu's internal factions had turned to outsiders who amplified differences in their own moral visions of native development. For all that seemed foreseeable, though, I had no idea why this dispute turned violent or why the Agato solution worked so swiftly.

When I am in Ariasucu, I spend hours trying to understand such conflicts, what the stakes are, and what the implications are for future projects. The contentiousness of small town politics, though, is part of a larger truth. Almost all these fights bespeak an arc of accomplishment. In this sector, residents have worked with state agencies to cobble Ariasucu's paths, build its community house, pave its volleyball court, and flatten its soccer field. Year in and year out, Ariasucu secures some material progress. And still, the problems hold. Most projects also air or deepen differences in outlook and interests. Community business brings dissidents out of the woodwork. Thus, collective action rests on an agonistic unity. Neighbors may not see eye-to-eye; they may in fact be deeply divided on basic issues. Yet they turn to techniques that build relationships and allow things to get done. Residents, as Mauss (1990, 82) once put it, have "learnt how to oppose and to give to one another without sacrificing themselves to one another."

Community Politics, Episode 2

In July 2001, a red and white bus of the Imbaburapac Cooperative rounded its last uphill turn in Ariasucu and began its long, slow trip back down to Otavalo. Some locals sat scattered among the seats. Apart from the rest, four men perched together on the carpeted engine cover. Where the men from Ariasucu seemed slightly tattered, wearing T-shirts and windbreakers, sneakers and old fedoras, these four looked sharp. They sported pressed, navy-blue ponchos, bright white shirts, white, creased pants, and clean *alpargata* sandals. One man held some envelopes, conferring with the others about the addresses. After five minutes, one of the four stood, received an envelope, took leave of his comrades, and called out his stop to the driver. He disembarked at the base of a footpath and hustled off out of view.

The bus then wound its way down the road and a second man received his envelope. Hopping off the vehicle before it had come to stop, he strode away up a steep dirt track. The route then picked up the cross-mountain, cobbled road and angled down to the Pan American Highway. A third man asked for a stop and left with his envelope. I had been sitting next to the door observing this scene and now figured out the timing of the departures. Each exit matched entry into a new community territory. The men must have been charged with communicating with local officials. Something was up.

Since the 1970s, Ecuadorian indigenous peoples have transformed the political links among their communities. They have not only fashioned them as instruments of development, they have also made them ligaments of a national movement. Indeed, eighteen months prior to this bus trip, national indigenous organizations had realized their brashest political maneuver yet. In January 2000, around-the-clock indigenous-led, anti-government protest attracted support of dissident military officers. Together they pushed President Jamil Mahuad from office. If the junta swiftly fell apart, the political ambition did not dissipate. It was no secret that native activists disliked the president who replaced Mahuad. Watching one man after the other dash off with his letter, I worried another uprising was in the making. When I spoke with the remaining courier, he confirmed that he worked with FICI, the Federation of Indigenous People and Peasants of Imbabura. The group was hosting a visit of the ambassador from the Netherlands and the vice president of CONAIE, the Confederation of Indigenous Nationalities of Ecuador, the country's largest indigenous organization. These activists were out drumming up interest among communities.

Even with all that had been written about the role of rural sectors within the indigenous movement, it took this bus ride to awaken me to the complexity of community power. These human-borne dispatches signaled a politics that was both piecemeal and systematized. Logistical skill played out within a richly jumbled cultural landscape of maize plots, multi-story houses, adobe huts, weaving shops, health clinics, schools, churches (Catholic and Protestant), volleyball patios, and soccer stadiums. Some neighborhoods had grown and merged with others; some had seceded through constructing their own community houses. Yet amid the clutter, collectivities had lined up in a political order that matched the organization of this corps of messengers. Each letter indexed a jurisdiction, a leadership, and mechanisms to deliberate, decide, and mobilize. The political significance of FICI's upcoming cultural event now depended on the response of local councils.

*   *   *

In this book, I examine both sides of community power at work in these episodes, the internal and external, and how they have come together to create a new capacity for political and economic action. The topic has its champions inside and outside of universities, among defenders of global capitalism and its critics. Consider, for example, the words of Jeffrey Sachs, Ivy League economist and UN advisor, and Wendell Berry, farmer and essayist. Sachs (2005) has recently rethought the possibility of villages. If he has kept his faith in global capitalism as a means to end poverty, he has increasingly made room for the role of local self-governance in his development models. Indeed, his advocacy for sound anti-poverty policy starts with "decentralization" and the recognition that

> investments are needed in hundreds of thousands of villages and thousands of cities. The details will have to be decided at the ground level, in the villages and cities themselves rather than in the capitals or Washington (Sachs 2005, 278)

Sachs argues for local collectivities on grounds of efficiency. The poor can not only govern themselves responsibly, but they will insure that "any help that they receive is used for the group rather than pocketed by powerful individuals" (Sachs 2005, 242). Capital of all kinds—economic, social, human—could be profitably grown through local initiatives.

In contrast, Berry sees in local communities the last chance to heal the damage done by Sachs's capitalism. Having witnessed his region of Kentucky lose its farms, sacrifice its soil, forget its stories, and seek out the garbage of cities as a source of revenue, Berry details the kinds of impoverishment an industrial economy has delivered. Like Sachs though, Berry (1990, 168) looks for change in rural communities, "not because of any intrinsic virtue," but because they have "lived for a long time at the site of the trouble." He concludes his essay "The Work of Local Culture" with a statement of faith: "I know that one revived rural community would be more convincing and more encouraging than all the government and university programs of the last fifty years, and I think it would be the beginning of the renewal of our country" (Berry 1990, 169). For Berry, a restored community would bring life back to the countryside, to be sure, but more than that, it would restore diversity and pleasure to work, scale exploitation to the powers of regeneration, and recover the mutual helpfulness of neighbors. Since the 1970s, native Andeans have organized, protested, and campaigned for principles such as these. The indigenous movement, in fact, is dedicated to the proposition that these are not merely local values, but national ones.

This book also covers the shortcomings of community power: the dissension, the missed opportunities, and the rivalries. There is nothing particularly Andean about such strife. Indeed, Berry's Kentucky is home to (half of) the U.S. archetype of bitter, small-town conflict: the Hatfield-McCoy feud. In the heart of Appalachia, the decades-long, deadly fight kept coming back to a familiar set of issues: land, romantic relationships, and miscarriages of justice. In the Ecuadorian Andes, the community conflict I have witnessed seems, at times, similarly endemic. However, these run-ins have been less family feud over past wrongs and more political clash over future directions. Indeed, Ecuador's recent history of urbanization and circular migration has splintered the forms of life in rural places. The nation's compact geography enables dense connections among town and country so that differences can concentrate and grow in provincial places. To return to Berry's observation, rural communities are important, not because they are refuges from capitalism and globalization, but because they are the "site of the trouble." In these locales, people must confront the wider economy's social costs with little of its material gains.

Anthropologists have long recognized this. Since the 1950s, they have increasingly seen peasant communities as defensive forms, coping with markets, states, and cultural norms anchored in North Atlantic capitalism. Describing the root causes of peasant unrest around the world, Eric Wolf (1969, 279) insisted that "what is significant is that capitalism cut through the integument of custom, severing people from their accustomed social matrix in order to transform them into economic actors, independent of prior social commitments to kin and neighbors." And having recognized the way national economies shaped rural places, many anthropologists largely dismissed rural collectivities' capacity to fight back. After a career of analyzing peasant society and politics, Wolf distilled the mismatch between community and capital into a new typology of power. If people within specific localities exercised personal control over others or organizational power, the localities themselves were the result of a remote "structural power" (Wolf 1990; 1999). Under the circumstances, those who aspire to make history had to become trans-local and class-based, not place-based.

Andean anthropologists, in fact, have been singled out for a misplaced concern with localities. Starn (1991; 1994) insisted that researchers pull back from communities and their deep symbolic structures and complex ecologies in order to take note of the poverty, violence, and political consciousness at work in the circuits that link villages and shantytowns. These connections created, in his terms, "the enormous pool of radical young people . . . who would provide an effective revolutionary force" (Starn 1991, 64). The implications were clear: you cannot have your local culture and your national actor, community-based politics and structural power.

The goal of examining the recent fights of Andean communities is to rethink this opposition. More to the point, I make the case that these collectivities were not merely defensive outcomes of distance forces, but a current of structural power in their own right. They have elevated the capacity for political action and have done so through a kind of vernacular statecraft. I derive the term from James Scott's (1998) thoughtful *Seeing Like A State*. He argues that modernist states grew their power as they found ways to simplify and standardize information about populations, landscapes, and natural resources. This mode of governance, call it high statecraft, could be consolidated through force and implemented in huge projects that attempt to remake society to conform to the ledgers and maps kept by the state. The useful insight here is that power can arise from certain strategic simplifications.

Today's native protest could be seen as the power of the "people's political standardization." Elaborating the apparatus of local government without much money or guidance from the state, communities have made the most of list making, council formation, boundary drawing, and interregional contacts. The bus-based communication system described at the outset of this chapter suggests some of the uniformities of this new order with its identically clad men delivering photocopies to councils within parallel jurisdictions. The peasant *comuna* and the trade *asociación*, two state-sponsored organizational forms, stand at the heart of this effort. Each organizes politics amid human-scaled collectivities. Both entities defend domains of economic value—specific mixes of labor, resources, and material desires. And each confers political intelligibility on the leadership and constituents involved. This embracing of state ideals of organization, though, has not locked in state power, but rather unleashed something more complex. When communities arrive at a consensus to act, they frequently mobilize to oppose state policy, rather than speed its implementation. Furthermore, standardized organizational forms allow opposition to scale up quickly. Demands become national political programs, not just local pleas for favors or exemptions.

But the truly interesting issue here is how standardization came to be embraced. Rural residents had in fact long opposed the presence of state officials in their territories and were deeply suspicious of locals who assumed the prerogatives of government office. As an alternative, most rural localities had their own authority figures and customs for collective affairs and local disputes. Since the 1960s, though, residents have formalized their leadership and membership along the lines laid out by the state—even if at times they have not bothered to register with the state. Indeed, the move to create councils and jurisdiction speaks to urgent concerns that may be tangential to the interests of elites who have long run the state. Ariasucu's electrification project raised some of these matters: bringing material improvements to rural sectors, challenging the forms of marginalization internal to native society, and making choices among alternatives of indigenous self-determination. Here, then, is the underlying impetus of vernacular statecraft. In the everyday work of communities, leaders must develop the tools that will allow them to administer, persuade, and at times coerce residents to move toward a common purpose. At its heart, this book argues the simple point that the organizational measures developed to manage differences within communities have set up the power wielded outside them.

In the remainder of this introduction, I spell out the terms and implications of this organizational dynamic. I begin with a short synopsis of political changes among Ecuadorian indigenous peoples. This sets up a challenge to scholarly orthodoxy that has reduced indigenous activism to an emblematic form of identity politics. I make the case for the plurality of values at work and the political work of moral choices. I then take up the special circumstances of Ecuador's indigenous civil society, a political space that has been largely constructed by the state, rather than through voluntary associations.

Ecuador and Its Indigenous Peoples

For nearly two decades, indigenous activists throughout Latin America have grabbed headlines. In 1992, a Guatemalan Mayan, Rigoberta Menchú won the Nobel Peace Prize. In the same year, Payakan, a Kayapo leader from Brazil, appeared on the cover of *Parade Magazine* for his environmental activism. Two years later Mexican Mayans donned ski masks and formed the backbone of an armed rebellion in the state of Chiapas. Surveying the new presence of Indians in the global political spotlight, Brysk (2000, 20) observed, "Latin America's indigenous peoples have made notable relative long-term gains in a single generation."

In all this, Ecuador's movement stood apart. Embracing street protest, negotiations with transnational oil companies, constitutional reforms, and electoral politics, their activism amounted to a transformative model of democracy. Indeed, the director of a national, pro-democracy NGO prophesied, "In the thirty years since land reform, Ecuador's indigenous people have gone from sub-human to political subjects. In thirty years more, they'll be in power" (Brysk 2000, 20). The move from "sub-human" to political vanguard in fact began long before land reform. Such change had to first overcome deep regional differences among peoples of the Pacific coast, the Andean highlands, and the Amazonian region. It also rested on the political transformation of communities within each region. I will elaborate briefly on each.

Ecuador is a compact nation of nearly 13 million people astride an astonishingly diverse geography (see map 1). To the west lies the coastal plain, *la costa*, with both Ecuador's largest city, Guayaquil, and its fastest growing one, Santo Domingo. A banking and shipping center, Guayaquil is an industrial hub whose elites have a long history of supporting free trade and liberal policies. The coast's economy, and especially its crop exporters, have relied on the labor of the Afro-Ecuadorian descendents of the original enslaved plantation workers. This workforce also draws on men and women whose parents or who themselves have migrated down from the Andes. American banana eaters have been the most faithful customers for this economy, helping make the Ecuadorian coast the largest banana-exporting region in the world. Still further to the west lie Ecuador's Galapagos Islands. Famed for their biological diversity and the insights Darwin gained from them, the islands count as one of the world's top ecotourist destinations.

MAP I Ecuador and location of primary research communities

In the center of the country, the highlands, or *sierra*, run north-south from the Colombian border to Peru. The most densely populated region, the Andes, is home to both the capital, Quito, and a string of provincial cities such as Ibarra, Latacunga, Ambato, and Cuenca that have grown with migrants from rural areas. They come to work in apparel industries, food processing, and street commerce; they also seek the high schools, water systems, electricity, and phone service that is unreliable or absent in rural areas. Indeed, the Andean hinterland and its *haciendas* (large farms or estates) have reproduced many of the inequalities of colonial society up to the present day (Lyons 2006). Even though formal debt servitude was abolished with the 1964 land reform law, the cultural memory of abuse endures; the economic inequities still go on. Ancient haciendas now sustain industrialized cut-flower operations, and the roses romantic young men and women in the United States buy for Valentine's Day have a high chance of having been cultivated and clipped by an Andean indigenous woman on a sprawling equatorial mountain estate.

To the east lie the Amazonian lowlands, a region known as the *oriente*. This territory is home to diverse indigenous nationalities and growing numbers of colonists, primarily impoverished residents of the Andes who have moved seeking land to farm. Home to less than 5 percent of the national population, the oriente is nonetheless the cradle of the elements shaping Ecuador's economic and political future. With the discovery of oil reserves in the twentieth century and the sharp increase in their exploitation in the 1970s, Ecuadorians took a step toward fulfilling their dreams. Now, with American commuters filling their cars with the refined products of Amazonian crude, the country is South America's second largest oil exporter and 50 percent of the national government's budget comes from oil revenue. And it was the ecological destruction owing to colonization and oil exploitation that provoked a backlash from the region's native peoples. Their response set in motion a truly national native movement.

Ecuador's physical geography contributes to the shape of its social landscape of race and ethnicity. The word *mestizo* refers to the majority of Ecuadorians whose identity blends Amerindian and European physical and cultural heritages. In daily discourse it is an exclusionary identity that is ethnically white and closely identified with the dominant, Spanish-speaking national culture of cities and provincial towns (Stutzman 1981; Whitten 2004). Afro-Ecuadorians make up a separate 5 to 10 percent of the population. They too have their history of blending European, indigenous, and African peoples, but in ideological terms, they are excluded from accepted ideas of Ecuador's mixed cultural heritage (Rahier 2003).

The term "indigenous" covers most of the rest—those who have some claim to being the original inhabitants of the land. They identify as different nationalities. In the Amazonian lowlands alone live the Shuar, Achuar, Siona, Secoya, Cofánes, Huarani, and several lowland Kichwa groups.

Many continue to exploit ancestral territories, combining gardening with foraging in the forest and wage work in towns or with oil companies. If the highlands is home to a single group—the Kichwa—that group subdivides into thirteen separate peoples who differ in dialect, trades, clothing styles, and practices. The coast, though largely depopulated of native peoples during colonization, still boasts at least three nationalities.

The different indigenous fights against racism, loss of territory, and neglect by the state have drawn from diverse sources in the different regions. In the highlands, indigenous activism was intimately connected to class struggle and peasant activism for land (Pallares 2002). In the early twentieth century, Kichwa localities had few political resources. Yet despite such limitations, in the 1930s and 1940s, indigenous activists in the northern highlands allied with the Ecuadorian communist party in order to reclaim holdings haciendas had seized (Becker 2004). In 1964, the military government worked to pass the nation's first serious land-reform laws, outlawing debt peonage and enabling legally recognized communities to sue for underutilized land. Indigenous organizing began in earnest. Many communities sought official recognition, more land shifted into indigenous hands. Agrarian economies, however, never properly developed; smallhold farming rarely delivered livable incomes. From the early 1970s on, new organizations emerged to lead first the struggle for land and then the wider defense of Kichwa peoples against new hardships.

In some ways, highland organizing was catching up to Amazonian groups. An indigenous people from the oriente, the Shuar had been the first to form an indigenous federation. With assistance from Salesian missionaries in the late 1960s, they formed a council to unite disparate local communities and secure rights to land threatened by an influx of colonists. The invasion by oil companies in the 1970s spurred other groups to organize as well. Individual Amazonian groups themselves came together under a new umbrella federation.

Finally, in 1986 Amazonian and Andean regional organizations, along with a new group representing coastal native people, came together to form a single national group, CONAIE. Led by Luis Macas, a Kichwa man from the highland Saraguro people, CONAIE first concentrated on cultural activism and especially finding resources for bilingual education. The 1990 *levantamiento* (uprising) shifted the group's priorities. Demanding progress on land claims, leaders also protested chronic neglect and mistreatment by government officials. The mobilization flooded provincial cities with marchers and shut down highways throughout the country, stunning the nation with the new scope of indigenous power.

Identity Politics and Value Conflicts

This brief review hints at the complexity of just one of Latin America's indigenous movements. Across the region, differences multiply. In Mexico, for example, the Zapatistas and their Maya supporters militarized their conflict. Yet in Guatemala, where government forces massacred Mayas during its genocidal civil war, pan-Mayanism hews closely to a cultural agenda featuring language revitalization and the defense of Maya religious practices. In South America, Amazonian groups can have more in common with other lowland native peoples than highlanders in their own country. As disparate as these movements are, though, scholars have reached some provisional generalizations about indigenous organizing (Brysk 2000; Van Cott 2000; 2001; Yashar 2005).

First, whatever else it has accomplished, indigenous politics symbolizes Latin America's new identity politics (Hale 1997, 568). Indigenous activists gained attention by breaking with national class-based movements in order to elevate their cultural distinctiveness as both source and object of their activism (Hale 1994). In particular, they sought to reclaim native history and to celebrate their communities as part of their fight against racism and mistreatment (Pallares 2002). Not only did national peasant organizations fail to address these concerns, but too often they replicated them, discriminating against indigenous activists within their own ranks.

Second, identity did not simply motivate indigenous politics. It became woven into the fabric of politics (Warren 1998b). As Alvarez, Dagnino, and Escobar write (1998, 6), "new social movements were those for which identity was important, those that engaged in 'new forms of doing politics,' and those that contributed to new forms of sociability. Indigenous, ethnic, ecological, women's, gay and human rights movements were the candidates of choice." Participating in the movement became a new way of being indigenous, while self-conscious, overt displays of indigenous culture became a new way of being political (Selverston 1994; Selverston-Scher 2001). In Ecuador, for example, CONAIE has made much of an alternative indigenous morality. Adopting the Inka greeting *Ama shua, Ama killa, Ama llulla* (K. "Don't steal, don't be lazy, don't lie") as a motto for their organization, they linked a past empire with a modern movement.

The Kichwa words do double service as both a symbol of nativeness and a marker of a hoped-for, public morality.

Finally, indigenous people open up a new international world of alliances by emphasizing pan-native values: the primacy of kin relations, the importance of their land, respect for the natural world, and embracing of equality (Allen 2002; Brysk 2000; Conklin and Graham 1995; Niezen 2003). In return, international courts used human rights law to support self-determination claims of those peoples with clearly demonstrated indigenous identity.

While mostly persuaded by these assertions, I think they beg important questions. To start with, race and racism in the post–land reform Andes break more than one way. As the social world of the haciendas dissolved, the countryside bore the full brunt of urbanization, migration, the spread of schools, and influx of missionaries. With these changes old racial markers did not so much disappear as metastasize. The polarities that once defined the Indian/White boundary—rural vs. urban, Kichwa vs. Spanish, illiterate vs. educated, peasant vs. professional—have become acknowledged internal differences of native communities. Racism endures, and for middleclass indigenous people may even have worsened (de la Torre 1999; 2000). Yet, in this new era, do indigenous communities really challenge racism or replicate it, hoarding opportunities among prosperous sectors and isolating poorer ones? A paradox crops up here. Scholarship on native movements that dwells on the importance of identity implies an enduring sameness of a people. Kichwa people, though, are at a peculiarly unsettled moment of their history. Sameness is in ever shorter suppy.

Kay Warren has raised similar concerns about difference and power relations within the Pan-Mayan movement in Guatemala. Noting that Pan-Mayanist leaders exert power over publishing, language standardization, and other matters, she asks (1998a, 182) whether they are "an emerging class-ethnicity." And beyond this privileged group, Jackson and Warren (2005, 566) recently observed, "any indigenous community will be riddled with conflicts—some ongoing and others resolved but not forgotten—as well as factions, hierarchies and decision-making mechanisms that exclude and marginalize some members." While suggesting the need to engage these conflicts, they despair that such scrutiny will only give ammunition to opponents of native people. Their worries acknowledge a real vulnerability. Mestizo elites seem to insist on unity, commitment, and numbers as the measure of the rightfulness of the native cause (cf. Tilly 1998). Internal dissent signals pathology in this view; squabbling has been used to justify neglect. But however inconvenient, these internal fights pattern politics in fundamental and creative ways.

In her chronicles of the Colombian indigenous movement, Rappaport (2005) has offered a way to address such issues. While not neglecting the problem of identity, she highlights how differences come to be managed at the intersection of cultural and organizational issues. Thus, a crucial aspect of her analysis entails understanding the mobility of boundaries, the changing way "insider" and "outsider" come to be understood both in activist lives and tactics. Similarly, in Guatemala, Watanabe (1992) has focused on what it takes to be a Maya insider. He argues that belonging to Maya localities depends not on a moral agreement or conformity, but connection, a willingness "to engage those nearest at hand in the immediacies of life" (Watanabe 1992, 12). Tracking the fortunes of Mayas caught up in export agriculture decades later, Fischer and Benson (2006) still argue for the centrality of moral projects amid the differing desires of living in a globalized economy.

Morality in these discussions both allows for connections across differences and pushes cultural matters toward hard political choices. Even in a small community—or rather especially in such a place—people hold more moral commitments than they can reconcile. Richard Shweder (2003) has emphasized that the plurality of values forces choices. As he puts it, "there are universally binding values, just too many of them. . . . When it comes to implementing true values there are trade offs" (Shweder 2003, 38). Interested in recovering a general respect for cultural pluralism, Shweder foreshortens the political implications of his insight. He raises the question of abortion, for example, to contrast U.S. practice and values with ones in India (Shweder 2000). But, whatever differences it might reveal between the United States and other countries, the abortion debate has long been a profoundly American site of value conflict. Indeed, commentators now territorialize this conflict with the hard boundaries of an electoral map that pits red, pro-life peoples against blue, pro-choice peoples. As Ginsberg (1989) has shown through fieldwork in a small Midwestern city, though, the abortion conflict is explosive not because it is between two peoples but because it is within one. Further, in Fargo, North Dakota, those on both sides of the debate hold other values in common, especially for the defense of women and their roles as mothers.

Among Andean indigenous people, polarizing and overlapping moral issues can play out with the same intensity of family-values debates in the United States. Thus, a woman refuses to speak Kichwa to her youngest son, hoping that Spanish proficiency will allow him to get ahead; her neighbor condemns this act as cultural betrayal. A man insists on accompanying his *compadres* (ritual kinsmen) through all days of a wedding; a cousin rejects such loyalty as backward drunkenness. A married couple sends their child abroad as an apprentice to a rich handicraft reseller; others see such an act as a blow to the future of a farming community. More than personal decisions, these are moral dilemmas for a people and raise issues of mutual obligations and, ultimately, authority. The historian of ideas Isaiah Berlin understood this. He wrote that "values may easily clash within the breast of a single individual; and it does not follow that if they do, some must be true and others false" (Berlin 1991, 12) Most importantly, Berlin saw this conflict as a deeply political problem. He argued that a troubled but necessary liberalism follows. It entails a politics predicated less on rational choices that promote universal well being than on radical and costly choices among equally worthy ends. His liberalism openly recognized the costs of moral conflict and sacrifice of rival moral goods (Gray 1996).

For me, contemporary indigenous politics is so important because it confronts such choices in a distinctive way that departs from Berlin's liberal analysis. If men and women remain moral agents engaged in acts of self-creation, the success of these projects rests on collective defense of cultural and practical resources—not the individualized rights offered by the state. For this reason, communities have maintained an unusually compelling place in peoples' lives. They can shelter the personal effort to build and defend a life and then fight to gain respect for that life nationally. Understanding the work of such politics is the chief task of this book. The focus of analysis consequently expands from the cultural differences of Kichwa peoples to structures of their civil society.

Civil Society and Vernacular Statecraft

That is not to say that shifting indigenous politics from the language of identity to that of civil society offers an obvious analytical payoff. In introducing a volume on civil society in Africa, the Comaroffs (1999), seem to delight in the incoherence of the term. They observe that "in the face of more exacting efforts to pin down its habitations, civil society often melts into air" (Comaroff and Comaroff 1999, 7). At a minimum, the notion refers to voluntary groupings, which taken together are "a part of society which has a life of its own, which is distinctly different from the state and which is largely in autonomy from it. Civil society lies beyond the boundaries of the family and the clan and beyond the locality; it lies short of the state" (Shils 2003, 292). Yet this sort of formulation raises immediate questions for the Comaroffs: "Does civil society exist as the antithesis of the state, in struggle with it, or as a condition of its possibility?" (Comaroff and Comaroff 1999, 7).

Historically, an overreaching state has precipitated such worries and propelled debates about civil society (Robson 2000). In Latin America, for example, civil society has been credited with opposing and helping to move beyond authoritarian rule (Alvarez, Dagnino, and Escobar 1998, 17). Yet, here is where difficulties begin to arise in linking arguments about civil society developed in Europe to the experience in Latin America. Civil society in the latter region often seems to act not as a defense against an intrusive state, but as a means to fill in for a seemingly absent one (Yúdice 1998). The historic link between community and state means that Andean communities, in fact, fail to fit the common definitions of civil society.

Indeed, in the Andes, community and state are impossible to disentangle. After the Spanish invasion, for example, the most far-reaching schema for local communities emerged during the rule of Viceroy Francisco de Toledo in the mid-sixteenth century. Seeking a steady flow of tribute, colonial administrators demarked *reducciones*, or concentrations of indigenous populations, and recognized an indigenous authority figure, or *Kuraka*, within these territories. Abercrombie (1998, 214) observes that the "life within Toledan era settlement towns brought about a simultaneous 'destructuration' (Wachtel 1973) and 'restructuration' of indigenous life, leading not to 'acculturation' but to new kinds of indigenous cultures."

In the post-colonial era, ambitious, new leaders of the Ecuadorian republic pledged to abolish the Indian tribute in order to modernize the young state and its national finances. Yet, as Guerrero (1989, 327) points out, the new state quickly found out that attacking the Indian tribute put into "play the whole system of social, political and mental structures." Rather than risk the world of Spanish-speaking privilege, authorities shored up an Indian tax and its local administrative units in a different form. The old colonial Indian elite might have been dropped, but indigenous men were still recruited into new local offices of the state. Once again, such indigenous authorities enacted a three-way mission: they used their local knowledge to insure taxes were paid; they leveraged their influence on Spanish speakers to defend indigenous autonomy; and through

their daily work as cultural translators, they preserved the division between Creole nationals and Kichwa peoples (Guerrero 1989).

In brief, deputized natives, vested in state authority, enabled the sedi-
mentation of government forms as local culture. Bits and pieces of the
state steadily accrued as indigenous custom. The stamp of external designs
on local practice, however, does not mean that locality is simply the final
stop for the trickling down of institutions and ideas authored in distant
capitals, a "remote and bounded terminus of a global web" (Orta 2004
9). Rather, as Orta (2004, 8) observes, locality is "never self-contained or
self-containing; the local emerges in a complex interrelation with other localities and overarching structures conditioning these engagements." The
task, then, is to discover not just what communities take on but what they
then give back through structures that span locations.

In Ecuador in the twentieth century the most significant external influence came in the form of the *Ley de Organización de Regimen de Comunas*
or more simply the *Ley de Comunas* of 1937. Intended to both defend old
prerogatives of indigenous communities and to modernize them, the Ley
de Comunas envisioned new efficient, productive cooperatives. Spelling
out a clear line of authority between the national government and rural
peoples, the law pushed to have settlements of 50 or more individuals to
form a comuna, or peasant commune. To do so, residents had to establish
the limits of their physical territory, elect a *cabildo* (Sp. council) headed by
a president, and create a list of inhabitants. All in turn had to be registered
with the Ministry of Social Welfare (Ministerio de Bienestar Social).

In this book, the "vernacular statecraft" that I document relates specifically to indigenous peoples' adaptations of the Ley de Comunas. The requisites of the law offered rough and ready administrative tools for promoting
local development, for dealing with antagonisms among neighbors and kin,
and for linking up with other communities in a struggle for resources and
civil rights. Characterizing this organizational work as "vernacular," I am
thinking more architecturally than linguistically. In vernacular architecture,
builders imitate and appropriate standard elements of widely used design,
adapting them to local conditions. Additionally, vernacular architecture is
"ordinary and domestic rather than monumental" (Oxford English Dic-
tionary). Translated into political terms, it combines replicable form, local action, and an absence of sustained state intervention. At times and
from afar, the profusion of vernacular structures looks like a massive single, complexly detailed form; up close it can be treacherous to navigate.

Speaking of community politics as "statecraft," I am borrowing from Scott's (1998) analysis of the state. Arguing that the modernist state gained steam as it made its citizens and resources "legible," he observes that maps, lists, and other techniques to regularize society are the "basic givens of modern statecraft" (Scott 1998, 3). Mandated at the center of power, some methods of administration have been embraced in the margins. Three techniques interest me in particular. First, I examine the power of community rolls, the lists councils keep for the projects they organize. Such rosters are deceptively simple tools that in fact mobilize crucial economic and political resources. Indeed, used skillfully, lists can convert disparate labor, cash, and raw materials controlled by myriad separate households into collective capital deployed for the community benefit. Further, lists can be managed to create and defend independent domains of value over which communities retain sovereign control. The well-kept list can back a variety of political ambitions.

Second, I examine the way communities inscribe and legitimate separate jurisdictions into the provincial landscape. While a native community may appear an "organic jurisdiction," a natural outgrowth of ancient habitation and social interaction (Ford 2001), many are in fact both recent and arbitrary. Groups in established communities secede from neighbors. Loose, unnamed settlements formally declare boundaries, and old-time communities assert new control over lapsed territories. The struggle for jurisdiction relates to the pursuit of autonomy and the defense of residents' rights. A jurisdiction can be so politically nettlesome, though, because "it is simultaneously a material technology, a built environment, and a discursive intervention" (Ford 2001, 201). Communities have used jurisdictional claims to parry other native sectors' power grabs, to fight crime, and to maneuver against the state.

Third, I take up the topic of how local authority comes to be codified in councils. Formally defined by the 1937 law, councils are but one mode of leadership among many. In years past, a community may have turned to different men or women because of their family seniority, sponsorship of community celebrations, church leadership, class position, or personal virtue. Further, of all the leadership forms, council offices in the highlands once were most suspect. They were an arbitrary, generic form linked to the outside, not local achievement rooted in community institutions. In recent decades, though, the formulaic nature of council positions has proved a useful source of legitimacy. The more contentious the community fight, in fact, the greater the value of a uniform corps of office holders who could reframe disputes, elevating them from family rivalries or interfaith conflicts.

The focus on bottom-up administration does not deny the continued importance of the state. "Vernacular" builds itself in its relations with "high" statecraft. Yet the state's influence varies. Post-colonial Latin American states have in fact long cycled through weakness and strength. In Venezuela and Colombia, anthropologists have detailed the "magical" appearance of the state that projects itself as a unifying force "by producing fantasies of collective integration into centralized institutions" (Coronil 1997, 4; Taussig 1996). In Venezuela's case, oil revenues inflate the state's god-like appearance (Coronil 1997). Flush with petroleum wealth in the 1970s, the Ecuadorian state also intervened widely in rural politics. Designating peasant communities, coordinating land recovery, the state both advanced the agenda of land reform and co-opted its grassroots leaders (Striffler 2002). However, the collapse of oil prices, government fiscal crises, and the move toward market liberalization in the 1980s finished off meaningful land reform and curtailed broad development schemes.

This lurching from strong activism to minimal involvement resulted not so much in a weak state as an "absent/present" one (Reddy 2001). It continues to be intrusive, laying down rules for community recognition, tracking paperwork, and sending out ministry officials to preside over projects. It also endlessly raises expectations. At the infrequent inaugurations of new development initiatives, elected officials and government technocrats alike orchestrate spectacles of dignitaries and cultural performers against backdrops of school supplies or community house furnishings to be given away (see figure 1). Yet when the state finally delivers, a project drags on through tortuous negotiations amid levels of government and with degraded results. Bootstrap administrative practice fills the gap between state spectacle and penury.

A few clarifications about the notion of "community" in this book. Unlike recent scholarship on the Ecuadorian Andes, I do not take "communities" to be synonymous with Andean indigenous people (*pace* Guerrero Cazar and Ospina Peralta 2003). Native society is too diverse, mobile, and urbanized to be pinned down with the term. Thus, I refer to Kichwa peoples in various ways, from urban migrant communities to Andean natives depending on the context. This book's conception of community is related to, but distinguished from, an "imagined communities" perspective (Anderson 1991). Having long ago lost the certainties of shared work, worship, and residence, Andean communities have elaborated rituals and other means of the imagination to restore bonds of memory and identity (Wibbelsman 2005). Their imagined affinities, however, hit up against fractious, day-to-day community business. Indigenous collectivities thus are also "produced communities" where imagination yields to persuasion, coercion, and resistance.

This study is also related to but distinguishable from research on social capital. The notion of social capital, and its connotations of cooperation, reciprocity, and trust, has received strong intellectual support from many economists and sociologists concerned with rural poverty (Putnam 1993). Indigenous communities have drawn praise for their apparently high stock of social capital, due in part to the kind of self-management I detail here. Recent studies of cooperation in highland communities, however, have shown that, while the social ties may be dense, they may not be amenable to economic exploitation (Martinez Valle 2003). In the chapters that follow, I raise additional doubts by illustrating how collectivities build social bonds *to limit* how either the state or individuals could profit from the resulting social capital.

Careers, Cooperation, and Protest in the Ecuadorian Andes

This book is divided into three parts. I begin by looking at the careers of three men, an artist, a capitalist, and an activist, who each pioneered assets or institutions for their communities. Through them, I want to humanize the history of the post–land reform era. They are from two distinct Kichwa groups. Julio Toaquiza (the artist) and José Vega (the activist) are from the Tigua Valley in the western ridge of the Andes about an hour away from Cotopaxi's provincial capital, Latacunga. Cotopaxi's hardscrabble Kichwa peoples have had long and intense contacts with both *haciendas* (highland estates) and coastal *fincas* (commercial fruit plantations). The third man is Alfonso Chiza,[1] from the community of Agato near the town of Otavalo in the northern Andes. Indigenous Otavalos have long been known for their weaving and commercial success (see map 2).

---

1. A pseudonym. Because much of this book looks at public figures—people known either through their political activism or artistic successes—I use their real names. In accounts of private events or descriptions of regular community members or in situations where revealing identity might place a person at risk, I use pseudonyms.

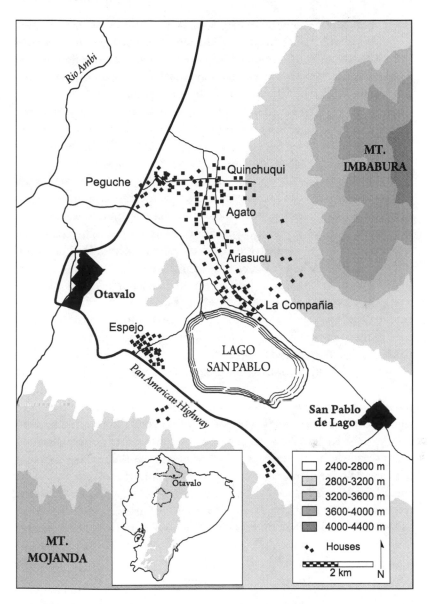

MAP 2 Otavalo region

In talking to me, the three men described a legacy, what they created from their travels, their work, and the distance covered from their parents' lives. The men all left home as boys, the Otavaleño to peddle crafts in Colombia, the Tiguans to box fruit on the coast. The alienation of these labors played out against ruptures at home: many young people had left, little state money flowed in, and the diversity of crops and livestock that once sustained a rural household was slipping. Each had lived in "gray zones" (Kleinman 2006) where the effort to sustain a fulfilling life against poverty and in the informal economy posed specific problems: how to stand by one's mother, how much sacrifice an individual should make to get ahead, and what one owed one's community.[2] As they recounted aspects of their stories to me, these men conveyed the commitments that built their lives. And as they suggested how these commitments transcended their lives and applied to others, I was struck by their incompatibility. Indeed, the third interview started when the subject sought to contradict the first and explain why a move to the city, not a return to the country, was a triumph.

These cases offer specifically male perspectives on late twentieth-century Andean lives. Modernization has often left women in highland Latin America marked as "more Indian," more outside the contemporary nation, and more removed from the modern economy (de la Cadena 1995; Smith 1995). Men, in contrast, have had the chance to "de-Indianize" in their move to the cities, to struggle directly, as de la Cadena (2000, 320) puts it, "against the wretchedness implicit in the dominant definition of Indianness." This has entailed trying out life beyond the racial markers of ponchos, the Kichwa language, and rural residence. Yet de-Indianization is not so much the abandoning of native identity as the remaking of it as modern. And for men, the effort is necessarily diffuse. Where a woman's Indianness becomes specified in her body and dress, a man's emerges in relation not only to his appearance but to that of his wife, to the practices of his family, and to the politics of his community.[3] In fact, the life course

2. Kleinman (2006, 17) observes, "it is especially instructive to examine the gray zones where the separation between acts that sustain a moral life and the inhuman ones that destroy it is thin, because these zones of the most troubling moral experience show just how difficult it is to live." Where his "gray zones" reach from war to sexual obsession, my concern is the narrower inhumanity of seeking meaningful work where it is next to impossible to find.

3. The indigenous mayor of Otavalo has found his own identity challenged because of his mestizo wife: "The problem is that Mario Conejo no longer thinks like an indígena. He is with his wife and his agents and has changed his way of thinking. He is with the mestizos," observed an Otavaleño man when explaining his doubts about Conejo's political commitments.

of each man becomes inseparable from the growth of institutions—from artist cooperatives to a Mormon Church—within their respective home territories.

Having described divergences in values in part 1, I then turn in part 2, "Communities," to episodes in which people work through them. Chapters 5, 6, and 7 follow the story of three sectors tackling both mundane and extraordinary events in their development. In Tigua, they rebuilt a footbridge. In Otavalo, two different communities caught and whipped thieves. All events sparked arguments among locals; some pitted the community against outsiders. In each, I show how people shaped a specific technique of community—whether list, jurisdiction, or the council—in order to orchestrate the situation.

In part 3, I widen my vision of community fights. By calling this third section "Statecraft," I highlight several things. To begin with, these final episodes involve indigenous people and state agencies at loggerheads. In one case, municipal authorities threaten to eliminate Tiguans' market in the city. In the second, Tiguans cope with the arrest and incarceration of a prominent member of the migrant community. In the third, a nationwide, indigenous-led strike against free trade with the United States withered to a tense standoff between the army and communities at a few diehard blockades in the Otavalo area. By framing the negotiations in all these instances as "statecraft," I underscore that, at one level, the encounters carry an implication for the self-determination of native peoples. The ideal of autonomy colors negotiations, even when no party has an interest in territorial separation. "Statecraft" also directs attention to the ceaseless tactical choices made. Community organizers put jurisdictions, council leadership, and membership rolls into play at various times in order to hammer out a consensus within the community

The first and last section end with chapters on national protest. In raising again the seminal uprising of the modern indigenous movement, the Levantamiento of 1990, and the most recent national uprising, the anti-free trade strike of 2006, I want to accomplish two things. First, the events allow me to explore a theme of this book—indigenous politics without unity of identity and values—on a national scale. While I do not want to tackle the national movement, I want to be careful not to set up a false inference: communities fight locally, but during national strikes big organizations step in and local disagreements are resolved. Instead, in looking at the national strikes, I want to recover the pluralism in action beyond community and associations.

Second, in my discussions of the two protests, I want to cede intellectual ground back to the importance of the indigenous movement. Having pushed the power of communities, I do not want to oversell it. Yet my deferment to the politics of the movement comes with an agenda. Turning from conflicts at the community level to community participation in national politics, I hope to show how indigenous power in Ecuador is not pyramidal, with the national organizations presiding as "leadership" and communities lumping along as "base." Rather, the most powerful mobilizations blend massed communities, connected through the new possibilities of civil society, and national visionaries. The chief contribution of this book will be to show how potent, and how plural, this politics can be.

PART I

Careers

FIGURE 2 The potato minga, Quindicilli, 1999

CHAPTER ONE

The Artist (Don't Forsake)

The Wind, a river of air, roars out of his cave in the *puna* [high grasslands], rushes about the mountainsides, and returns again to his home. The river of blood circulates through the human body. Human energy flows out in labor and returns in *ayni* [neighborly aid]. Generations pass into the same soil from which their ancestors sprang and from which they will nourish future generations.—Catherine Allen, *The Hold Life Has*

The Potato Planting Minga, June 1999

Across the way, Segundo[1] raced down from the neighbor's house, his legs churning to keep up with the steepness of the hill. Once down on the main path, he ran around the contour of the community before arcing back up toward where I stood on the edge of Alberto Cuyo's patio. The boy's route nearly covered the whole of Quindicilli, a settlement of fifteen or so houses cradled high up in the last fold of the Tigua Valley. The interprovincial highway cut into the slopes just above the homes, connecting back to the larger community of Tigua-Chimbacucho and carrying on over the ridge to a few more Quindicilli houses before dropping down to the town of Zumbagua.

I had arrived in Quindicilli four days earlier, leaving a month's research in Quito among migrants from Tigua. In the capital, I had been interviewing

---

1. A pseudonym, like all the names in this section.

Tiguans who had moved to the city to paint and sell scenes of rural Andean life. Now it was early June and the annual Corpus Christi celebration had started in Zumbagua. My host in Quito, Marco Cuyo, worked it out for me to travel back with a family member to see the fiesta. I also harbored the hope of finding Julio Toaquiza, the man who started the painting tradition and who is still revered as one of the finest practitioners of the art.

Upon my arrival, Alberto set up a bed for me in a concrete-block, tin-roof house built by Marco a decade before with his first painting profits. Marco had never returned to live in the house and the building had slowly accumulated boxes of clothes, arrays of hoes, and sacks of grain. Alberto still lived next door in an adobe-walled, straw-roofed home with his wife Mercedes and their adopted daughter, a plump toddler who was years younger than any of Alberto's five grandsons who all lived down in Quito. Another older woman, an *upa* (K. mute), also lived and worked with the family.

In my first days in Quindicilli, Segundo had stuck close by me and seemed a part of Alberto's household. We breakfasted together in the old house and Segundo accompanied my explorations. During afternoon meals he kept urging me to walk with him up the grassy mountain above the community to see the whole valley. As I got caught up in the fiesta, though, Segundo seem to move out of the house and across the way, eating with us only once in two days. Puzzled, I asked why Segundo was no longer at breakfast. Mercedes laughed and said he did not live here. "Where does he live?" I wanted to know. "He is an orphan," she replied.

When I had been learning Kichwa five years earlier, my teacher in Otavalo, Ecuador, taught me *wajcha kawsay* (K. an orphan's life) were other words for *yanga kawsay* (K. poor, humble, worthless life). Segundo's clothes, though, were always clean, his hair tidy, his legs tireless, and his round face quick to shift to a smile. As well off as any child I had met in Tigua, he seemed less to me "no one's child" than "everyone's child" or better said, "Quindicilli's child." I was happy to see him running back up to the house.

Segundo was returning this day for the same reason that I was hanging around instead of heading down to the fiesta. Alberto and Mercedes had organized a collective work party, or *minga*, among a few neighbors to help them plant potatoes. Segundo answered the call along with a chatty friend of Mercedes' who lived close by and a lean compadre from the top of the community. Having watched me fuss over my new Nikon camera (the kind Tigua artists paint on the tourist figures in their compositions),

Alberto came to me the night before and asked me to take pictures of the minga. After Segundo arrived at the patio, he and I ducked under the straw eaves into the house where Mercedes handed us tin cups of steaming water. Following the others' lead, I stirred in spoonful after spoonful of *machica*, or sweet, toasted, ground barley, until I had a dense, porridgy drink to fortify me for the climb to the field.

Once we arrived with sacks of seed potatoes, hoes, fertilizer, and camera, Alberto directed me to stand in the middle of the rows of black soil that he had hoed into the hillside the day before. He composed the photo—the five *mingueros* fanned up the field, the seed potatoes up front, embraced in three sacks—and I snapped away (see figure 2). As I recorded the scene, the familiar anthropologist's worry struck me: how long can this go on? Migration had cut the muscle out of Quindicilli. Adults in their prime and growing adolescents had departed. The life of these fields rested instead on the labor of grandparents and on these seed potatoes and on the fistfuls of fertilizer patted into the ground with the tubers. And there was no one but an orphan to learn the art and carry it into the future.

Yet, here again I was missing the point. Alberto himself was celebrating. Life offers up a few photo-worthy events: baptisms, weddings, fiesta sponsorship. On this day, though, Mercedes and he had added to them with their minga—a ritual of field, family, and their valley's fertility. For him, things were not falling apart, they were coming together.

An Ethic of Loyalty to the Land

Devotion to the land is both an obvious native Andean value and an elusive one. Obvious because indigenousness is fundamentally about being from some place. It is an identity bound to a people's control of land that derives, in turn, from their status as the original people of that land (Niezen 2003, xv–xvi). And convenience alone would not induce a people to stay put, to weather the tensions of human social lives that are so closely intertwined, and to assume the responsibilities of passing down the workings and knowledge of a place. Devotion captures the weight of it, the affection and moral commitment that makes communal longevity possible. In more human terms, devotion seems obvious to me because my compadres have always been clear about it. When I moved in with a family in the Otavalo community of Ariasucu in 1991, my host walked me around his neighborhood, shaking his head at a weedy field bordering on his own and neglected by a migrant family. He told me that his mother had always taught him, "You must farm. Never give up your fields."

Devotion to the land, however, is also elusive. In writings about the highlands, three issues get frequent mention as the cause of enduring ties between Kichwa communities and the land: the economic necessity of subsistence farming, the spiritual pull of powerful mountains and a nurturing earth, and the enduring ethnic identity demonstrated by working the land. Yet, economics, faith, and identity are three good reasons to quit the countryside.

The subsistence argument for staying on the land, for example, only makes economic sense when people have, relatively speaking, a lot of land. In a World Bank assessment of rural poverty in the sierra, researchers found a subsistence economy thriving in one of the four indigenous communities selected for study. In the sector of Jatun Era, residents had been able to buy land from the hacienda where they once worked and consequently owned on average between five and ten hectares. This amount allowed them to farm, meet their needs, and sell a little surplus (Hentschel, Waters, and Vandever Webb 1996). Few people migrated out. Indeed, only 20 percent of households reported members who had gone to the cities for work compared to over 50 percent in other study communities. The Jatun Era land holdings, however, were more than three times the average farm size of indigenous households.

In fact, between 1954 and 1974, the minute size of *minifundista*[2] land holdings in Ecuador fell by 10 percent to only 1.9 hectares. At this size, subsistence income alone supports no household. A crop from family fields may be the "most essential component of household reproduction" (Hentschel, Waters, and Vandever Webb 1996, 20), but it will always leave people short and will never promise the cash incomes that bring consumer comfort. Between the allure of modern commodities and the meagerness of farm incomes exists an uncloseable gap of desire. It is this breach that gives indigenous men and women no rest.[3] Put another way, for the vast

2. Minifundista holdings are defined as farm size of less than 10 hectares. Data based on two national agricultural censuses, the first conducted in 1954 ten years before the 1964 land reform law was passed, the second in 1974 (Wilkie, et al. 1990).

3. Phrasing borrowed from Kundera's description of the restlessness of infidelity: "but between the approximation of the idea and the precision of reality there was a small gap of the unimaginable, and it was this hiatus that gave him no rest." Milan Kundera, *The Unbearable Lightness of Being* (New York: Perennial Classics, 1984), 199. The forsaken in the novel is a spouse, not land.

majority of peasant households who commit themselves to farming they are de facto committing themselves to day labor, temporary migration, craft enterprises, animal husbandry, and other jobs.

Living from the land, of course, is for many not just an economic act, but a spiritual proposition brought to life in little, daily rituals. The Kichwa leader Quimbo (1992, 211), for example, observes how Kichwa salutations flow from children to parents, in-laws to in-laws, people to guardian mountains and the *allpa mama* (K. Mother Earth). He argues that the greetings are like a "school of culture or a school of rights." Discussions of self-determination can frequently invoke this sort of ethic, offering a fertile ground for discussions of Pan-American native unity (Warren and Jackson 2002, 13).[4]

The problem with territorial spirituality, though, is that it is now one religious tradition among many. Indeed, spiritual options have proliferated for Kichwa people. In La Compañía in Imbabura province, for example, evangelical Protestants, Mormons, liberation-theology Catholics, and nonaligned Catholics not only oppose each other but frequently break down into further factions (Andrade 1990). These changes can amount to far more than political infighting. Andrade has observed that when evangelical churches get the upper hand "cultural and economic change accelerates" toward a more individual mentality and a capitalist ethic: "the traditional religious manifestations with Catholic inspirations become restricted, which places ancient schemes of identity in crisis" (Andrade 1990, 71). With such intense and sustained proselytizing, any blanket statement of shared indigenous faith invites skepticism. Spiritual motivations, even about the land, need to be demonstrated, not assumed.

Regardless of its spiritual or economic rewards, though, working the land itself confers ethnic legitimacy. In retelling his life history, for example, the president of CONAIE, Luis Macas, cuts events down to their agrarian bone. He glosses over his high school experience, his first effort to join the church, his subsequent flight from seminary, and his university degrees and instead dwells upon his time spent in his own community: "what is important is that half my life was in the community plowing, working" (Macas, Belote, and Belote 2003, 223). Indigenous authenticity lies in the soil and the unity of those who work it.

4. The native spirituality embodied in a well-met Mother Earth travels internationally. At a 1991 Guatemalan conference convened to unite Indian peoples from the Americas with popular classes, an Aymaran Indian from Bolivia introduced his delegation with a long prayer to *Pachamama* (K. Mother Earth). "By carrying on our religious tradition," he explained, "we are resisting" (Hale 1994).

Binding oneself through story and deed to the soil, though, does more than affirm identity. It triggers a deep set of racial reactions. From the hacienda's big house down to the market town's fly-blown restaurants, mestizos have forced an endless performance of deference and respect from those stained by their labor in the earth—lowered eyes, elaborate greetings, self-humiliation (de la Torre 1999; de la Torre 2000). Mary Weismantel (2001, xxviii) recounts one wrenching scene she witnessed when a mestizo woman drove a man in a poncho and his young son from her simple restaurant with kicks, blows, and racist curse words, only to praise the father moments later as a "good little Indian" when he remained outside and begged to be allowed to buy food to eat with his child in the street. Little wonder that current indigenous politics cultivates racial pride by stressing that "Indian" includes a wide swath of nonrural peoples: migrant workers, merchants, and urban professionals (Pallares 2002, 21). Living from one's fields restores indigenous people to the most vulnerable and marked position in Ecuador's racial hierarchy.

Briefly stated, subsistence incomes, spiritual power, and identity can be unreliable inducements to stay on the farm. The exodus of a generation from Quindicilli underscores the stronger attraction for some of better schools, more wage opportunities, and simple conveniences of plumbing and electricity. Consequently, finding out how attachment to the land can outweigh urban promises of progress requires working through the obligations of specific lives. After all, people grapple with their commitment to place in a whole set of boring or aggravating or amusing or loving encounters with their family, compadres, and neighbors.

How such interpersonal connections sustain devotion to place is my concern in this chapter. I explore these themes in the life of just one Tiguan resident, an indigenous artist named Julio Toaquiza, whom I got to interview after the potato minga. His effort to stay put in Tigua-Chimbacucho, Cotopaxi, revealed how down to earth community loyalty is. Indeed, Julio wove his devotion out of the ups and downs of his production: his farming, his craft-peddling activities, and his improvised art techniques. Not forsaking Tigua meant he had to step in and regenerate the fruitfulness of the work there for him and others too. Through his labor and imagination, he created new folk art commodities. As he passed on his painting techniques to others, art became a trade and a new reservoir of community wealth. Hundreds of other households have turned to it, either to shore up their lives in the country or to buy their ticket out.

Julio Toaquiza and the Start of Tigua Painting

The public face of the indigenous communities of Tigua Parish is a painted one, hawked in the parks and streets of Quito or carefully illuminated in expensive folk art galleries in the northern business district. The valley's landscapes shine out through bright enamel colors, thinned with gasoline, and brushed on sheepskin stretched over square wooden frames. Most compositions contain simple, precise figures of men in ponchos and white pants, women in dark skirts and bright shawls, and costumed dancers at fiestas posed against backdrops of green and yellow fields held in place by brown, vertical planes of gully walls and cliff faces. The white-capped volcano Cotopaxi presides in the background. The glossy pigments, careful details, and decorated frames now offer such a coherent visual style that even when Tigua artists such as Juan Cuyo Cuyo copy the works of Frida Kahlo and Fernando Botero the result shines with an indigenous authenticity. By the late 1990s, some meticulously rendered paintings were selling for over $500 a piece.

The thumbnail historical sketch of Tigua painting given in catalog exhibitions, gallery materials, and Web sites emphasizes one man. Adapting a tradition of fiesta-based decorating for the ethnic-arts trade, Julio Toaquiza launched a new expressive form. As Jean Colvin and Alfredo Toaquiza (2001) have put it on Tigua's Web site

> Traditionally, the Kichwa people of the highlands decorated drums and masks for festivals and fiestas. Painting on a flat surface is a relatively recent development. This art form began in the early 1970s when Julio Toaquiza, encouraged by a Quito art dealer, began painting pictures of daily life using sheep hide stretched over a wood frame and a brush made from chicken feathers. Over the years, Julio has encouraged his children Alfredo, Gustavo, and Alfonso as well as many others in Tigua to paint.

In June 1999, in the midst of my third attempt to research Tigua painting, I finally met with Julio[5] for a three-hour interview at his home in Tigua-Chimbacucho. The afternoon after the potato minga, Alberto came and found me and told me that he had talked with Julio that morning. I asked if he thought Julio would still be around. Alberto urged me to go see.

---

5. I primarily use first names to refer to individuals because of the great redundancy in surnames.

With vague memories of a Web page photo of a handsome, mustached face and a brightly striped poncho to guide me, I set off walking down the road to find him. Once I got to Chimbacucho, I scanned some of the bigger new homes standing near the highway. I assumed that with earnings from his paintings, Julio would have set himself and his family up in such a place. Elsewhere in Latin America, newly invented craft traditions have made their founders rich by local standards. Michael Chibnik, for example (2003, 22) describes his visit to the founder of Oaxacan woodcarving as follows: "The maestro dressed nattily in a guayabera (a lightweight tropical shirt with clean lines, four pocket design, and decorative embroidery) and white pants, greeted us warmly and invited us into his showroom. Manuel apologized that he could not show us a video that had been made about his work; electricity was temporarily out in Arrazola. The walls of the showroom were covered in photographs and drawings of the artisan as a younger man. Art books and magazines with articles about Manuel filled the tables."

Having seen Julio's name in art books and his paintings in exhibition catalogs, I expected similar flair. Certainly the top Tigua painters who lived in Quito lived nearly as well. Yet, now I was unable to discern which house might be Julio's. I approached a man who had been standing on the edge of the highway observing me. He huddled beneath a dull, reddish and grayish striped poncho and kept a beige balaclava pulled low over his face. His feet sported some army boots, lace-less, with their tongues hanging out over the toes and the sides folded over and flapping around his ankles. Cautiously, concerned that I might be dealing with another upa, I asked in Kichwa where I might find Julio Toaquiza. After a long pause, the man answered, "I am Julio Toaquiza," and he led me back to his house.

The little building stood on the edge of the highway. It was a cement block structure donated by the Banco Ecuatoriana de Vivienda (the government housing bank) after the 1996 earthquake had damaged Julio and his spouse Francisca's main house. Inside, a salvaged Tae Kwon Do billboard with a silhouette of a man in a high kick divided a bedroom from the *sala*, or entry room. Another plywood and cardboard divider blocked off a third room on the opposite side of the sala. Next to the house, against the north wall, was a shack built of tin roofing that leaked smoke out in all directions. Inside, above a cooking fire bubbled a blackened pot of potato and barley soup. The day I visited, the only evidence of Tigua art in Julio's house was a few unpainted wooden masks lined up in the sunshine that slanted against the Tae Kwon Do wall. Destined to be sold to middlemen, these would earn Julio only a few dollars apiece.

Julio had been interviewed before, for a book, a documentary film, a thesis by his daughter, and other projects. As I started to talk to him about Tigua and my interest in the art, he seemed fed up with the whole role of interviewee. When he found out that I spoke a dialect of Kichwa from Otavalo, he switched back and forth between Spanish and Tigua Kichwa, speaking slowly, repeating words, urging me to get the pronunciation right and generally treating our encounter as a language lesson. When I got out my tape recorder, he got out a flute. He played snatches of songs into the microphone, music evidently trumping words as something Julio was going to commit to posterity.

Charles Briggs (1984) has critiqued the anthropological interview for the way it can run roughshod over other cultures' communicative norms. He observes that interviewers crudely control the process of turn taking and impose the wrong referential frames for the information they seek (Briggs 1984, 21). Charles clearly had not met Julio. Here was an informant adept at turning the tables. For almost an hour he disrupted all of my researcher's prerogatives, framed and reframed our conversation in multiple ways, and thwarted any initiative of mine to make it sound like an interview.

The encounter's tone switched, though, when I asked what he had done before he started painting. It seems I had finally raised the proper referential frame. Julio started telling a story that began years before his birth, making clear that for him, painting has its roots in an economic world of suffering, not an expressive world of handicrafts. To make me understand, he began describing an act of betrayal that happened in the 1930s and instructed me in the routes and occupations of Tigua peasant life in the 1960s.

From my earlier research, I knew the basics of parish history and social geography. A large hacienda called Rumichaca owned by the Riofrio family dominated the landscape. In the 1920s and 1930s, indigenous peasants worked as *huasipungueros*, indentured laborers who worked twelve to four-teen hour days on the hacienda in exchange for the right to raise their own food. This they did on borrowed plots of land that crowded up around settlements of one- and two-room houses on the ridges near Rumichaca. The fields petered out above the community in the *paramo* (high, wet moorland) and below against the edges of the estate. The demands of the hacienda made their own subsistence work hard. Fed up with the fruitless labor and mistreatment, workers began to organize. Finally, they staged a strike in 1929. The owner summoned provincial authorities who violently broke up the protest, leaving nine indigenous laborers dead (Colvin 2005).

As Julio told his story, though, he explained that Riofrio combined his cruelty to his workers with affection for an indigenous woman. As he fought his peasants' efforts to organize, the *hacendado* slept with this woman from the community. Over the years, they had several sons and a daughter. Riofrio looked out for his boys, recognized them as his sons, and allowed their baptism with his last name. He forsook his daughter, though, denying her his name and any of his wealth. She grew up Indian while her brothers grew up white. When the boys got older, the father supported the brothers' move over into Zumbagua where they set themselves up in the transportation business. The sister, Maria Victoria Tigasi, never left Tigua. She married a man from the community of Tigua-Chimbacucho. Julio was Maria's second child.

"She had nothing," Julio said of his mother, contrasting her life with the lives of her siblings, "The brothers sell gasoline. They have money." Maria Victoria was widowed young and left alone to raise her children.

During Julio's childhood, the power of hacendados like Julio's biological grandfather, so secure in his mother's time, had begun to weaken. On the coast, the banana plantations of the United Fruit Company and others fueled a racing economy starting at the end of the Second World War. Coastal population doubled in twenty years (1942–62), drawing individuals and households from valleys like Tigua. If hacendados like the Riofrio family in Tigua clung to the old ways, they gained less by them. Cities expanded, reorganized, and sought water systems, housing, and schools. Urbanization undercut the political clout of landed elites with their ancient adobe chapels, tapestry-hung manor houses, and settlements of rebellious/obsequious peasants. Even down on the coast, landowners' fortunes reversed. Plant disease and labor activism crushed the authority of once-dominant foreign corporations, leading to the peasant takeover of one of the largest operations (Striffler 2002).

Under the leadership of a reformist military government, the Ecuadorian state adopted an agrarian reform law in 1964. Debt peonage ended, and state lands in some regions passed into smallholders' hands. Elsewhere, peasant sectors geared up to fight in the courts for territory designated as expropriable under the law—underutilized estate holdings, former common pastures illegally seized by landowners, and other tracts. Estate owners fought back. They did not merely release former workers from debt but purged them from the estate's economic and moral accounts. They rid their high pastures of peasants' bony livestock, kept water from the Indians who had once dug the irrigation ditches, and reserved work opportunities for a dwindling number of full-time employees.

In addition, a landlords' organization, the Chambers of Agriculture and Livestock, controlled the staffing of the new court system of the Instituto Ecuatoriano de Reforma Agraria y Colonización (the Ecuadorian Institute of Agrarian Reform and Colonization). Consequently, many peasants' legal claims for land went nowhere. Describing the changes that came to Tigua's neighbor, the parish of Zumbagua, during the 1960s and 1970s, Weismantel (1988, 74) writes, "The death of the hacienda brought an end to many of the structures that had enabled hacienda peons to satisfy their needs without cash. Yet they were also left without the wherewithal to enter the cash economy fully." This impoverished emancipation put men in motion in search of other income. And once on the move, they had to contend directly with the forces that eroded estate power—urbanization, population growth, export agriculture, and workforce modernization.

As Julio described his life, he illustrated the uncertainties of growing up at this time. He had begun his working life at the age of eight, a child laborer on the hacienda, only to join others migrating to the coast at the age of eleven. In Quevedo, he found work with a sugarcane mill making *raspadura*—a roughly processed sugar with a grainy, toasted taste. After spending a year there, he returned to visit his mother for All Souls Day at the beginning of November. He promptly headed back down to Quevedo and improved his Spanish. A year later, barely a teenager, he arrived in a rapidly expanding Guayaquil and worked in Salon Chifa, a Chinese restaurant where he washed dishes, bused tables, and eventually learned to stir fry rice, potatoes, and chicken. He quit and returned to help his mother in Tigua, planning to get back to Quevedo where he had a lead on a job in a lumberyard.

"Then I fell in love," he told me. Barely fifteen years old, he married his sweetheart, a girl named Maria Francisca Ugsha, and they settled down in Tigua to try to live by farming the land owned by their parents. But within a few years, their crop failed, "the grains did not produce well." Renting two rooms in Quevedo, they opened a restaurant. Julio could still remember the prices. Francisca sold *café*—a breakfast of bread, eggs, and hot sweet herbal tea or instant coffee—for six *reales* and *almuerzo*—a lunch of rice, meat, and fried plantains—for one *sucre* to the other men from Tigua and Zumbagua who lived in town. Julio worked at the lumberyard. At the time, they had one son, Alfredo, who was a year old, and, partly out of concern for him, they gave up their work in Quevedo, returned to Tigua, and tried to raise sheep. He also began to buy drums, crosses, and other peasant artifacts in the valley, reselling them to folklore dealers in Quito. When wool, lambs, and antiques failed to bring a return, Julio returned to Quevedo to work in the lumberyard, stacking heavy poles in the back of the trucks. One day when his back was turned, another loader mistimed his throw and caught Julio square in the shoulder, costing him (temporarily) the use of his arm and (permanently) this job. Once again he rode back to Tigua to find a way to live from their land and peddling peasant artifacts.

Despairing over years of wasted effort and his battered body, Julio visited a *yachac* (K. shaman/healer) who lived near Santo Domingo de los Colorados. The yachac went to work, cleansing Julio with mouthfuls of *trago* (K. cane liquor) blown across his shoulders, back, and chest and deep drags of tobacco smoke puffed about his head. When he had finished, the *yachac* offered a prophecy. Julio repeated his words to me: " 'Julio,' he said, 'you will have work. Before, you suffered. You will now have your own work. You will not have to go around suffering like you have.' " Julio recalled the shaman going on and explaining that a dream would reveal his work and that he must not let go of that dream: " 'Julio, you have suffered a month, even longer. With this dream, you will know how to be well there at home. You will not suffer as before if you get hold of this dream.' "

Not long after returning to Tigua he did indeed dream powerfully one night. Amid the images that came to him, he saw himself standing in his home, bent over a drum, drawing on its top. In the dream, his wife sat beside him (in recounting the dream amid the masks in the sunshine of the sala he reached out his arm and patted the air where he dreamt her shoulder to be). She had her own work, yet she was right up close to the drum.

Gripped by this dream, he reentered it through the odds and ends that laid scattered about his house—the drum he played at fiestas, some "white powdery dust" (perhaps lime), water, chicken feathers, leftover packets of wool dyes, a stick, and thread. He mixed the water and powder into a thin, milky paste and whited out the shiny, stained patina on the top of his drum. As it dried, he bound the chicken feathers to the stick and assembled a delicate paintbrush. When ready, he blew away the excess powder on the drum top, dipped his brush into the dye, and started to paint boxy figures in ponchos dancing during a fiesta.

Days later he brought this scene to life when he took his drum down to the market town of Pujili to dance with some friends in the Corpus Christi celebrations. As Julio made his way up the street playing the flute

FIGURE 3 Julio Toaquiza Tigasi, untitled painting, c. 1998

and drumming, he caught the eye of an American staying in Pujili. The foreigner invited Julio back to his house where he telephoned the artist and folk art dealer Olga Fisch back at her store in Quito.

Fisch had arrived in Quito decades before. She was a refugee from Hungary who claimed to have escaped Europe in a dirigible bound for Brazil, from where she made her way to Ecuador.[6] Her own fiber art drew on German expressionism and in the spirit of early twentieth-century aesthetic movements, she passionately explored and supported the craft practiced by native Andeans. She and Julio struck a deal for the sale of the drum over the phone. Later when Fisch met Julio and saw his work, she said she would buy any more like it. In the months that followed, he shifted his folk-art trade from reselling to creating. In our interview in

6. Personal communication, Marion Stegner. Stegner worked as a Peace Corps volunteer in Quito from 1971 to 1973, when she collaborated extensively with Fisch in working to develop trade in indigenous artisan products.

1999, Julio insisted that a second dealer, not Fisch, urged him to concentrate simply on his paintings and to frame sheepskin so that his art could hang on the walls. Whatever the origin of the idea of the paintings, Olga Fisch kept her word and bought all of Julio's output.

Here, finally, was an end to his suffering as the shaman had promised, Julio's "own work." Painting income now could hold Julio and his wife's precarious household together, when combined with cultivating crops and raising livestock. Ironically enough, after the era of fixed ties between patrons and peons had ended Julio found security in patronage. His art, though, often celebrates a more fundamental bond, the tie of a married couple. In 1999, when sorting through a pile of Tigua paintings stacked up in a folklore shop, I came across a small painting by Julio. In the composition sheep move one way, a man mounted on a llama follows, a woman tends her animals in a field, and a man on horseback has arrived waving a bottle of *trago*. All crowd around the central figures: a woman spinning and a man standing just behind her, close enough to be able to reach out and touch her shoulder as they stand there (figure 3).

The Enigma of Julio's Land Allegiance

My interview with Julio left me nonplussed by his dedication to Tigua. His land promised so little; it rewarded his devotion so spitefully. His household seems to have spent years being pulled down by the gravity of post–land reform provincial capitalism, worn away first by insufficient land holdings and then by inadequate wages and finally through brutal work on coastal commercial farms. And yet when deliverance came in the form of a new, creative art form, Julio and Francisca sacrificed much of its earning potential. Rather than move to Quito or some nearby provincial town with electricity, hardware stores, and buses that would make it easier for him to create and sell his paintings, they settled for their fields, those worn vestiges of inequality, racism, and patriarchal discrimination.

If this dedication is remarkable, it also takes us back to the arguments that invited my skepticism: the economics of subsistence production, the power of Andean spirituality, and the depth of indigenous identity. In his telling, each of these factors drew Julio out of himself and his coastal jobs and back to Tigua and into his bonds with others. In Julio's narrative, subsistence farming, spirituality, and identity name social fields, not simply individual motivations. Thus, for Julio, farming meant a measure of freedom for his household. When he was a younger man, what his working life had failed to deliver and what the shaman promised was his "own work"—independence unavailable to hacienda laborers or coastal workers. If they delivered little else, the fields let Julio and Francisca work for themselves.

Spiritually, at least in our conversation, he revered not the fertility of Pachamama, mother earth, but the power of a lowland shaman. It took a strong faith in this man to move from a dream to chicken feathers, wool dye, and a drum. By acting on his belief, though, Julio turned these items into stepping stones to economic stability as a farmer. Finally, in talking about his journeys, Julio linked his returns to Tigua with his desire to visit his mother, to establish a household with his wife, and to find a better place to raise his son. His land allows Julio to fulfill his duties as son, and as husband, and as father, and in each as Kichwa. Indigenous identity is achieved not by directly embracing the land, but by forging his bonds with his family by means of the land.

Julio Toaquiza's case is idiosyncratic. Few individuals create an art form in order to be a peasant. His life story, though, illustrates a basic point. Devotion to the land in the rural Andes is an achievement, not a given. Further, this is an achievement of indigenous social ties: allegiance to farming and the land comes about as part of recognizing the claims kin have to one's respect and duty. Riofrio disowned his daughter and recut a racial divide into his family and the landscape; Julio kept faith with his mother and inherited those divisions. By not forsaking, he has never fully escaped the suffering those exclusions entail.

Finally, though, in sticking by Tigua, he has widened the possibilities for his neighbors. He painted and sold and cultivated a relationship with a gallery in Quito and through it all developed an expressive form with commercial value. By teaching his family and some of his neighbors, Julio turned the earning potential of his craft into a new economic reserve for the community. Tiguans tapped it, fought over it, and built new political connections through it. In the coming years, defense of the art became the work of councils and cooperatives (as detailed in subsequent chapters). Julio left such organizing largely to others, though. He has channeled his energy into his fields, his household, and his art. In contrast, the next two men to be profiled have built on their own careers to construct new community institutions.

FIGURE 4 Indigenous capital, indigenous labor, Otavalo, 2006

CHAPTER TWO

The Capitalist (Don't Be Backward)

[The Bourgeoisie] has created enormous cities, has greatly increased the urban population as compared with the rural, and has thus rescued a considerable part of the population from the idiocy of rural life. — Karl Marx and Frederick Engels from *The Communist Manifesto*

"Progress," "development," "modernization," and "advancement" all ring with the idea of evolutionary ascent, the scaled march up and away from being native or tribal or Indian. Arturo Escobar has critiqued "development" discourse in particular for its ethnocentrism. Using Colombia as his primary case, he observes that in the wake of World War II international agencies promoted "a normal course of evolution and progress" based on the affluent west (Escobar 1995, 26). Western scientific knowledge would be the means; native peoples a target; growth, capital, and enlightenment an outcome. "Indigenous peoples had to be 'modernized,' where modernization meant the adoption of the 'right' values, namely those held by the white minority or a mestizo majority and, in general, those embodied in the ideal of the cultivated European" (Escobar 1995, 43).

Escobar admits, though, that development was less a radical new program than a reorganization of older words and ideals. Indeed, fully a century before, Latin American elites had aimed their countries' material and social ascent toward Europe. In this earlier formulation of progress, material form shaped goals and measured outcomes. As the historian Bradford

Burns noted (1980, 20), "The more the capital city architecturally resembled Paris, then *ipso facto* the greater degree of progress that particular country could proclaim." The upshot of this rush to materialize Europe in the Americas was an "ideological flood, which swept before it most American originality" (Burns 1980, 18). Away went diverse homegrown development. In its place, universalized values dictated an industrialized, national course. Indigenous peoples became the "Indian problem" and rural places were monitored as refuges of ignorance.

In the Andes, the geography of progress has remained constant to the present day. Cities represent the future, the country, the past. The more rural the setting, the more tenuous the claims on modernity. Gudeman and Rivera (1990, 123), for example, describe the Colombian journey from Cali ("a major city with direct air links to North America") to Cumbal ("a one-sector economy") as a trajectory of technical decline. The farther one goes from the city, the more limited the technology and the more likely the economy is organized around the house and the reproduction of a family economy, rather than profit.

Yet, ironically, provincial residents had a knack for becoming swiftly and passionately modern. At the turn of the twentieth century, for example, in Chachapoyas in northwestern Peru, wealthy landowners reigned with a petty tyranny. Beginning in the 1920s, urban mestizo artisans, muleteers, petty shopkeepers, and Indians fought this aristocratic despotism. Modernity was the premise of their challenge. Nugent (1997, 316) writes that momentum grew as popular classes touted "modern notions of discipline, order, hygiene and morality. For these 'personal' characteristics were seen as the antithesis of the violent and abusive behavior of the decadent aristocratic elite."

Decades later, in Túquerres in mountainous Southwestern Colombia, residents' rejection of the contempt usually shown them by urban elites was likewise rooted in a subordinate group's shared sense of modernity. The challenge, though, came in the kitchen. A government program in the region had pushed the adoption of modern gas stoves to clean up rural hearths, citing a report that declared "kitchen hygiene is 98% negative. . . . Since *cuy* (guinea pig) excrement adds to their scraps of greens and water, it obviously produces a nauseating smell" (Antrosio 2002, 1112). For locals, though, state efforts were beside the point. Independently of the program, Tuquerreños had long been buying imported Ecuadorian stoves and already were remaking their lives, in their own words, as "economic, fast, and clean" (Antrosio 2002, 1120).

Certainly, to embrace modernization as a social value is to submit, at some level, to a hierarchy born of European ideals, to the city, to the dictates of efficiency, and to evolutionary schemes of improvement. However, these hierarchies arrived centuries ago and have been taken up by enough generations and locations to permit diverse groups to organize in competing ways toward progressive ends. Modernization has become its own vernacular, one that plenty of indigenous people adopt and enrich. In this chapter I take up the discussion of progress among its most famous Kichwa representatives, the Otavalos. I focus, in particular, on Alfonso Chiza,[1] an entrepreneur whose manufacturing plant, capital equipment, and urban property was valued at more that one million dollars in 2001. When asked about his successes, Alfonso emphasizes his hard work, sacrifices, and credit-worthiness and he insists on the importance of these ideals for indigenous people. Indeed, putting time and money behind his words, he worked for years to build Mormon churches that could reinforce such values in the impoverished community where he grew up.

Otavalo

An online search for "Otavalo" in 2008 returned about 640,000 pages, mostly dedicated to the tourism and crafts found in this city of 40,000. The city's official municipal Web site leads the way, featuring the "Plaza de Ponchos," the open air market with its hundreds of handicraft vendors. Sidebars offer bios of the "tourist of the month" (February 2005 featured Scarlet Ortiz, a young Venezuelan soap opera star), explanations of eleven different handicrafts, and lists of public Kichwa festivals. Indeed, the once majority mestizo residents and even the mundane business of government have all been crowded out of Otavalo's cyberspace. The promotional bias hints at indigenous Otavalos' well-documented affinity for commerce (Chavez 1982; Colloredo-Mansfeld 1999; Korovkin 1998; Meisch 2002; Walter 1981).

Unlike native artisans in Mexico, Guatemala, Panama, and elsewhere, Otavalos did not cede the lucrative wholesale or retail trade to whites, ladinos (a Guatemalan term equivalent to Ecuador's mestizo), or foreigners (Stephen 1991; van den Berghe 1993), but instead have captured trading profits. Their commercial ambitions took an international turn in the

1. A pseudonym.

1940s when Rosa Lema, an indigenous woman from Peguche, a peasant artisan community just north of Otavalo, accompanied the president of the republic on a trip to the United States. By the 1960s, Otavalos had begun traveling regularly to Lima and Bogotá to sell goods. In the 1970s and 1980s, families moved to Amsterdam and Barcelona.

The children of these pioneers, joined by thousands of other Otavalos, now form a wide trade diaspora. This combination of risk taking, industriousness, and ethnic pride has won wide respect for Otavalos within Ecuador, where they are often held up as the "truly national" ethnic group (Hurtado 1980; Whitten 1985). Some of this praise is invidious. Touting the Otavalos' success offers state officials a backhanded way to pin the poverty of other indigenous groups on their own failures. Faith in hard work, however, is not simply outsiders' projections; an entrepreneurial ethic lies at the core of many Otavalos' own self-identity.

Those most articulate about sacrifice and advancement tend to be producers or artisans and not just vendors. They are the men and women running the mechanized workshops churning out sweaters, hammocks, blankets, and ponchos. Among these is Alfonso Chiza. In 2001, I met Alfonso when I began investigating the impact of Ecuador's "dollarization" reforms on artisan trades. Implemented in 2000, the dollarization entailed the abandonment of the national currency, the adoption of the U.S. dollar, and the reduction of electric subsidies among other fiscal reforms. One of the trades I studied involved twenty-one family-owned firms who made acrylic-fiber sweaters. Their combined production capacity reached over one million sweaters a year, although in 2001 most workshops operated at only a fraction of their potential. The first producer I interviewed, in fact, had shut down his three huge knitting machines, which together had cost him over $120,000. He sent me to talk to Alfonso.

Alfonso Chiza: Capital, Responsibility and Success

The Chiza family's building was a discrete block of retail space and family apartments on Otavalo's north side. In the 1970s, the neighborhood was little more than a grid of low adobe houses, walled gardens, or open land grazed by sheep brought down by women from surrounding peasant communities. By the 1990s, indigenous entrepreneurs had developed block after block. With the relocation of the bus station to this northern neighborhood, buses, cars, tricycle-carts, and pickups now congest the streets as they move people and goods between the market and the transportation terminal.

Amid all the action, the three-story Chiza building was surprisingly difficult to find. It had a discrete commercial sign hanging between the second and third floors and most of the street level windows were shuttered with steel roll-up doors. Delivery trucks pulled up to the south end of the building where large doors swung inward on a passage that led through the house to a paved patio that connected to an industrial building on the back of the lot. Ignoring the casual gringo tourist, the family sold almost exclusively to indigenous resellers. These young men and women stock up on sweaters before the European summer tourist season and the U.S. and Canadian Christmas sales season, often bundling and shipping diverse crafts to partners whom they join abroad. On a typical weekday, these intermediaries dropped in on the austere showroom, viewing the samples stacked on the floor, before sitting in the chair in front of Alfonso's small desk and chatting with him about the terms of a sale.

When I took my position by the desk in June 2001, I explained I was an anthropologist from the United States interested in Otavalo's current economic problems. He quickly offered to help. He said, "I know all about the old ways, the 1940s, 1950s. People planted their grains, they wove, they drank. They did not have their education; they did not have their profession. It is not like you, professor, anthropologist. People were not aware."

I nodded. I wrote it in my notebook, figuring I would let him establish his expertise about anthropologists and my supposed interests before I would steer him to today's issues. Only after I had written this litany down two more times during subsequent meetings did I begin to understand his suspicions about anthropology that prompted him to open our conversations this way.

"In 1953, I began," he said. And then he suddenly rocked back in his chair and started to pump his legs up and down and swing his right arm in a fluid elliptical motion, conjuring the posture of a twelve-year-old boy weaving *fachalinas* (Sp. shawls) on a treadle loom. Back then, he lived in Agato Center, a community up on the slopes of Imbabura about an hour's walk from Otavalo. In a day, he could make one or two products on one of his family looms. "For my father this was sufficient." But not for Alfonso. "I wanted ten to twelve products, but this was not enough. I wanted one hundred, then one thousand. For this reason I mechanized."

His machinery, though, would wait. In 1962, he went to sell handicrafts in Colombia. He had very little inventory. "What I had was loaned to me," he said. In Bogotá, though, he got a break when a hotel let him sell on their premises. "I sold and sold and sold. From this point, I had my capital."

He returned to artisan production in the late 1960s, but soon made two big changes. First, he moved from Agato to Otavalo. Second, he bought an electric loom in 1970 in Quito and set it up to weave acrylic-fiber ponchos. At this point he began having labels made for his goods carrying a brand named for an indigenous folk hero. He dates his real expansion to some twelve years later. Beginning in the early 1980s, he started to visit the United States to learn about the market and to export directly.

Utah had been his destination on four successive trips over five years. Religion, not business, motivated his travels. As one of Otavalo's early and avid converts to the Church of Jesus Christ of Latter-day Saints, he went to Salt Lake City to learn its doctrines. For Otavalos like Alfonso who were looking to change their lives, Mormonism shared with other Protestant faiths several advantages. The church supported those who sought to avoid drinking and the ravages of alcoholism. Encouraging saving over spending on fiestas, Protestant church membership morally reinforced the redirection of resources away from community celebrations and toward private enterprise (cf. Andrade 1990; Annis 1987). Churches themselves became a target of entrepreneurial effort. Indeed throughout the 1980s and early 1990s, Alfonso worked almost as much to push Mormonism as his own products. He led the effort to build the first Mormon church in a rural Otavaleño community. Although at first he was not able to plant his faith back in Agato where he grew up, he succeeded in establishing a small Mormon complex not too far away in La Compañía.

In these years, Alfonso saw great potential for his manufactured products, especially if he could convert to modern machinery that would expand sweater making, rather than poncho output. At first, he tried to get a local bank to back him, but here old prejudices blocked his way. He spent three days filling out paperwork, declaring his net worth, offering collateral. In the end, the loan officer congratulated Alfonso, informing him that he qualified for a $500 loan. Looking for credit elsewhere, he borrowed $30,000 from the machinery vendor, a factory representative who was selling remade German equipment. Alfonso paid off the loan within a year. With his sales growing, he maintained the confidence of his creditor and he assumed five more such loans over the next five years. By the late 1990s after a second wave of expansion, he had over a half million dollars worth of knitting machines, and more money invested in industrial sewing machines, overlocks, and other equipment. His daily production capacity stood at 450 sweaters if the shop worked a single shift, 900 a day when they ramped up to meet peak demand.

When I interviewed him in June 2001, he reported that in the prior week he had had three sales: 447 sweaters, bought by an Otavaleño intermediary bound for Uruguay; 400 sweaters, bought by an intermediary bound for Chicago; 800 sweaters, bought by an intermediary bound for Chile and Argentina. "It is a lot," I observed.

"No, it is nothing," he answered. "They used to come and buy 1,000 units, 1,500 units," he lamented. We then got onto the subject of what it would take for young men and women to revive the Otavalo economy.

Alfonso complained that the young resellers do not want to work hard. "They want to travel, to know the world; they buy hardly 500 sweaters. They do not want to work. They buy from others and sit in the market." He contrasted this with his current effort as a manufacturer: "It is difficult to work. You must sacrifice well. There is little profit. But I like to struggle. I like to sacrifice, to produce."

Mistaking his point, I asked whether he meant that young people should invest in being artisans, not resellers of others' good. He said, "No. You need to know the market. But, they leave to sell with only 500 sweaters. They have no capital. They need to take 5,000 and 10,000 and stay a year or two or three. They will become known, their clients will learn to trust them and they will get capital. With 500 nothing happens. They travel, sell a bit. Nothing. They are bankrupt."

For Alfonso, capital marks a fundamental difference. Before one has reputation and respect, one is without capital. He reminded me again of when he first went as a young man to Colombia: "We did not have capital; we did not even have shoes." He returned, though, with capital and his success followed from its possession. As we talked, though, he made a careful distinction about where capital's power lay. He told me, "Here in Ecuador, capital is dead. Machines are dead. We earn only from our labor." His words partly reflected his frustration with the dollarization and his underutilized equipment. But they also indicated continued awareness of human exertion at the heart of the economy. In this view, capital does not breed money on its own but rather magnifies the economic power of individual effort. In part, this potency is a matter of leverage: with ten times the capital a young woman or man could sell fifty sweaters where her or his peer sold five.

Capital, though, amplifies a personal, moral capacity as well. Its presence reinforces discipline; its absence indicates a lack of commitment.

This view came up in several related comments about young vendors. He worried in passing, for example, that "They do not have capital; they do not have responsibility." Likewise, he observed, "They do not want to sacrifice. When they do not have capital, then that is even worse." He despairs that young Otavalos do not have reputation, savings, or reserves of credit to get them through these hard times of the dollarization.

If capital is important, Alfonso does not reduce advancement to it. In a later interview, I switched the topic from the dollarization to the economic growth and political empowerment of Otavalo's indigenous society. I wanted to know, in particular, what he thought of the native control of development programs in their communities. Philosophically, the call for self-determination rejected the universal ideal of progress long ingrained in the idea of modernization. To create alternatives to Eurocentric models of development, CONAIE (1994, 55) built its political program around autonomy, "the capacity of indigenous communities and nations to decide and control in our own territories, the social, cultural, and economic order with the existence and recognition of our own authorities in coordination with central authorities." In 1998, the national movement finally gained constitutional recognition of the right of indigenous autonomy, although what rights and resources would devolve to communities was not specified. Did Alfonso think that native control could bring native advancement?

He sidestepped the question. Instead, he argued that the first step toward real improvement was education: "These days, young people must study. Handicrafts are not enough. Otavalo could be much better with students studying at the elementary level, high school, and university. If we do not study, we are just locals." Being "just locals" was a consequence of past self-destructive behavior and remained a pitfall for future indigenous politics, especially programs of autonomy. He explained,

> We could not enter the city, and why? Because there was a lot of drinking, a lot of fiestas. So the people in the city did not need this type of problem, while in the country it was nice: "Ufyashun Compadre, salud, ischcandi nishun." (K. Let's drink, cheers, I say we drink together.) But here in the city there is no way to enter with this mentality. One must enter with another type of mentality, to be kind, to do business, to study. But in the country they only want to drink, to make a fiesta. They do not want to send their kids to elementary school, to high school. And so, for me, I do not like autonomy.

I followed up by asking, "So should there be autonomy?"

"No," he answered.

"Why?"

"Because we all have free capital in order to have an open market. Thus we all progress. This is the way it has been for me. The people here have always thought that indigenous people form cooperatives only for indigenous people. So they invite me, always saying, 'Sr. Chiza, please join.' And so I have said, 'What is the plan of study, with how much capital, how many people, how much production, how much profit?'" He paused and shrugged, implying he never got any answer, and then went on. "So it does not function. This is the way of autonomy."

Being local for Alfonso signified indigenous people turning in on their own poverty-stricken world. It meant cutting themselves off from the city, refusing to change, to learn from others, and to work across cultural boundaries. Being local brought with it an insistence on sharing—forming cooperatives—without considering how to grow. He would hear people out when they proposed schemes for local development, but unless he saw a chance for progress as he defined it, he opted out.

His rejection of autonomy, though, was not a rejection of the indigenous movement or of indigenous politicians. In fact, in 2002, he thought Otavalo's new indigenous mayor to be vastly superior to the previous mestizo mayor. He pointed to the creation of pedestrian malls in the center of town, the new traffic circle on the north edge of the city, and a rebuilt bridge with improved sidewalks and street lighting near the historic water mill. The bottom line in all of this was "better service for the tourists." Alfonso also voiced strong support for national leaders like Nina Pacari, an indigenous lawyer from nearby Cotacachi who later would serve as Ecuador's foreign minister. "She is well prepared, well educated," he said with obvious pride.

With his talk of free capital, open markets, education, and hard work, Alfonso had tempted me to claim the triumph of neoliberal discourse. All the free market promises that began with President Febres Cordero's first wave of market deregulation in 1984 and culminated in the dollarization of 2000 seemed to have percolated into his everyday speech. However, Alfonso's perspective predates neoliberalism. Undertaking fieldwork on the Otavalo worldview in 1977–78, Leo Chavez (1982) wrote a doctoral dissertation explaining the importance of "rationality and honesty," "innovativeness," and "independence and self-reliance" for Otavaleño artisans' self-image. Indeed, those raised amid the looms and corn fields of Imbabura seemed to epitomize the rational peasant once idealized by

Popkin (1979, 4): individuals who are "continuously striving not merely to protect but to raise their subsistence level through long and short term investments, both public and private."

For Popkin, a history of colonialism, market expansion, and state formation conspired to make the peasant into "a rational problem-solver, with a sense both of his own interests and of the need to bargain with others to achieve mutually acceptable outcomes" (Popkin 1979, ix). If such terms seem to fit Otavalo well, the case I am making for indigenous Otavalos' entrepreneurship differs from Popkin's in two fundamental ways. First, where Popkin saw a value-free economic orientation—something akin to the maximizing individual—I see a profoundly value-laden stance. Rationality for Alfonso is deeply moral: the self-made man or woman overcoming poverty's defects through his or her own responsible behavior. Second, what Popkin offered as a universal proclivity of small-hold farmers is, in Ecuador, a limited one. Or rather, it is a partial one. If many Otavalos profess rational hard work's importance, many also recognize alternative ideals of peasant self-sufficiency (pursued so intently by Julio Toaquiza) or collective struggle (championed by José Vega).

The assertion that the pursuit of rational accumulation is a moral project is hardly a new idea. Indeed, Alfonso's insistence on capital as a measure of personal reputation rings with the urgings of an older puritan voice. His words had called to mind a text I assign in my classes:

> The most trifling actions that affect a man's credit are to be regarded. The sound of your hammer at five in the morning or eight at night heard by a creditor makes him easy six months longer.
>
> It shows, besides, that you are mindful of what you owe; it makes you appear careful as well as an honest man and that still increases your credit.
>
> For six pounds a year you may have the use of one hundred pounds, provided you are a man of known prudence and honesty.

The lines are Benjamin Franklin's, the source Weber's *The Protestant Ethic and Spirit of Capitalism* (Weber 1992, 49–50). Alfonso's insistence on sacrifice, on hard work, on reputation begetting capital, and on capital protecting reputation takes us step-by-step into the "tremendous cosmos of the modern economic order" described by Weber (1992, 181).

Alfonso's vision of work and accumulation, however, suggests a rereading of the colonial morality or at least a redirection of Weber's claims. Weber reaches back to Franklin's writings to find evidence for the ways the

FIGURE 5 A Mormon church, near Otavalo, 2005

pursuit of money became morally sanctioned, the roots of a "philosophy of avarice" (1992, 51). Yet, in the lines Weber cites, Franklin most directly worries about credit, not money. If Franklin's *Advice to a Young Trades-man* foreshadows a morality of capitalist accumulation, it more immediately addresses the problem of credit, trustworthiness, and obligations, which are concerns that Franklin shares with Alfonso. For both American Puritan and the native entrepreneur, worries about credit and capital spring from a desire for orderly, binding, and profitable social relations. Money and a new communality of fruitful work go together.

The promise of such relations is ever present for Alfonso and speaks to a second difference between his spirit of capitalism and Weber's. Behind the German social scientist's modern economic order is the monastery. From here, the dreary moral codes of callings and thrifty asceticism emanate to sink the routines of work into a dull grind. In contrast, behind Alfonso's vision is the city, whose schools and open markets can rationalize an unruly country life. Upon entering the city, indigenous people can realize their true potential. They can be well educated, kind, and sober. With their new preparation, they are becoming national leaders, effective mayors, and successful capitalists, and they can accomplish these specifically as indigenous people. In biographical terms, in fact, the Church is not origin but destination. As Alfonso and his fellow converts adapted to the city, learned its ways, and prospered in its economy, they diverted some of their gains to building a new house of worship as culmination of their success. By erecting a bright, modern cinderblock church in a trim, fenced compound that contained a lawn and sports court, Alfonso ultimately transplanted his urban values back to a rural parish (see figure 5).

Progress, Anthropology and Indigenous People

For Alfonso, being progressive seemed to entail not just being a capitalist and a Protestant but also being an anthropologist. His repeated offer to explain native life suggested a wish to join with me to construct (rural) Indians as Other.[2] He too had an urge to record and explain *comuneros* (Sp. community members) out there in the corn fields, to encapsulate them in a cultural complex that linked values, customs, and achievement. Yet he had little interest in anthropology's well-honed relativism. Pitting urban, rational, and prosperous against country, drunken, and poor, Alfonso Chiza not only described but blamed. Such language made his economic victory seem socially Pyrrhic, a new replay of racism that now divided indigenous people internally. Such a division mapped easily onto economic class. He was rich, profiting from the labor of poor indigenous people, yet spurning his shared ties of culture and kinship.

Yet this simple resolution of Alfonso's convictions into class ideology misses the pull of progress in Native American communities that cannot be reduced to economic position. Other ethnographers have also encountered indigenous informants who roundly denigrate the life around them while holding onto the possibility of both radical change and Indianness. In the course of his fieldwork in the Mam (Mayan) community of Chimaltenango, Guatemala, for example, John Watanabe (1992, 24) asked a man what he would write if he were to author a book on his community. The informant then drew a diagram with two columns, one labeled "Ladino" and the other "Indian." Then under Ladino, he listed "Wealth,

2. Charles Briggs offered this insight in a conversation we had about Alfonso.

Exploiter, Literacy, Religious Faith, Medical Curing, Self-Improvement."
Turning to the Indian side, he wrote "Poverty, Ignorance, Illiteracy, Traditional Beliefs, Magical Curing, Alcoholism." Watanabe then watched as
the Maya man drew an arrow from the Indian column to the Ladino one.
His book would spell out this change. Struck by this, Watanabe asked if
there would still be Indians. The man replied, "Yes."

The vignette, one that foreshadowed a similar encounter in the course
of my own fieldwork (see chapter 5), presents an anthropologist with
three problems. Having affirmed so many negative stereotypes, Watanabe's friend is still a loyal, sympathetic, Maya voice. Having emphatically
claimed all the qualities of the first category, the informant insists that the
second category still remains apart. And seeking to modernize in terms
that seem both Western and ethnocentric, Chimaltecos are still and would
remain, at heart, Mayan. Anthropologists fumble the indigenous vision of
progress that makes these distinctions possible. Alfonso Chiza understood
this failing well. His formulaic response to me—"Anthropology? Sure, I
know about farming, weaving, country life, fiestas, drinking"—reflected a
doubt. He could not see that an anthropologist would ever inquire into the
details of crossing over from a category of poverty to one of wealth, of how
an indigenous man runs a factory with half a million dollars of knitting
machinery to make a profit in an international handicraft market.

Andean ethnography bears him out. When confronted by men and
women bent on junking the old ways, anthropologists become their most
skeptical. Rhetorically, they pursue one of two strategies. Writers can
challenge the columns, erasing the boundaries and insisting on a mixed,
middle identity. Such a hybrid character, though, does not arise either in
the analysis offered by Watanabe's informant or Alfonso. In their schemes,
native people can radically remake themselves by adopting others' practices and still remain categorically native.

Conversely, anthropologists can discredit the Mam's arrow to progress
and wealth as hegemony at work—the blind acceptance of evolutionary
discourses of modernization. Thus, for example, a recent analysis of Ecuadorian indigenous politics dismisses one particular leader for his desire
for change. In *Crude Chronicles*, Sawyer (2004) investigates why a splin-
ter group of Canelos Kichwa communities in Pastaza province has allied
itself with the ARCO oil company and against the wider indigenous organization OPIP (Organization of Indigenous Peoples of Pastanza). When
visiting with the dissidents, she is told by their leader, "[OPIP's leaders]
don't want us to be educated and work. They don't want us to wear shoes.

They want to keep us poor and oppressed." He feared that the federation deceived his people and would keep them "*salvaje* [Sp. savage, wild], manipulable, submissive." With ARCO, he felt that "el indígena will prosper, progress, and produce."

In Sawyer's account, this man has been duped. She glosses his faith in work as "Smithian logic" and credits it to ARCO, who provided this leader with an office, secretary, and stacks of the *Economist.* Describing his "slick new haircut and shiny new shoes" Sawyer all but writes him off as a hollow shell fabricated by the oil company. She is right, in a way. ARCO *is* using him to divide indigenous people in order to embark on hugely destructive tapping of oil reserves. If they succeed, though, it is not because they have planted false, nonindigenous ideals among the Kichwa. Rather, ARCO is falsely playing up to very real ideals of work and betterment held by some, perhaps many, within indigenous communities. They want to shift out of the shoeless, submissive, and nonworking column and into the prosperous, productive, and non-manipulable column. The oil company cynically capitalized on these longings.

Having realized such longings themselves, Otavalo's merchants and capitalists have learned that their wealth does not buy them out of Ecuador's racism. In Alfonso's case, he had to jump through every hoop the bank set in front of him, only to be offered a loan worthy of a glorified street peddler. He, however, doesn't dwell on the discrimination. For him, progress and advancement are there for those who embrace them. They serve as personal guideposts and for grounds of greater indigenous unity. In helping to build La Compañía's Mormon church, Alfonso hoped to remake a community around a commitment to a rational, kind, and prosperous way forward. A disruption of traditional practices is a price he is willing to pay for such progress. The next chapter, though, features a man who found a less contentious way to bring urban values and resources to his home community.

FIGURE 6 Kusawarmi (husband-wife) work in a Quito painting studio, 1996

CHAPTER THREE

The Activist (Don't Suffer)

Well organized, complete, that was good. People meeting, people listening in our sessions. People believed. Now nothing is happening. People do not believe. — José Vega, June 1999

When he discussed the spread of Tigua painting, Julio Toaquiza insisted that he did not teach anyone from Tigua-Quiloa, a rival peasant sector northwest of his own community. During our interview in 1999, Julio speculated that his brother taught one of the Quiloans, most likely José Vega, noting that they were compadres (relatives through the baptism of one of their children). A week after that interview, José saw a transcript of Julio's words in my notebook. He pointed at the tape recorder in my backpack and told me to turn it on. He wanted to set the record straight. Once I got the recorder set up, he tapped it twice asking, "Is it functioning?" then offered his account.

In fact, he did not contradict Julio. Rather, he repeated a story of laboring, suffering, and economic salvation through painting that was much like the original painter's. In the mid 1960s, José left home to work near Quevedo in the warm lowlands to the west when he was fifteen years old. He packed fruit in crates and did other work on commercial farms. He returned to Quiloa after six years, got married, and stayed put.

Speeding through these facts, he then slowed down to explain how things fell apart: "I planted the potato field that lies on the backside of

Quiloa, lower down. There I planted. The frost came. Those potatoes were finished, not one did I get. I was angry about that, that potato field. I went to Quito for a month. Are you noting this? Is it recording?" He went on to say that the next trip to Quito came within a year and lasted six months.

The Uruguayan architect Guillermo Jones-Odriozola had anticipated his arrival. In 1942, Quito municipal authorities hired Jones-Odriozola to help plan the city's future. Offering a vision of modern efficiency, Jones-Odriozola mapped out a way to rationalize the city, creating functional divisions among homes, work, and parks (Carrion and Vallejo 1994). These zones in turn would fit within a broader class-based, tripartite division: upscale residential neighborhoods out on the expanding northern edge, the middle-class areas closer in toward the city center, and new neighborhoods south of old colonial Quito where rural migrants could come and live. José lived in the south.

Drawn up in the architect's urban plans as working-class neighborhoods, the southern barrios became very familiar to José. He favored them not for the social order they offered within Quito, but for the easy way they allowed one to get out of the city. José seemed to pick places according to the names hung on the route placards that sit in the lower right corner of bus windshields: Marin, Mira Flores, and Guamani. These neighborhoods were transportation hubs that made it simple to find a ride in and out. Even years later, when I first visited his rented apartment in 1992 in Guamani, it had a bus terminal feel. Stretched out like a boxcar, the flat's four rooms looked out onto the Pan American Highway and trembled with the traffic.

Although he began in Quito by working construction jobs, he looked for his own economic edge among migrants. When the Toaquiza brothers started to paint, José saw a way into the antiquities and tourist business. Picking up the basics from Julio's brother, José made sure he had a few paintings with him each time he went to the city. He lacked, though, the Toaquiza name and contacts. With little idea of what to do, he sold haphazardly to tourists he encountered near the El Ejido Park in the center of the city and along the broad commercial avenue Rio Amazonas. Then in 1979, acting on a long-shot tip, he went looking for the museum at the Banco Central (Ecuador's central bank). He had been told they collect indigenous art and he hoped to sell them a painting of a fiesta scene. Once at the Banco Central, he talked his way past the guard, discovered which floor the museum staff worked on, and accosted a young curator, who would turn into a loyal ally.

She advised him to enter his painting in a national art competition that was sponsored by the bank and open to any Ecuadorian painter. When the judging was over, José Vega had earned a certificate of special recognition for his composition *Fiesta de 15 de octubre* and the honor of having his painting installed permanently in el Museo Mitad del Mundo. And months later, when the woman from the Banco Central finally found his home in Tigua, she delivered a cash prize. José took the money, showed it to his wife, and within weeks they had packed up their belongings. Long before the next actual Fiesta de 15 de octubre rolled around, they quit the countryside and moved to Quito. Twenty years later, sitting in his house on land he owned just south of the city in Santo Domingo de Cutulagua he announced to my tape recorder that he had moved so as "not to suffer."

He has yet to fully escape the shadow of suffering, though, or to lose the restlessness that comes with it. I had first met him in 1992, and then stayed with him in his new home outside Quito for a week in 1996. I interviewed him extensively in 1999, then lost touch until we had time to catch up at his market stall in Otavalo in 2004. Some years I found him painting ambitiously, working on scenes that were more than a meter wide by a meter high; other times he simply churned out simple tourist souvenirs. In 1992 he was deeply enmeshed in working his nongovernmental organization contacts in Quito to support a project in Quiloa. In 1999, he declared his painting to be at a dead end and was commuting down to the coast to see about finding some other work in Guayaquil. In 2004, the sparkle was back in his eye and he spent fifteen minutes trying to enlist me in a new scheme to develop a trade association for the women of Quiloa who had moved to Quito. In a way, José is similar to Alfonso Chiza in seeking in the city the means to redress the problems that burdened native peoples in both town and country. But, for José the move is more tactical than moral. Being based in the city taps funding resources not available at home. Further, for José, the way to get ahead is to work collectively as much as individually.

Urbanizing Country People

City life can mean a cultural unmooring for Andean peoples. Indeed, from the beginning of the colonial era, the arrival of Indians in the cities has worried nonindigenous observers. Already in 1594, Catholic Church authorities recorded what they construed as urban life's corrosive effect on indigenous society:

... and all the cities, and towns, and places are full of these *naturales* [Sp. Indians] and in the shadow of the Spaniards and with their favor, they do not want to return to their land, making of themselves *yanaconas* [tenant Indians] which many are not. .... With the same freedom they want a trade and to read and to write, being certain that as an Indian who can read or who has a trade or who rides a horse is then exempt from obligatory labor service.[1]

The author offered these observations to support the reform of rural settlements into reducciones, nucleated communities subjected to tighter colonial control. The words speak to a practical concern with preserving a rural labor force. When read centuries later, though, they foreshadow the postcolonial republic's racism. The need to pin down labor dissolved into a social preoccupation with keeping Indians in their place—and a generalized contempt for those who supposedly forget it. The observations of bygone yanaconas set up contemporary assumptions about the blending away of Andean culture: in the move to the city, new customs erase old identities.

Andean natives who have settled in towns came to be labeled *cholos* or *cholas*, terms once defined as those who "have abandoned their Indian identity without effectively gaining acceptance as Hispanics" (Pitt-Rivers 1965, 43) or more succinctly "'in-between' beings" (Seligmann 2004, 129). These terms imply fundamental cultural change along with some social mobility. Seligmann's informant Lucila Chawar Ronda, for example, is a Peruvian woman who was born in the countryside but has long lived in Cuzco. Lucila reports to Seligmann (Seligmann 2004, 129), "My mother and I are both mestizas, not campesinas [peasants/Indians], because we have moved up and are a little more than they are." Indianness is past, mastery of urban life may yet lie in the future, yet the social gain is achieved.

Weismantel (2001) has argued, though, that the terms cholo and chola, in fact, have a deeply conservative element. For all their suggestion of cultural change, they reproduce again and again the binary of race. To call someone cholo or chola asserts a kind of superiority over those labeled Indian while actually denying privileges of race assumed to come with that mobility. Whiteness is unobtainable, yet even so cholo/a identity is irreversible. It marks a move into an unsettled urban social world in which

1. From chapter fifty-three of the synodal constitutions of 1594, (cited in Ortiz Crespo, Alfonso, and Rosemarie Teran Najas 1993).

new habits, skills, and desires will only measure the distance one has come from being a "real Indian."

The scale of change in the post–land reform Andes, however, invites rethinking the equation linking city, cholo, and change. Indeed, the equation sets up a geographic miscalculation. As Escobar points out, since the 1940s, state ministries, international agencies, churches, and universities targeted rural areas for a profound project of modernization and cultural reordering. What was labeled "development" from above was in fact a form of "cholofication" from below. The major initiatives tied to education, transportation, hygiene, and productivity were premised on consigning Indianness to the past *in the countryside*. New rural schools created during development programs such as Misión Andina in the 1950s taught basic Spanish proficiency and literacy. The division between monolingual Kichwa speakers and bilingual speakers thus starts not with the arrival in town but with hopeful parents in the country. Supporting schooling, they sought to release their sons (especially) and daughters from the toil they knew. Subsequently, boys who stayed in these rural classrooms, then became men prone to migrating (Preston, Taveras, and Preston 1981).

Protestant churches joined the state in equipping rural people with a modern outlook. Missionaries taught Kichwa peasants that formal education, cleanliness, and an "enterprising personality" were Kichwa values. Thus, Muratorio (1980, 51) observes that "the very basis of their new Kichwa identity may lead them to assimilation." Even where their presence was small numerically, the Protestants' impact spread widely. Not the least, it spurred greater activism in the Catholic Church, including a need for priests to likewise support literacy, dignity, and economic improvement.

Meanwhile, during the 1960s and 1970s, Ecuador's improving networks of roads and oil-led growth stripped the boundaries off the industrial economy that was once tethered to Guayaquil, Ecuador's largest port. With its control of oil revenue, Quito offered a highland hub that could rival the coastal power of commodity export capital. Intermediate-size sierra cities such as Riobamba and Ibarra experienced their own high growth rates. Consequently, many more peasants found city work to be closer to hand. In much of the sierra, the expansion of the urban economy did not relocate whole reserves of destitute small-hold farmers to the city so much as shore them up in the countryside. Migration took the form of circulation (Brown, Brea, and Goetz 1988; Waters 1997).

New urban geography, rural schools, and better roads opened possibilities for some careers to span cultural and geographic space. That is, if Julio and Francisca rejected town to farm, paint, and raise their children in the country, and if Alfonso Chiza and his spouse spurned the country to work, invest, and raise their children in town, José emulates neither. Indeed, unlike Alfonso, José divines few moral lessons from his move to the city that lead him to claims of extraordinary progress. Rather than link sacrifice, capital, and advancement, he highlights the more humble motivation of avoiding misery. And for José this reason is socially acceptable grounds to drop farming. Others followed for the same reasons and José directed me to interview some of his relatives.

Petty Advancement

When they began to paint, few of José's family harbored ambitions for substantial earnings. For example, one of José's brothers-in-law, Francisco Cuyo, had started laboring on the coast in the early 1960s before he was married. He earned eight sucres a week (at a time when a simple lunch in a restaurant would cost him one sucre). Each year, he would catch a ride on a truck back home, stopping in Pilalo to buy some *mishki* (roughly processed cane sugar) for his parents. After several more hours' travel up the road, he disembarked in Quindicilli on the ridge that divides Tigua from Zumbagua and hiked down and across to Tigua-Quiloa. There he turned and made his way high above the core settlement to his family's home, made of bound straw, and nestled into the paramo. Invariably it was dark and he would rouse his parents to share with them a lump of rough sugar and a few sucres. After twelve years of these trips, Francisco asked José to teach him to paint when he saw that mishki and sucres could be had with only short stints in the city and longer periods sitting at home quietly at a table.

César Ilaquiche learned not from José but from one of José's first pupils, Manuel Cuyo. César was born in the sector of Yanapata below Quiloa. He went to Quevedo in 1971, the year his father died, when he was fourteen, and he packed fruit for five years, "suffering, suffering," he said. When he married Manuel Cuyo's oldest daughter in Quiloa in the late 1970s, he moved briefly to his in-laws' compound. Manuel urged him to paint and offered to teach him. Cesar said, "My father-in-law asked, 'Why do you go to Quevedo to suffer?'"

Even when earnings from painting became hard to come by in the late 1990s, Francisco Toaquiza explained to me that Tiguans would stick with it: "What else are we going to do? We are schooled in it; we cannot change. More than anything it is soft work. It's not like working outside. That's very tiring outside. Working construction is other work. When it rains, you have to be working. This art is inside the house. We are not so exhausted anymore."

When the topic shifted from why one should paint to how one succeeds, painters' stories diverged. In gathering career histories of twenty urban painters in 1999, I expected to be told the market ran on reputation and contacts such as those formed by the original painter. Indeed, some confirmed their importance. Francisco Toaquiza, for instance, told me that to succeed, "one must have contacts. One needs to export." A second painter noted, "One needs a little capital and to have a sales post [in El Ejido Park] . . . [There is] the possibility to export directly if there is someone there to receive the paintings out there in another country."

More painters, however, emphasized the importance of working hard to come up with new ideas. One painter put it this way: "I must analyze [the compositions]. I must paint more with the folktales. If I lower my standards, I am left with less." Prosperity comes from careful observation. As another said, "I must think about the countryside. I saw a rock in this way or a hill in this way or a beach along the edge of a river that is flowing. That I must record in my ideas. For me I like that all the painters go on prospering little by little because the painting is getting better. I like this a lot. Yes, bit by bit a few have improved. But those who have not improved their painting seem to me at this moment a bit of a failure."

These observations on getting ahead, not surprisingly, sound like trade advice—useful professional tips. The men who offered them counted among the successful minority who lived from their painting. Of the approximately 300 members of Tiguan painters' associations in 1999, only eighty or so earned enough to fully support their households. Such success encouraged faith in both their own skill and the rewards of the market. Yet, if the comments carry a tone of self-affirmation, they are a far cry from Alfonso Chiza's triumphal capitalist maxims, which would sort winners and losers according to rational effort and moral progress. Indeed, the difference between the painters' view and Chiza's parallels the distinction economic anthropologists make between the petty commodity form and real capitalism. Scott Cook (1990) observes that petty commodity production involves maximizing choices, competitive markets, and cash returns—but it is never fully capitalistic. It never sustains the rational cost accounting and wage-labor practices that make ceaseless profit the guiding principal of economic life. The petty commodity producer's modest aspirations are captured in the oft-repeated words "Don't suffer" and "improving oneself, little by little." If a more robust sense of advancement does crop up in Tiguan narrations of their artistic careers, it is in the one sphere that is least emphasized by Alfonso Chiza: the importance of collective organization.

Artist Associations and Households

Already by 1980, more people had started to paint than the market could support. Tiguan artists were in essence gambling, staking a lot of time and effort for wildly uncertain payoffs. More than a few painted crudely, sloppily copying people like José, and contributed nothing to the development of the art. On the business side, few Tiguans in the 1970s had experience selling anything but their labor to outsiders. Most new painters unloaded their paintings for low prices at the back door of folklore galleries or in chance encounters with tourists or during new Sunday "Art in the Park" events held in El Ejido Park. Many returned home to Tigua with unsold inventory. Others left paintings to be sold by José or the few others who lived in the city. In those infrequent instances when the item sold, the painter would then be paid during his next trip.

José Vega began to give up some of his painting time and started to organize the painters. He could have been moved by the frustration he saw, or inspired by the efforts of many peasant communities in the 1970s who organized for formal recognition from the state. Conversely, he may have simply tried to enlist allies in an attempt to elevate his own sales effort and insure that he would not lose rights to sell in the park. When I interviewed him, José was more intent to explain the form and location he chose for his artisan association than his reasons for pushing it.

He started from scratch. In 1983, residents from Tigua-Quiloa had no other formal association. They had neither registered their community as a comuna with the Ministry of Social Welfare nor formed a narrower agrarian cooperative dedicated to joint cultivation and marketing. José eschewed both of these forms. Intending foremost to give a legal voice to Tiguans who wanted to sell in El Ejido Park, he sought jurisdiction in the province of Pichincha (Quito). His decision was reinforced by his lawyer, who said that if they organized as a peasant organization, they "should go

back to Cotopaxi." In 1999, he continued to emphasize to me the importance of establishing a business organization:

> Father Julio was the first painter, but he had nothing. On the other hand, I came
> second, and got our association here in Quito with its official judicial statute.
> This was not for the peasant community. I am a handicraft promoter and a
> businessman. After our sellers' organization, the rest of the Tiguan associations
> came.

He officially named the group "The Association of Indigenous Small Traders of Paintings and Handicrafts of Tigua" and built it up by recruiting the
painters who regularly arrived in Quito from Quiloa and by signing up a
core of about ten migrant households who lived in the city. Within a year
they had met their primary objective. The city recognized the organization
and granted them the right to continue selling in El Ejido. This space then
catalyzed the transformation of the art, its economics, and the household
relations of those who grew to depend on it.

Having established a steady weekly market, the Tiguans could now
wait for tourists, collectors, and dealers to come to them. Moreover, as the
painters regularly congregated, they realized gains independent of meetings with clients. Artists now spent time face-to-face, painting-to-painting,
stealing ideas seen one week in others' work, putting out their own innova-
tions in later weeks for others to take back. The gatherings materialized
in more creative art. Looking back, Francisco Cuyo, president of Quiloa's
main artist association in 1999, said, "We came to the park and tried to
make a good presentation. There was a lot of improvement."

Turning from the early motifs depicting uniform figures against styl-
ized rural scenes, artists began to display a sophisticated cosmopolitanism.
They composed scenes interweaving Catholic ritual with subtle Andean
symbolism or else layered richly textured images of bullfights, dancers,
and musicians in crowded snapshots of Cotopaxi culture (Whitten 2003).
Some experimented with painting urban markets, capturing the world into
which they were moving; others portrayed country life in a fresh way, by
rendering interiors of peasant houses.

Paintings improved and incomes rose but the advancement rested as
much on the household and the gendered reorganization of artisan work as
on individual inspiration. Many Tiguans followed Mercedes Cuyo and José
Vega's example and moved their households to the city. Relieved of farm
chores, women in the city often joined their men at the paint-splotched

desks. They took up routine tasks of filling in background colors or completing repetitive details or decorating the frames. Some women also produced their own compositions, keeping them simple so they could be multiplied and sold to tourists looking for inexpensive souvenirs. Such sales allowed steady earnings and let men embellish more visible, larger, and expensive *cuadros* (paintings) that could broaden their reputation. Making still more time available for their husbands' painting, women covered the commercial routes. Many left the house almost daily to sell in Quito's tourist districts and to tend selling places in El Ejido on Sunday. The *kusawarmi* (husband-wife) division of labor that emerged in Quito in the 1980s took the art to a new level of artistic detail and commercial output.

Children had to adapt to the new intensity of both parents' work. The administrative demands of schooling, for example, often fell to older siblings who had to handle the registration, exam fees, and report cards of their little brothers and sisters. Frequently, a mother's absence to sell meant children would have to fend for themselves at meal time. In one household that I lived in for six weeks, three brothers ranging in age from eleven to sixteen shared an evening meal with their parents only once or twice a week. The rest of the time the boys left cooking up to their youngest brother who would boil cauldrons of rice with thick slices of onions, boil some potatoes on the side, and set out another pot to cook some noodles. When all was ready, he mounded the rice, potatoes, and onions together and draped the pasta over the top. While the meal was gratefully consumed night after night, the boys did delight in their mother's return and the chance to have fried fish, chicken soup, or occasionally some lamb.

Quito residents turned rural household roles upside down, with men passing their days indoors, women commuting and selling in the city center, and, occasionally, with the children occupying the kitchen. In the process, men's reputations as painters grew, women's work intensified inside and outside the home, and households earned more. Largely invisible to outsiders, women slowly gained recognition as painters within Quiloa. A growing number of them became members of the artist association in their own right. They spoke up at the meetings, participated in sporadic training programs and had a say in who would lead the groups. And as the membership broadened and became more inclusive, the agenda of the group reoriented toward the welfare of Tigua-Quiloa.

FIGURE 7 José Vega, Mercedes Cuya, and their family at home on the edge of Quito, 1999

When I turned off my tape recorder during our interview in 1999, I got out my camera and asked to take some pictures of José. He posed awkwardly for a bit, then called his family over to join him for some more snapshots. I went back a few weeks later and presented him with a set of prints. He flicked through the portraits and close ups, shaking his head and declaring, "ugly, ugly, ugly." Finally he stopped and said, "This. This is good." I stepped over to see what caught his fancy. He carefully held a photograph of him in a lineup with his daughter, son-in-law, granddaughter, and wife. Compared with the clarity of the portraits, this picture seemed poorly composed. No one could be made out that clearly owing to their distance from the lens and the shadows and bright light of the equatorial sun; the granddaughter had been distracted and had looked away (see figure 7). Yet the print captured how he wanted to be pictured, not as a lone painter but as a member of a household. The photograph was a historical document, his own account of what Indians were doing in the city centuries after his ancestors were condemned for being there, reading, and riding horses. It bore witness to the social world that he helped create in Quito through the labor and art and organizing that had taken place across three provinces and over the course of a lifetime.

Translocal Community Development

Indeed, José and the other urban artists went beyond creating meaningful individual lives in the city. They exploited the recognition they earned with their art to bring development projects back to Quiloa. In fact, despite José's insistence that the trade association was an urban institution, the leadership made sure that the group's meetings rotated monthly between Quito and Quiloa so that people back in Cotopaxi would not be left out. Further, the first funds ever raised by the group were used to build a craft store in the middle of Quiloa. They purchased cement blocks, tiles, metal window frames, and glass panes to erect the sector's first modern building. Members stocked it and kept it set up as a store for the next two years. They never made a sale; no road served the community and no agency promoted tourism in Quiloa. Eventually they converted the store to a general community house.

Over the next eight years José obtained three other projects, all for the rural sector. They got seedlings to reforest part of the community with native species; they received materials and technical assistance for a soil-building project involving great wooden crates of worm-infested straw. Most ambitiously, they obtained funds and technical support for the construction of forty new adobe homes equipped with a special room brightened by a large window and designated as a painter's studio. The project lasted nearly three years in the early 1990s. Although some of the houses were never completed, most were, and Quiloa thickened with architecturally uniform, carefully engineered, whitewashed homes.

The new buildings, along with the community house, the soil project, and other efforts, shaped Tiguans' sense of the importance of collective effort. In subsequent years, painters sometimes referred to this string of projects when explaining what it took to succeed as an indigenous artisan. As one young Quito migrant put it, "One person alone cannot do it well." From procuring raw materials to assisting sales efforts to defending the park's sales posts, he listed tasks that the association previously helped people with. By the late 1990s, painters began to pin the lack of further growth in the artisan trade on a lack of cooperation. As one Tiguan migrant lamented in 1999, "They are badly disorganized, these indigenous painters. No one can organize in this form. If there is one association, there are six or seven. There is no one who will support us in this form."

Where Alfonso Chiza, a successful Otavalan manufacturer, touted sacrifice, capital, and responsibility, José Vega, a prize-winning Tiguan painter and association leader, noted suffering and sought unity. But it would be inaccurate to contrast them as polar opposites. José and other Tiguans' early economic success required their own modernizing measures. Many painters sought advancement by moving to the city. They reorganized household routines, resulting in a new division of labor between husband and wife and new intensity for both. Gudeman and Rivera (1990) note how house-oriented production can develop in the city, preserving livelihoods that do not subscribe to a market-maximizing logic. With the painters, I have seen the opposite: assembly line–like production at the kitchen table, commercial trades in the place of subsistence work, and gendered complementarity configured by market routines. All combine to remake the "house" as business.

From the 1980s on, Tigua-Quiloa diverged sharply from Tigua-Chimbacucho. If Julio Toaquiza developed his art to survive in Tigua, José Vega cultivated his to flee. Getting ahead meant getting away from Quiloa. Yet here, he and the members of Quiloa's association evaded the rigid spatial categories of progress proclaimed by Alfonso Chiza. During the 1980s the trade organization of the migrant community overrode distinctions between a pristine "peasant" domain and its opposite. Such crossings of the rural-urban boundary, in fact, have been noted by Jane Jacobs (1969, 16) as an intrinsic part of urban development. A critic of the grand, rationalized planning of the kind that the Uruguayan Jones-Odriozola used to lay modern Quito, she challenged not just the compartmentalization of urban life but the more basic conceptual division between city and country when she wrote that "both in the past and today, then, the separation commonly made, dividing city commerce and industry from rural agriculture, is artificial and imaginary. The two do not come down different lines of descent. Rural work—whether that work is manufacturing brassieres or growing food—is city work transplanted."

Through most of Tigua's modern history, the transplanting of urban work has been the purview of the white-mestizo oligarchy that devised property laws, land reform, road systems, and civil regulations to fit the visions of the modernity they pursued. Migration into the cities in the 1970s and 1980s, though, created new urbanites, many of whom were indigenous and a few of whom worked as self-made development professionals. People such as José Vega emerged who were articulate about community needs, newly versed in NGO culture, and sufficiently effective in community politics to operate across urban and rural milieus. By coming to own a piece of the city, he and other Tiguans broke the past monopoly on directing rural development. Paralleling Alfonso Chiza's effort to build churches and spread his faith back on Mount Imbabura, José Vega and his associates constructed a communal house and transplanted a slice of Quito's artisan-tourist economy back to their parish.

So is José a cholo? In Weismantel's (2002), Seligmann's (2004), and others' accounts of racial geography, José's permanent relocation to the city alone jeopardizes his Indianness. Biography, though, does not support such hard and fast cultural distinctions. Development programs and church missions have long facilitated the abandonment of indigenous culture in the country; large-scale circular migration interweaves urban and rural experiences; and urban Indians have led the effort to revitalize rural indigenous culture. This does not mean that the cholo/a identity is no longer an accurate social category. Rather, the opposite. It is possible to be cholo/a in more ways and more places. And, likewise, it is possible to be indigenous in more places, and in fact, in the same places once claimed for cholos.

In José Vega's case, he narrates his life as economic hardship surmounted first through migration and then through political organization.

Responding to Julio's transcribed words in my notebook, José wanted an opportunity to promote the city and painting's untold urban side. His later activist career exploited his city base to advance Quiloa's economic growth. It not only injected urban resources into a rural parish, but implicitly affirmed indigenous people as town residents. At the same time, he neither repudiates his past as backward nor embraces his present as culturally enlightened. Put another way, his story does not do the same racial work of others' narratives, those tales in which speakers claim to be "a little more" than peasants simply because they moved to town (Seligman 2004, 150). José fails to sell the ideal of progress on the backs of his brothers and sisters who have not left Quiloa to join him. In José's life, city and country became a more unified field of action. At a national level, indigenous leaders were to show just how politically powerful such integration could be.

FIGURE 8. Friends and families

CHAPTER FOUR

Uprising, 1990

This is not a workers' strike.
This is not a teachers' strike.
This is not a students' strike,
THIS IS AN INDIAN UPRISING.
—Protest Chant, Chimborazo Province, 1990

Committing three chapters to explore three men's lives, this book has taken the long path into the topic at hand: protest, popular mobilization, and Indian-led activism. In part, I do this for the lesson that I learned from Julio Toaquiza. He did not want the story of Tigua art told without having the history of laboring and suffering documented by me. I too do not want to set out the recent events of community politics without building a deeper understanding of Andean careers in the mid-twentieth century. In a somewhat simplistic way, I have made these three lives stand in for the multiple livelihoods that native people put together in the contemporary Andes. Versed in CONAIE's motto, "Don't Lie, Don't be Lazy, Don't Steal," I have also cast these lives in moral terms, coming up with supplemental commands that struck me as fitting the lessons dictated to me: Don't Forsake, Don't Be Backward, Don't Suffer. And having taken care to underscore the discontinuities in their lives, I want now to finally see what I can make of their common ground.

Who Are the Indians?

Near the midpoint of their book on Ecuador's indigenous movement, the Quito-based scholars Fernando Guerrero Cazar and Pablo Ospina Peralta (2003, 120) open up the whole problem of classifying people as indigenous. They begin with an anecdote about being surveyed in the 2001 national census. For the first time in decades, the census included a question that asked the respondent to declare his or her own ethnicity. One of the authors recounts how the young woman doing the census in his building entered his apartment, sat down, worked through the questions, and got up to head to their neighbor. The author pointed out that she had omitted the ethnic question. She smiled and returned to her seat and carefully reviewed the form. After checking the data, she confessed that she had the information; she had already classified the household as white. Guerrero and Ospina draw a double moral. First, no organized effort to arrive at objective classifications of people can escape such projections, short-circuiting, or outright biases. Second, the criteria for identification are not all clear.

Political groups vary widely when asserting what distinguishes ethnic heritage and estimating the number of indigenous people in Ecuador is contentious. CONAIE has routinely placed the number at 40% of Ecuador's 13.5 million people; meanwhile a longtime leader of the conservative Social Christian party claims that they are no more than 10% of the population. Guerrero and Ospina show an inclination to use language as a starting point for discussions of identity. They carefully work through a survey of over 14,000 households from 2000 that asked how a respondent would categorize himself among six ethnic categories (blanco, negro, indígena, mestizo, mulato, and otro). The survey recorded which languages were used in the home and which languages were used by parents. The results showed national indigenous self-ascription reached little more than 6 percent. However, when self-ascription and history of Kichwa language use are aggregated, 17 percent of the population could be considered indigenous.

No sooner were these numbers out, though, than did Guerrero and Ospina's various informants pick them apart. Committed to the idea of a mixed-blood nation, for example, some blond, blue-eyed Quiteños reject the idea that any Ecuadorians, including themselves could be white (Guerrero Cazar and Ospina Peralta 2003, 121). In other cases, Kichwa speakers reject other individuals' Indian self-ascription if the claimant appears too physically white.

Three decades earlier, Pitt-Rivers anticipated these disputes in his essay "Who Are the Indians?" (1965). He observes, "The judgment of who is and who is not an Indian varies according to the social position of the speaker," noting that for someone descended from the old colonial aristocracy any nonaristocrat is an Indian. In fact, among all social classes, the term "Indian" can be used as an insult "without any literal ethnic connotation" (Pitt-Rivers 1965, 45). Meanwhile an Indian from the highlands of Peru would place all cholos, mestizos, and blancos in the category of white (Pitt-Rivers 1965, 43).

Having described the social hierarchy that produces itself through the idea of the Indian, Pitt-Rivers nonetheless fixes the identity in a few aspects. He claims that Indian peasants "show a tenacious attachment to their culture and to their community," that their worldview is geographically defined and "rooted in the earth," and that they are too often "poor and uneducated" (Pitt-Rivers 1965, 47–48). Asking "Has the Indian a future?" he implies that they do not. Migrating in great quantities,

> An indigent rural population is exchanged for an under-employed urban one. The fact that the former are largely classed as "Indians" and the latter are not, once they have been assimilated, hardly changes the insecurity of their situation. This might be called integration without redemption. But at this point the problem has ceased to be "the Indian problem" and has become the social and economic problem of the nation. (1965, 48)

Pitt-Rivers's essay appeared at the time land reform got underway in Ecuador and the moment when Julio Toaquiza, Alfonso Chiza, and José Vega launched their working lives. In light of their experiences, Pitt-Rivers's basic point rings true. His emphasis on Indians caught up in national folklore, poverty, and stigmatized identities spells out the social limits they faced. And yet, he got the future wrong. Julio, Alfonso, and José do not disappear as Indians. Moving from past to present, they remake themselves as indigenous people, not unredeemed urban proletariats. And while I have dwelt on the moral divergences in their careers, I also concede the shared elements from which they compounded their different lives. For the generation who came of age in the twilight hours of the hacienda's social power, lives have been oriented by the unyielding trilogy of race, place, and work.

Race in Ecuador, for all its connotation of epochal clashes between European invaders and America's original people (Gose 1994), lives in the trivial "attacks and responses" of everyday life (Cervone 1999, 137). Emma Cervone (1999) argues that no public self is possible for Indians to this day without tactics for an ethnic defense, without, that is, symbolically or spatially rejecting derogatory stereotypes and claiming respect. And yet, in the lives of the men I interviewed, these tactics never included trying to erase race itself as ongoing terms of social relations. In fact, Julio Toaquiza's response to racism is to pick at the scab and reopen racial wounds. Unprompted, he laid out his mixed heritage and he spelled out for me the differing fortunes of people from his valley who were white and who were Indians. Further, he and Francisca have reproduced their lives in intimate proximity to the hacienda that caused so much pain. Julio painted images of it, farmed near it, and looked down on it from his house along the highway.

In an entirely different tactic, Chiza's "ethnic defense" borders on offense; the rejected becomes the rejecter. He shifts racist terms inward. Distancing himself from the stereotype of uneducated, undisciplined, and backward, he reinscribes this same social division among indigenous Otavalos. Only in the stories that José Vega dictated into my tape recorder does the discourse of race become muted. To be sure, like the census taker, I could quickly move his household into a ready-made racial category. Yet his talk of organizing, uniting, living in the city, and being *comerciantes* (Sp. business people) speaks to class identities—both peasant and urban working class—that would be overlooked in a simplified racial scheme.

"Place" more obviously unites the three men's experience. Each is from a rural community; all invest their time and effort as adults in improving its fortune. Thus, Julio teaches a new trade to family and neighbors in Chimbacucho, Alfonso leads a group to build a modern Church near Agato, and José forms an association that promotes the development of Quiloa. More tellingly, these men earn their living specifically by being from some place. Julio paints and sells Tigua art, Alfonso manufactures Otavalo crafts, José solicits projects that are funded because they involve a rural, Kichwa community. Against the placelessness of the modern economy—the flow of capital and commodities—these men are pinned down. They still make their way in the world according to their ability to demonstrate their authentic ties to some specific and out-of-the-way place.

The work found in these places is itself often a defensive tactic. The appeal of subsistence agriculture and craft production for Julio has been the way it has enabled life outside menial urban wage work. The others, too, have sought an economic autonomy, one that has been made possible through the domestic organization of their work. Indeed, as different as running a factory or raising barley or selling to tourists in Quito are as jobs, households stand at the heart of these occupations, pulling together contributions from a married couple and older unmarried children to make a success of each venture. Since land reform divorced these household economies from haciendas, they have articulated with new markets in new ways. Forming alliances, they gain resources from diverse outsiders—folk art gallery owners, industrial equipment sales representatives, Mormon Church authorities, central bank officials, and development agency technicians. Years of migration broke indigenous isolation to make these connections more likely. And as contacts grew, so did earnings and payoffs of other sorts.

As they met others, struck deals, worked for their families, and sacrificed for their communities, Julio, Alfonso, and José pulled off their homemade projects of remaking Indian identity. The efforts were "homemade" because their identity is as much a joint feat of their households and the social ties made through the joint labors of the hearth as it is of individual self-creation. "Homemade," though, also refers to the idiosyncratic, handcrafted nature of these three de-Indianization projects. The choices they made led them in different directions and they narrate their lives in different terms that single out different goals. If all bear witness to the suffering of Indians and each has contributed to the greater good of his community, each has his own take on how he prevailed. Large-scale efforts to reclaim indigenousness were absent as these men came of age and common scripts had yet to be written. They had to find their own words to tell their own tales.

Three decades later, things changed. "Who are the Indians?" was borrowed to title another essay written on Latin America's indigenous people in 1994. In this essay the author, Les Field, insists that politics, resistance, and partisan language are moving to the center of defining who or what is Indian. While Field is reviewing recent scholarship in the essay, he is clearly also moved by events that he had reported on in Ecuador (Field 1991). In 1990, Ecuador's national indigenous movement orchestrated a levantamiento (uprising), a moment which forever changed the politico-cultural landscape in which a de-Indianization project could take place.

The Modern Movement's First Uprising

Angered about the government's apathy toward their mistreatment, growing poverty, and lack of land, Indians took action at a national level in 1990. The uprising began when indigenous leaders from CONAIE and other activists occupied the Santo Domingo church in Quito at the end of May to protest the failure of the legal system to process land claims. CONAIE leaders also saw a general strike for land as a rebuff of values underlying Ecuador's mestizo-dominated political system. Coming up on the 500th anniversary of Columbus' first voyage to the Americas, Miguel Lluco of CONAIE said, "We were rejecting the celebration of the 500 years. We said, at least make it to 500 years with land" (Leon 1993, 137).

Spooked by the extent of CONAIE's organizing and the show of support for the Indians among some non-indigenous sectors in Quito, the police encircled the church. They turned back those trying to bring food and cut off all communication between the occupiers and the outside world. Then, early in June, as those in the church began a hunger strike, indigenous peasants from the central highlands left their fields, hearths, and workplaces by the thousands in order to block highways with tree trunks and boulders, shut down commerce, and march on provincial government offices. Their goal was not only to force the government to negotiate seventy-two stalled land claims but to protest specific abuses by local civil authorities. As the strike continued, a group of communities in Chimborazo enacted a long-planned takeover of a hacienda, further intensifying events.

Unable to contain the strike with the police and army, the Social Democratic government of Rodrigo Borja agreed to negotiate with the leadership of CONAIE at a national level. In the provinces, authorities received delegates from indigenous organizations who presented lists of grievances. The bargaining went beyond community efforts to recover their fields. In Quito, CONAIE's sixteen-point memorandum guided the dialogue, whose starting position was the need for a "public declaration that Ecuador is a plurinational country (to be ratified in the constitution)." Once negotiations ran their course, gains were slight. CONAIE came away with few concessions on any of their sixteen points. Lawsuits for land redistribution remained mired in the courts. Only at the local level did more land start to move into indigenous hands, mostly through private sales by nervous hacienda owners.[1]

By political standards, though, the protest accomplished a lot. The events in June inserted the ethnic question into national politics. Rural activism had moved "from peasant struggles to Indian resistance," in the words of political scientist Amalia Pallares (2002). In explaining this transition, a certain conventional wisdom has emerged among scholars and activists alike. I want to review and challenge this standard account, an awkward task because my conclusions resemble much of what is written. Yet, if I agree on central facts, especially the primacy of communities, I see a far more diverse social and economic world that set up the protests. Consequently, I argue for a very different role for the civil society that continues to emerge alongside the national movement.

The case for ethnic politics started with the premise that land reform failed Indians: "The communities lost the game in terms of access to economic resources"(Korovkin 1997, 32; Selverston-Scher 2001). Without having received sufficient land, Ecuador's rural population divided and Zamosc (1994, 43) shows that full-time small farmers were far more likely to be mestizo than indigenous. For the meagerness of their holdings, indigenous peoples increasingly became "semi-proletarian migrants," leaving the land as Julio, Alfonso, and José all did, for months or years or permanently.

Most agree, too, that the urban experience was largely fruitless. Pallares observes that, destined to circulate endlessly from their communities to cities, Indians suffered continual mistreatment or *maltrato*—the abuse and contempt of civil authorities, rip-offs by mestizo merchants, and the scorn of town residents. Indeed, in the midst of the 1990 uprising, Alberto Taxco, an indigenous yachac, held a mock trial of public officials

---

1. Sales were predicated on rupturing indigenous unity. Blanca Chancozo, a CONAIE leader, observed (Leon 1993, 134), "There is an [indigenous] minority that says: 'Ah no! Those others are communists, we are not.' They approached the government in order to say, 'we do not agree with [CONAIE]. We are not going to rob land. We are not thieves.' They said they were not going to join in with us and that it is better to buy the land. So the government or the landowner took advantage of this form of pressure to say, 'To you, I will sell,' in order to put us in conflict among ourselves." Yet, while Chancozo clearly saw the insidiousness of these sales, she saw triumph in them too. This other group exploited the uprising to express their needs in peaceful terms, she notes. Further, this "parallel group" reaffirmed the same basic necessity at the heart of the events: land.

in Latacunga (the capital of Cotopaxi province where Tigua is located) for their racism and abuse. Taking advantage of the police's vigilance of this protest, Taxco turned and spoke directly to the police chief and said:

> If you take an Indian prisoner, you must treat him as you would treat a deputy. Would you kick the deputy as you arrested him? No! What would you do to the *runas* [Indians]? Kick them, kick them! If you caught a landowner's son, you would hold him by the hand and make arrangements with his father. This is neither just nor equal. (Pallares 2002, 19)

When it comes to work, authors portray a grim situation. "Towns and cities institutionalized a labor partitioning system that assigned Indians the most menial and underpaid tasks" as maids, porters, and bricklayers (Pallares 2002, 43, 64). When the bottom fell out of the Ecuadorian economy after the 1982 drop in oil prices, this tedious work became even more meager. Construction activity declined by 50 percent between 1987 and 1990; real wages across all sectors fell almost 30 percent between 1980 and 1985 (Zamosc 1994, 49). That is, in most accounts, Kichwa careers in the last third of the twentieth century were one long losing streak.

And with the material failure of land reform noted and new hardships of temporary migration and urban employment lamented, political analysts tend to pass the story of Indian consciousness from economics to politics. New leadership councils and formal political linkages that reached across parish boundaries promised hope in the absence of an economic future. "Reform initiated a dramatic growth in indigenous organizing" (Selverston-Scher 2001, 36) and in some places a "province-wide community movement" (Korovkin 1997, 32). Politics, moreover, fed off of a new awareness of culture. The children of *huasipungueros* (indentured laborers on haciendas) committed themselves to maintain community life and "to promote cultural revitalization and political organization" (Pallares 2002, 43). Only the economics of land ownership remained in scholarly accounts as a material preoccupation amid the celebration of community identity and organizing. It surged "as a constant theme and certainly one of the most contemporary and historical problems of the struggle" (Macas 2001, xiv).

To put it bluntly, I find this story of the peasant-Indian political transition too rehearsed. The narrative arc, woven alike into activist accounts and researchers' analysis, colors recent history with a triumphant inevitability. Indeed, it has a mythic ring: loss (the community-hacienda complex undone and the bleeding away of subsistence resources), crisis (failed peasant farming and descent to temporary urban wage work), and the rebirth (the renewal of active indigenous communities in pursuit of communal territories). In such a telling, a world of nearly landless peasants shuttling between their plots and fruitless jobs finds redemption through community, indigenousness, and activism.

I want to question several assumptions underlying this scheme. For example, conventional wisdom equates mistreatment and racism with a generalized failure of the indigenous urban experience. That would be news to Alfonso Chiza and the Otavalo entrepreneurs of his generation who moved into town. Even Pallares' own descriptions of indigenous mistreatment can be read against the grain as accounts of social mobility. She observes (2002, 64) "a substantial increase in the numbers of educated and professional Indians" and records the experiences of a few of them, including an indigenous medical assistant in Chimborazo and an engineer from Cotacachi. In fact, from the 1960s on, the sheer numbers of Indians seeking professional careers helped change a basic tenet of national culture. Education no longer had to be equated with assimilation. Indians could associate with other Indians in high schools and universities relieving the social isolation that helped force assimilation. Undeniably, racism did rob these careers of their real potential. Yet, the disdain of others did not undo the determination of many indígenas. Never certain, urban successes were significant anyway.

Second, writers repeatedly see rural organizing as a realm that exists independently of urban careers and built of longstanding indigenous values and practices. Zamosc, for example, writes:

> Among the peasants who had to organize in order to fight for the land, a sense of collective purpose emerged based on appeals to primordial loyalties. In reactivating the ties of extended kinship and reciprocity, this process reinforced (and in many cases even regenerated) the old Indian community as the natural organizational framework. (Zamosc 1994)

The words "primordial," "kinship," "reciprocity," and "natural" imply that an indigenous destiny is at work. Community organizing, however, especially in the decade leading up to the uprising, had less to do with ancient logic than 1980s ambition and change. Indeed, the appropriate model is José Vega's small business association of circulating migrants, not a primordial farming village.

The data Zamosc (1995) later compiled to estimate the size of Ecuador's indigenous population show this. Using a language census from the 1950s, he identified which parts of the sierra were predominantly mestizo and which parts predominantly indigenous. He then charted population growth rates, organizational trends, and other demographic indices. Among these, he recorded changes in the registration of *comunas* (peasant communities that hold some resources in common), *cooperativas* (narrower collectives of peasants using shared land for agricultural enterprises), and *asociaciones* (groups dedicated to shared economic activity or community development). His data show that through the 1980s, associations had actually become the preferred method of indigenous organizing (see figure 9). Encouraged by new legislation in the 1970s, indigenous groups coalesced around specific rural development projects, artisan trades, or urban marketplaces. Forming associations—becoming *socios* (partners) rather than *comuneros* (peasant community members)—did not require shared land holdings and afforded more flexibility. Yet, as José Vega's association of small traders demonstrates, these associations could be the vehicles for rural development.

The third problem that crops up in standard accounts is that the uprising itself comes to be seen as indigenous will made manifest—a single, powerful act driven by the political activation of Indian identity. The events in late May and June of 1990, however, were a composite of different protests. If each related to land and each coordinated to some extent through CONAIE, the different actions also showed other agendas, which themselves motivated some indigenous communities and left others unconvinced. The idea to occupy Santo Domingo church in Quito, for example, grew from a prior experience. The brief occupation in 1989 of the offices of IERAC, the government's land reform agency, by a group of indígenas was a revelation to activists schooled in rural protest (Leon 1993, 137). This seizure taught CONAIE activists that pressuring the central government directly could achieve results. Thus, seeking to bring about changes at the core of Ecuador's political system, some in CONAIE went ahead with organizing supplies and participants for the occupation—even as others thought it would undermine a peasant-based uprising for land.

In the provinces, the wider general strike attracted protestors less interested in constitutional matters than in ending civil servants' abuse of indigenous clients. They also wanted to restart legal proceedings in numerous land cases. Evangelical indigenous communities in Chimborazo, however,

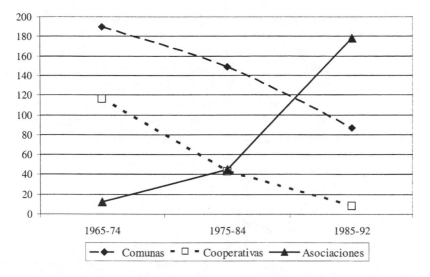

FIGURE 9 New registrations of comunas, cooperativas, and asociaciones in predominantly indigenous areas, 1965–92 (data source: Zamosc 1995)

did not sign on. Only as the strike gained momentum did a Protestant
radio station call out its communities to a meeting to decide whether to
participate. Thousands responded. And when the military tried to turn
them back, the evangelicos quickly converted to the cause, bringing about
rare unity between Catholic and Protestant communities and the mutual
support of their radio stations (Pacari 1993).

The most radical incident, the invasion of the hacienda Charrón in
Chimborazo would have happened with or without the other events. The
communities around the hacienda wanted to take it early in the year, but
indigenous leaders from Cañar and elsewhere counseled a delay to coordinate with the levantamiento. In the event, the coincidence helped to
intimidate authorities. At one point the hacendado arrived with trucks full
of soldiers and a bulldozer to open the way back to his occupied hacienda.
The activists from Cañar had sent a group to start fires over on a mountain
and they pointed these out to the soldiers, calling out, "Just wait! Many
more Indians are going to come." They let authorities know that, if they
did not hand over the hacienda's land, the protestors would expand their
invasion and take the town itself. Such threats carried all the more weight
for the mass protests happening elsewhere in the province.

At the same time, though, the leaders of the invasion did not fully
trust the leaders affiliated with CONAIE. When state authorities came to

mediate, Nina Pacari, who was a member of CONAIE's directorate, was with them. The invaders, however, treated her as just another lawyer. Nicanor Calle, one of the Cañaris, explained, "An indigenous leader would never come together with the authorities without first having consulted with the people" (Leon 1993, 119).

And even this variety in the levantamiento's events—symbolic protests in the capital, occupations of provincial governments, a hacienda invasion—was not broad enough to attract many participants in Imbabura or Cañar, provinces with some of the most active indigenous groups of the 1980s. Further, the Amazonian member organizations of CONAIE, some of whom had pressing land issues of their own, also did not get involved. If identity supplied many with a reason to join June's strike, it did not do so for all of Ecuador's native peoples.

*　*　*

So here, with the recognition of urban careers, of modest class mobility, of internal cultural divisions, and of important indigenous organizations' nonparticipation, a more complicated picture of the uprising emerges. But why quibble? The protest overcame many past weaknesses of native organizing. It revealed new powers to coordinate and a new vision, not just for indigenous peoples but for all of Ecuador at the end of the twentieth century. Indians had emerged to challenge the central government, not just local landowners. Given my agreement with much of what has been written, why point out fractures among those that have only recently come together?

Because these fissures reveal one of the greatest—and most overlooked—issues of modern Indian politics: creating potent political bonds among peoples who are going their separate ways. As jarring as his descriptions are, the Mormon entrepreneur Alfonso Chiza gets at a basic historical truth. The indigenous movement launched itself at a moment when Indians had begun successfully rejecting agrarian lifeways as well as holding them up. Activism picked up momentum when the post–land reform social polarities began to remake Kichwa communities and become manifest in trades, churches, and community organizations that were founded on rival principles. And it is here that the crucial task of indigenous politics lies. The levantamiento of 1990 forced Ecuadorians to ask, are we one nation or many? Whose values, culture, and laws should prevail? Yet this latter question has its own urgency among indigenous peoples. And the answer for both the plurinational character of the country and the future of Kichwa peoples themselves after 1990 came down to the same core issue: what it means, and what it takes, to be an Indian community.

Communities have come to matter so much for four different reasons. First, organizationally, CONAIE's power sprang from the relations it opened with and among local communities. The uprising succeeded because of the scale of unity among notoriously independent peasant comunas. This also left nonlocal leaders with an ongoing task. They had to listen to, develop plans with, and mobilize thousands of peasant community presidents, vice presidents, secretaries, and treasurers. Council members at the local level had the mirror image of this problem. Converting their neighbors' concerns into the sort of demands that CONAIE would fight for, they had to invest time in regional and national sessions to define a political agenda. Community leadership now sets up as an organizational bottleneck for national political development.

Second, the community was not only a means but the ends. Greater autonomy for separate communities lay at the heart of the alternative political model offered by CONAIE. But here another problem crops up. As discussed in chapter 2, CONAIE (1994, 55) argues that autonomy would guarantee indigenous communities the power to decide and control "the social, cultural, and economic order" in their own territories. Such self-determination seems workable for certain Amazonian groups largely in possession of their ancestral territory and living in important ways from the resources of that territory. Territorial autonomy, however, seems at best impractical, at worst totally misguided for a sierra community of a few hundred semi-proletariats on the side of the Pan-American Highway. Clear as an ideal, autonomy presents myriad problems as a practical matter.

Third, when Ecuador's indigenous movement does do important work building a new Indian identity, the resultant "indigenousness" itself frequently circles back to community. To be sure, leaders of the 1990 uprising saw identity in terms of history, captured in a shorthand way by the idea of 500 years of resistance.[2] And, broadly speaking, the Kichwa language,

2. "They have spoken much about the 500 years; this is present in the memories of all [protestors]. It was a history of exploitation. How do a people arrive at 500 years if we do not exist? We had to demonstrate that we were living," explained a leader from Cañar (Leon 1993, 142).

farming, and religious practices also define what it means to be native Andean. However, for many commentators, the integration of these elements that ultimately confers the status of indigenousness comes through community membership. When asked to comment on the role of women in general in the uprising, for example, Blanca Chancozo observed that women had always been present and participating in the politics of the community. In her testimony about women's leadership, however, she emphasized less their leadership than their identity as community member: "There was a woman killed. It was not that one could say she was the primary one or a leader, just one more member of the community and was, in that, the equal of all" (Leon 1993, 135).

Fourth, community confers an ethical legitimacy, especially in the struggle of minorities to gain full equality. Attaching the word "community" to a group underscores a "horizontal comradeship" among its differing members, a brotherly and sisterly common cause (Anderson 1991, 7). And unity contributes to the worthiness of rights claims in the eyes of outsiders. Indeed, the power of minority communities in particular depends on demonstrating large numbers of members united in their commitment to shared values over a long period of time (Tilly 1998).

Yet, here, too, Andean communities fit awkwardly into a paradigm of durable solidarity. Leaders avoid equating community with unity prior to some kind of dialogue among members. The right of dissent is taken for granted—hence the call for a meeting of all Protestants in Chimborazo to discuss whether to join the 1990 uprising, even as their Catholic neighbors and kin were occupying highways and marching on cities all around them. With growing religious divisions and migration, in fact, a single intrinsic moral good that all can call upon to unite members is hard to come by. Briefly put, the political worthiness of community unity that is important in the logic of social movement activism is not only elusive, but often openly disputed.

A deep pluralism is at work here. Indigenous communities, trade associations, provincial federations, and national organizations never cease having to adjust claims and counterclaims and deciding which point of view needs to prevail at the moment. The practicalities of agreement achieved in one instance, such as the levantamiento of 1990, need to be achieved anew in another, such as the 1994 national Minga por la Vida (Collective Work Party for Life). Put another way, rather than proving the enduring unity of a native way of being, moments of political agreement testify to the power to solidify relations and the skill to define circumstances in which one goal emerges as primary.[3]

In the remaining chapters, I make the case that Ecuadorian indigenous peoples have created these circumstances through their vernacular state-craft. They have set up the apparatus of local government keeping lists, forming councils, defending jurisdictions, and participating in regional federations. In all of this, differences and inequalities are not erased but organized, sometimes in lasting and iniquitous ways, sometimes in passing. Provincial, regional, and national organizations may contribute to this or-ganization. Outside activists visit, talk, listen, help develop demands, and then define appropriate contributions and work to track them and spend them. Yet, as intensive as such interventions may be, they depend not only on the prior existence of community institutions, but the constant leader-ship of residents to engage and legitimize the purpose at hand within the sphere of community politics. My exploration of both the weaknesses and the periodic effectiveness of this community-driven pluralism begins with a description of a single instance of the most emblematic activity of com-munity unity in the Ecuadorian Andes: the minga, or work party.

3. This description of community borrows Stanley Fish's (1980) discussion of interpretive communities.

PART II

Communities

FIGURE 10 Positioning the beams in Quiloa's new bridge, 1992

CHAPTER FIVE

Projects and Lists (Don't Shirk)

This community like any other, had to change and needed to change, but what if its own life, its own good had been the standard by which it changed, rather that the profit of distant entrepreneurs and corporations? — Wendell Berry, *Home Economics*

In 1988, José Vega took charge of his community's own good and sold a bold view of its future to representatives of the Spanish government's aid agency. Since painting employed ever more men from the sector, he argued, Quiloa's economy could grow through renovating its housing stock–building new homes with studios lit up by a bright window. Not only could painters improve their craft, but tourists would come to see a prospering community of whitewashed, tile-roofed adobe homes. Remarkably, the development authorities bought into the idea. In March 1991, forty Tiguan households (thirty-seven in Quiloa, two in Quindicilli, and one in Chami) began to receive materials, technical advice, and carpentry assistance from FUNHABIT (Ecuadorian Foundation for Habitat), an Ecuadorian rural housing NGO. By June all foundations had been dug, many poured and completed, and a few were crowned with chest-high walls made of specially engineered, compressed adobe blocks. The trade association president's new vision of his community was taking shape.

Ultimately, the success of this project depended on perpetually rallying community resources to match the donations. FUNHABIT had budgeted

the funds for the engineer, carpenters, adobe block–making press, timber, cement, glass, tiles, and whitewash. Yet, resources were tight. The
NGO was also managing the construction of a large communal house and
a childcare center in two other communities. FUNHABIT's directors depended on Quiloa's leadership for crucial organizational work. Allocating
the houses among contending families was left in community hands, as was
distributing the carpenter's time, dividing up materials, recording recipi-
ents, and elevating this project over other demands on residents' time. In all
this, the council would have to push for an endless series of mingas, or collective work parties, if the project were to stay on track for completion.

The promise of the mingas, in fact, had helped to secure outsiders'
funding in the first place. They signaled the seriousness of Quiloans' participation. Further, for donors, whether private or state agencies, such
work parties also give projects a native authenticity, the spirit of collective life that gets associated with indigenous people. For council members,
running a minga was a chore. It required identifying participants, organizing them according to project needs, tracking involvement over time, cor-
recting for substitutions and balancing accounts. All of this in turn hinged
on the most basic task of governance: keeping lists. This chapter follows
one work party and its tactical moves in detail. While indirectly linked to
the housing project, the minga had actually been called to rebuild a small
bridge. I review where the effort threatened to unravel, how it became a
vehicle for underlying resentment, and where it sparked new conflict. I
then go on to describe the minga's success and show the way lists helped
make it happen.

The Bridge Minga, Quiloa, 1992

In June 1991, I spent two days riding in FUNHABIT's pickup truck. We
were ferrying materials out of building supply businesses in Latacunga in
the central Andean valley, up through the *paramo* (high moorland) and
its shifting clouds and into the parish of Tigua. On the two-hour trip, fog
and mist closed the view down to the dark, scrubby vegetation and over-
grazed grasses at the edge of the highway. The road then twisted down
through the community of Casa Quemada and the Tigua Valley opened
out in front of us. After the paramo, it seemed to teem with agricultural
activity. Hundreds of peasant plots had been stitched into steep hillsides
with lines of cacti.

We coasted down to the valley floor and passed clumps of trees that sheltered farm buildings. These belonged to the hacienda, which was still largely intact among its flat bottomlands on the edge of the Yanacachi River. The wind whispered here, passing quietly through the farm's pine groves and across grassy fields. Only when it crossed the hacienda's boundaries did it seem to take a harder edge, scraping across the dusty plazas of peasant communities and rattling through the brown-grey eucalyptus leaves that offered thin shade to the houses clumped together up on the ridges.

Our destination of Quiloa on the valley's western ridge was notable for its continued isolation smack in the middle of things. In 1991, these homes had no electricity, no running water, and no road link. Most traffic in and out of Quiloa moved by foot on a rocky path that angled up more than a kilometer to meet the highway where it turned out of the Tigua Valley and began its steep drop into Zumbagua. When residents hired trucks to bring in building materials or ship out crops, the vehicles motored out of Chami up a grass path and along the ridge. The domestic water supply was a seasonal stream that flowed most of the year in a narrow gully that split the community. Among the communities of Tigua, Quiloa stood out for combining all the infrastructure deficits to be found in the valley in a single sector.

On our supply trips, we were bringing cement and roofing tiles. When I was not unloading, I toured some existing homes. Under their tin roofs and behind earth walls, the owners kept their hopes for progress protected. In all, I entered eleven houses whose *total* furnishings included seven gas stoves, six beds, five tables for painting, two benches, and one lidded chest for clothes. The stoves surprised me. Cooking-gas bottles weighed twenty-five to thirty kilograms and wrenched the arms and backs of those who had to lug them home. Quiloa residents faced a trek of over a kilometer or else had to pay more to hire a truck than the gas itself would cost. Little used, the stoves seemed optimistic wagers that a road would soon serve Quiloa.

I cannot say I shared the hope. After several trips to the sector, I gave up on research in Tigua when I realized the apparent busyness of the valley was the optical illusion of an overused peasant landscape. The hundreds of small fields did not translate into hundreds of toiling farmers. Crops had been left in the care of others to grow in the mists and winds of the valley. Migration had quieted the community and too many of the residents that I wanted to interview had left. I headed north and spent the rest of the summer listening to the ways Otavalos produced crafts, traveled abroad, and repatriated profits into their own brand of modern domestic architecture (Colloredo-Mansfeld 1994).

In July 1992, I returned to Quiloa, more serious about learning about Tigua and its art. I had an open set of questions about expressive practice—architecture, painting, family celebrations—and how people could use it to defend a community. The FUNHABIT project was still going on and I again rode up with a supply truck, this time with my wife, Chesca, to negotiate with council members about doing the research and finding a place to stay. The project engineers set up a meeting with Maria Estela Vega and her husband Manuel Vega.[1] While we sat eating hardboiled eggs dipped into little cones of salt on a tin plate, the engineer and Maria Estela worked out terms that led to us moving into a small spare house in their tidy compound.

In the first few quiet days, Chesca and I drew a map, learned about the community kitchen funded by a state program, and saw enrollment lists for the bilingual school. From all this, we calculated the population of the community to be about 300, living in seventy-two house compounds. During our stay, between sixty and seventy inhabitants were in Quito. Yet, Quiloa was unusually full at the moment. The FUNHABIT project had lured people back to the community. In our third day there, residents took advantage of the returned migrants and organized to rebuild the narrow footbridge that spanned the small central gully. With the president of the community in Quito, other *cabildo* (council) officers took on the project. Among these was a young man named Fausto Vega who sported a new haircut, a clean hat, and a thick denim jacket. Quiet spoken and quite formal towards us, Fausto was also very patient. In our initial days in Quiloa, I circled back by his family's house regularly to find out what was going on.

In retrospect, I see Fausto was in an awkward spot. While elected in Quiloa, he was a formal member of the peasant community of Chimbacucho where Julio Toaquiza lived. That was where his wife was born and where the two of them "paid their minga," as Fausto put it. That is, they participated in and got formal credit for collective work days in Chimbacucho's community projects. Fausto professed to like Quiloa best; he was born there and his parents lived there, and he would ultimately inherit land there. Chimbacucho, though, had its political and cultural act in or-

1. Maria Estela Vega, Manuel Vega, and Fausto Vega are all pseudonyms.

der. "It is well organized," said Fausto. His faith in Chimbacucho's political potential rested in one man, the painting cooperative president, Alfredo Toaquiza. Son of the founding painter, Alfredo had established himself among the foremost painters of his generation in a commissioned project for a chapel in Tigua in the mid 1980s. He also had organized painters to achieve greater aesthetic recognition and political clout. Just months earlier, Alfredo had led a parish-wide meeting of community *dirigentes* (Sp. council members). He used the venue to raise consciousness about Tigua's development. Fausto remembered Alfredo diagramming step-by-step the sharp distinction between mestizo and indigenous advancement. Using a staircase of development, he showed that while mestizos had education, cars, houses with floors, sufficient food, and hospitals, Indians had nothing (see figure 11).

Fausto's rendition of the two-sided sketch and his accompanying effort to explain it to me now strikes me for its similarity to the anthropologist John Watanabe's conversation with his Maya informant in Guatemala a decade earlier (see chapter 2). Each moment entailed an anthropologist being tutored in Indian deprivation. Each informant-turned-instructor emphasized the gap as prelude to insisting on change. And, they each mapped improvements that would seize the benefits of the mestizo world. Visually, though, the staircase schema credited to Alfredo communicated more than just emulation of mestizos. To begin with, the path ahead progresses, step-by-step. It begins with basic needs and ends with the luxury of a car. Second, with each pass up the line, indigenous people move away from mestizos to their own modern future. Third, councils preside over this change. Alfredo had insisted that indigenous people had to organize, sell their goods cooperatively, and force the government to bring in electricity and better roads. Alfredo's schema did not push capital and individual sacrifice so much as collective struggle. Fausto came out of that meeting recommitted to working for community development as Alfredo did in Chimbacucho.

And yet, despite Fausto's allegiance to this charismatic leader and his vision of progress, Fausto neither painted nor actually lived in Chimbacucho. Rather he and his wife and children made their home in Quito. There he earned a living as a member of a cargo-handling cooperative in the city's main bus station. Fausto, in other words, was nominally Quiloan, formally Chimbacuchen, and practically Quiteñan. He ratified all these identities through organizational ties. Being from three places, though,

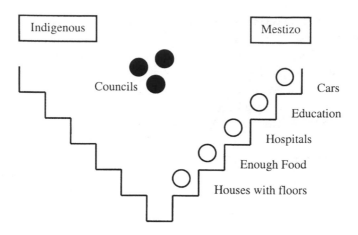

FIGURE 11 Fausto Vega's explanation of ethnic disadvantage

also means seeming to be from none. Fausto had neither a record as a
council leader nor a steady presence as a resident in Quiloa the day he
headed out to get the bridge rebuilt. One sign of his weakness was the
division of tasks that day. The vice-president, a stern, tall man with his hat
wedged so tightly on his head against the wind that his hair splayed under
the brim, took it upon himself to call people out to work. Fausto stood by
to see who would assemble.

Wincing against blasts of wind and dust, Fausto waited in the community plaza among a cluster of residents, writing participants' names
in his notebook. A group of men lost patience with the record keeping
and headed off and destroyed the old footbridge. Before Fausto and the
other council members could redirect them, the FUNHABIT supply truck
arrived. It carried the first shipment of long, thin, wooden tile runners,
enough to roof about two houses. The crowd abandoned the bridge minga
and individuals claimed priority for use of the runners. Unable to con-
vince any homebuilder to concede a share of this shipment, the engineer
and Fausto decided to subdivide the runners among all claimants. Almost
an hour was lost in carefully counting out each of the runners into thirty-
seven piles (it would not be the last time houses in the outlying communities would be deprived of materials). Recording who had received how
many, Fausto waited for the bundles to be carried off and stored before
pressing on with the bridge.

A FUNHABIT carpenter then discovered that the gas stove he had
brought up to his temporary housing had been stolen. The carpenter had

never showed much enthusiasm for the project. The unknown thief had now pushed the man to the point of quitting. Given the number of families who had been left out of the housing project, Quiloa had a long list of suspects who stood to gain more from a purloined stove than from a happy builder. More conferences among council members and FUNHABIT technicians followed the discovery of the theft. Finally a search party, accompanied by Fausto, set off to hunt for the stove.

Meanwhile wildcat parties of community members had fanned out across Quiloa armed with axes, looking for suitable trees that could be claimed for the bridge. One group swarmed across Maria Estela Vega and Manuel Vega's patio, making for their windbreak that was anchored by an unusually thick pine tree. Manuel pleaded with the vice president to spare the big tree. Maria Estela had no patience for the protocols of titles and councils. She shouted directly to the axmen about how her family needed the wood to carve masks to sell to tourists. They accepted her point and set off to bring down other trees.

Others who mounted a less spirited defense saw their timber crash. Four large trees with trunks measuring thirty to forty-five centimeters in diameter were felled by the end of the morning. Fausto explained they needed so much wood as their plan was not to simply replace the footbridge but reconstruct a new bridge that could handle cars. The residents wanted to make it possible for tourists to drive in from the road—a route now marked by braided single tracks that wove across tilted slabs of rock on a steep hillside.

The weight of large trees finally forced everyone to cooperate. Yet even so, the burden of carrying the logs fell unevenly. The wider work party cajoled two labor-worn men long accustomed to heavy lifting to step up. The peasant communities where I had lived in the 1990s had a few such men. Recognized back then by their stooped shoulders, patched polyester sports coats, buttonless shirts, and oversize shoes, they were socially, if not always occupationally, market porters. When the bitterly envious visited a *brujo* (Sp. witch) to curse away the fortune of some prosperous neighbor and reduce him to a life of "carrying potatoes," they had in mind such men as these.

Once community members had recruited two men to raise and shoulder the thick butt of the trunk, women and men lined up behind them and together dragged the log to the gully. Now the premature destruction of the bridge cost everyone. Had it been in place the new logs could have been ferried across and easily positioned. No bridge meant transporting the trunk down and out of the gully on paths etched by sheep hooves. The work party pivoted the log around and aimed for a narrow path. It proved too steep and the momentum of the large eucalyptus trunk ploughed the yoked men at the front end of the log into the gully's far wall. At this point, they had had enough. They quit, unwinding the ropes from their shoulders, and marched out of the gully. With the work stalled, people sat down and handed bundles of salty, boiled potatoes and toasted haba beans among family members.

In the meantime, a lone axman had set upon an especially large eucalyptus tree that held the gully wall together about 150 meters above the bridge location. He had cut a deep wedge halfway through the trunk before the vice president and others shouted him off, saying he was wasting his time and everyone else's. If the claim on the tree was legitimate, forcing all the mingueros to move one more trunk was not. The axman gave up, leaving the wounded tree standing.

In the afternoon, residents hauled four other trunks to the bridge site. With ropes and timbers, they managed to get two of the lighter logs to span the gully. People then called it a day, leaving two other logs on the side of the gully and the large one sticking up out of it. Finally, Fausto got out his notebook and duly recorded the participation of forty-two families (of approximately seventy-two potential households) in the bridge-making minga on the 27th of July, 1992. Absent families would be later approached and asked to make a monetary contribution toward the cost of materials and thereby get participation credit. Weeks later down in Quito, in fact, when Chesca and I distributed photos of the event to some of the participants who had likewise returned to the city, Fausto snatched up the extras. "With these," he said, "I will show how we worked together. I'll get some more collaboration." Our snapshots became one more tool of community administration (see figure 10).

On the day of the minga itself, we returned to our household compound. Over the next twenty-four hours, we witnessed the curious final allocation of the household resources that had been put in play during the work party. That night, Maria Estela boiled the evening soup over a fire kindled from the carefully counted tile runners that FUNHABIT brought up. The timber's productive life had ended not as a layer in a new roof but as a political token in a household's tenacious defense of its participation in a development project. The next day, Manuel chopped down their tall pine tree. Sawing it into ten chunks, he whittled two of them down to misshapen lumps before Maria Estela dismissed his effort and went off to

Zumbagua herself to buy unpainted masks from a carver. The tree's last real use had been achieved by Maria Estela when she used it as a bulwark to defend her household economy against an overreaching community project.

Over the next few days, the community finalized its work. When the FUNHABIT engineer returned with more materials, the council convinced him to drive them around to Zumbagua to buy cement for the footings for the cross beams. Within a week, work parties had mixed and poured the concrete, set the logs, spiked thick timbers across the top, and finished the bridge. Fausto, though, did not see the final achievement for months. He had left two days before its completion. He needed to get back to work in the bus station.

*   *   *

Mingas such as this one testify to a shared material life that emerges amid Tiguans' individual careers. This joint base is a kind of human-made commons that underwrites the continuing vitality of private holdings, largely by interconnecting them (Mayer 2002, 124). While I am using the idea of a base in a narrow way, I am drawing on Gudeman's (2001, 7) wider conception of a base as a community's "lasting resources (such as land and water), produced things, ideational constructs such as knowledge, technology, laws, practices, skills and customs." Indeed, among various mutual labors of Andean community life—planting, harvesting, house building, fiesta sponsoring—community mingas serve specifically to create, maintain, or upgrade physical networks of potable water pipes, electric lines, and paths. Councils may also call out mingas to prepare central meeting areas to receive important guests or spruce up soccer fields and volleyball courts for tournaments. In all these cases, community mingas are precisely those efforts, often called *obras* (Sp. public works; cf. Serrano 1993), that increase circulation of all kinds, whether of water, electricity, news, entertainment, or people.

Quiloa's bridge minga's full sequence of acts, though, went beyond removing the old bridge, gathering materials, and building a new one. It also entailed a woman shouting down unruly men to protect her tree, wildcat axmen spurning direction, the yoked porters in rebellion, and stove-hunting distractions. Neither accidental nor incidental, these conflicts speak of the varied interests of men and women, of urban laborers and peasant farmers, of project beneficiaries and the excluded.

Fausto, for instance, hoped to fashion himself as a community officer after his mentor Alfredo. To do so, he had to nudge Quiloa's development up a step. Yet, Maria Estela refused to grant him much respect. In the confrontation on her patio, she did not dignify him and his office with a direct appeal to defend her pine. The genders of the actors—male council member versus female dissenter—are not coincidental. International donors, national NGOs, and local councils have mutually reinforced each other's authority in ways that worked against women. Men came to dominate community organizations. As they lost jobs and commercial opportunities in the recessions of the 1980s, men looked for both new resources for their households and new channels for their careers. Serving on community councils often granted return migrants special access to development projects. In personal terms, such service recognized men for their Spanish skills, intercultural knowledge, and administrative know-how. Peasant organizations formalized a masculine public sphere. For example, although formal, registered membership in a comuna is open to all adult men and women, in the mid 1980s, less than 10 percent of comuneros were women (FIDA 1989, 166, as cited in Deere 2001). More telling, in an analysis of 2,253 comunas and over 3,000 other base organizations, the Ministry of Agriculture and Livestock found that women made up less than 1 percent of the leaders (Deere and Leon 2001 52n40).

Women's losses are particularly ironic. They had taken on increasing responsibility for the reproduction of the subsistence economy with the rise of male migration (Weismantel 1988). Moreover, even as men earned more cash and secured openings in the market economy, women had maintained equality and economic authority within the household (Hamilton 1998). Yet, their economic contributions within their homes did not translate into political power.

The minga disruptions speak to other latent divisions. Frequently, those on the periphery of active peasant jurisdictions—often poorer households more dependent on their farming for income—found themselves committed by councils to development projects that stopped short of their neighborhoods. Advantages accrued at the center; households at the edges never started up the staircase. This past neglect sets up skepticism toward new projects. If, for instance many painters with their new homes insisted on a car-worthy road, the men yoked to the log saw less urgency. No tourist would visit them; their meager market purchases would never warrant a delivery truck. Certainly a road would be public good they could use, but a project that brought in potable water, for example, would deliver much greater benefits. These geographical mismatches in time spent on a project and rewards gained can turn to fission, as marginal zones seek to elect their own councils, achieve their own legal recognition, and secure more appropriate projects.

Such power hierarchies within and between Kichwa communities were not simply vestiges of the pre–land reform era, but the expression of a new indigenous social world taking shape in the politics of comunas, cooperatives, and associations. In the course of their public works project, no single value related to land or community could be appealed to in order to unite people. Coordinating residents rested on the few lean resources that the council has: the authority bestowed through democratic election, the ability to levy fines, the incentive of some external resources, the personal charisma of leaders, and the keeping of lists of participants. In fact, the last of these may be the most useful technology.

To be sure, a list is a pretty thin mechanism to engineer feelings of belonging. As James Scott (1998) writes, statecraft, not community solidarity, features elaborate list making—tax and tithe rolls, property rolls, conscription lists, and censuses. To accomplish its tasks, the state has to find a way to systematize identities and "create legible people" primarily through the use of patronyms (Scott 1998, 65). Yet, in managing modern peasant community politics, lists have a hidden power to create a limited currency, minga points, and a distinct sphere of exchange, the peasant comuna, where such currency can convert individual resources into shared development. Lists achieve this power, not only for the way they single out and specify people, as Scott would have it, but for three ways that they generalize individuals into community members.

Lists

To begin with, in an Andean community, the use of first and last names supposedly makes people knowable to outsiders, but it in fact renders them anonymous to insiders. These are too redundant for everyday use. A Quiloan ledger, for instance, offers an unceasing array of Cuyo Vegas, Vega Cuyos, and Vega Vegas. In practice, only officials and anthropologists use these. Real people use nicknames. My personal queries often required back translation into these monikers:

RCM: Did you serve on the council with Fausto Vega?
RESPONDENT: Which Fausto Vega?
RCM: "Potato Blight"
RESPONDENT: Oh, no, not with him, but . . .

Second, if lists seem to rob people of the individuality that their nick-name so pithily communicates, these records also strip history down to its barest minimum. Traditionally, in Andean scholarship, the founding assumption of community studies was historical continuity, and the in-digenous concept used to guide inquiries into it was the *ayllu* (Orta 2001, 199). In the broadest sense, ayllus were "named, landholding collectivi-ties" (Salomon and Urioste 1991). The act of identifying with an ayllu located the individual, not only in physical space but in the flow of time. For theoretical and political reasons, current ethnographic study has dis-tanced itself from the ayllu; scholars want to avoid essentializing Andean communities as timeless, kin-ordered places (Weismantel 2006). Even so, in writing on the movement, activists and researchers alike continue to take the kinship and social ties of rural communities as a starting point for modern organizing (see chapter 4).

Conditioned by such assumptions, I found list keeping jarring to ob-serve. The lists cut membership down to discrete moments of community development. Work in past projects may set someone up as a potential participant in the next one, but it does not guarantee it. Indeed, many projects start with leaders tramping around their sector reassembling their community on paper. They find some residents in the core have switched allegiances and work for other sectors; households from elsewhere may opt in. Finally, only a steady stream of volunteered labor, materialized as a line of "Xs" recorded by the secretary, will substantiate membership.

Third, lists also level status in a way that makes people convertible. One woman might be a fifty-four-year-old grandmother, an experienced farmer, and leader in past confrontations with the hacienda. Another might be sixteen, unmarried, and living with her parents. Both, however, are alike on the rolls. Households frequently make use of this reduction-ism to adapt whatever disposable resources they have to get on the list (see Mayer 2002, 125, for similar observations about Peruvian communal work). I know a family in the Otavalo area, for example, who routinely call their youngest son home from whichever town he is selling crafts in to work in the potable water mingas. The father has Parkinson's disease; the mother sells cooked potatoes on minga days to the other laborers.

The young man is chronically underemployed. By working in his parents' stead, he can convert his idleness into water rights. On the other hand, in Quiloa, a few families who have cash from profits on painting sales often choose to pay the minga fines rather than work. They buy credit on the lists without giving up a day's painting.

Lists are thus a device to strip away individual uniqueness to create a generalized resident made exchangeable through labor value. A new legibility? Peasant list making is more about an old commodity: the minga point. Fausto Vega clearly conceptualized the minga in this way when he told me that he "paid the minga" in Chimbacucho even as he recorded mingas for Quiloa. This commoditization lets communities gain power from their rosters and ledgers to defend their territory. The councils can convert the diverse economic and social capital of individual households into a common labor pool, creating a mechanism of public finance through their notebooks. The minga lists, in fact, have added power. They limit further circulation of resources and residents. If you pay your minga in Quiloa, you get nothing in Chami. If you work for the bridge, you do not have a claim to electricity. If you work hard now, you nevertheless must return to work hard later. Credit does not carry forward to the next project.

That is, minga lists tackle the problem of conflicting interests by creating a special domain of value. Belonging to Quiloa does not mean having to subscribe to a single unifying idea of the "Quiloan." Rather, it entails pledging time and effort to accumulate the narrow currency needed to improve one's life within the sector. Different resources can be used to get ahold of these points; different interests can be served by them. The state or an NGO can trigger the organization of a minga by putting up materials and expertise that the community must in turn match with their own contributions. Yet Quiloans themselves are the arbiters of the value that is put in play. Neither rival sectors nor the state itself can divert the currency of participation to other projects. The lists offer leaders of a community an instrument to channel action, lengthen or shorten commitments, and raise or lower their cash value via fines.

The lists activate possibilities of local control. In his analysis of the modern use of *khipus*, or knotted cord records, in the Peruvian community of Tupicocha, Salomon comes to a related conclusion.[2] He argues that more

2. An intriguing example of a list form that bears aesthetic, ritual, and social potentialities is the khipu. Khipus are bunches of dyed knotted strings, most famously associated with Inka record keeping (Urton 2002). Khipus, though, predate the Inka and continue to be used for

FIGURE 12 Quiloa's bridge, seven years later in 1999

than being simple recording devices, the khipus were operational devices (Salomon 2002, 315). They were a means of strategy—game boards—not just a series of events or objects. Throughout the contemporary Andes, where cheap school supplies have taken the place of artfully tied cord accounts, record keeping can still allow a community to operate on terms its members influence.

Community work, the kind that moves people up their staircase of progress, is costly, contentious, and administratively demanding. The col-

---

complex purposes today. Residents of San Andres de Tupicocha in Huarochiri province in central Peru, for example, still use cord records to materially link community organization and social identities. Elements of their practices have been recorded in the only textual source on a preconquest Andean religious system written in Quechua, the Huarochiri script. Intriguingly, the text mentions khipus used for the similar task of census taking at community gatherings, for which today's minga lists are used. Frank Salomon (2002) reports that from the manuscript "we learn that when the people of Concha Village went to visit the lake deities that owned their water, they 'took a quipu account of all the people who were absent and began to worship'" (Salomon and Urioste 1991).

lective, unpaid labor mobilized in a minga is too tightly pledged to the construction of desired services, too carefully tracked by households, and too systematically monitored by community authority to be glibly described as a voluntary, cooperative effort. Indeed, the bridge minga suggests that the central task of collective work is better thought of as negotiation than cooperation. Of course, people do come together, sacrifice household resources, and build up their community's infrastructure. In Quiloa's case, people take real pride in their accomplishments—often because they know what has to be overcome to make the minga go. And making it go is the work of the list keepers. If communities create lists; the lists themselves are the hidden ligaments of community bonds. Yet, for all that, the political presence that communities maintain in relation to one another and the state needs a more public and unified quality than what lists provide. Consequently, the growth of any community comes to depend on the practices of territorial jurisdiction, a topic taken up in the next chapter.

FIGURE 13 Symbols of indigenous sovereignty: flag of multiculturalism, werewolf mask, wrist-watch, and rooster, La Compañia, 1994

CHAPTER SIX

Justice, Jurisdiction, and Race (Don't Steal)

Self-respect is a question of recognizing that anything worth having has a price.
—Joan Didion

This chapter and the next one examine two instances of popular justice that occurred in the Otavalo countryside in 1993. In the first episode, I explore how the interplay between place and politics organized Otavalos' confrontations with "outsiders" to unify the sprawling community of La Compañía. In the second event in Ariasucu, I illustrate how even in moments of convergence, the symbols of intra-ethnic subordination are worked out. In both cases, I am concerned less with the content of indigenous law and judicial ritual than I am with the consequences for community statecraft of pursuing justice locally. "Rough justice" creates leaders and fixes the territories of their power, even as it scars bodies and scares authorities.

Judicial practice brings into sharp focus a central question of community self-determination: what is the practical extent of community authority? The tactics of Latin America's social movements since the 1980s have elevated this issue. By insisting on cultural recognition and by redirecting broad civil rights struggle toward narrower legal battles for land, native and Afro-descendent groups linked politics and territory in intimate ways. Bettina Ng'weno (2007, 31) notes, "In Latin America, the political reforms that have recognized multi-cultural, pluri-ethic nations . . . have invariably recognized special territorial and property rights for specific groups defined by cultural distinction." The linkage solved an urgent problem as both native and black peoples in Andean nations moved from being "legally silenced racial groups to legally vocal visible ethnic groups" (Ng'weno 2007, 13). The successes, though, create two new problems: How can collectivities inscribe politically meaningful territories on the landscape? When they do, does such a territory ultimately serve the people or the state?

Indeed, blacks and Indians have pushed demands for local autonomy as far as they have, in part, for the way states have advanced their own agendas through empowering communities. Nikolas Rose (1999, 167) argues that "community" is an "element in particular styles of political government." Because of the importance of communities in keeping order during the second half of the twentieth century, "a whole array of little devices and techniques have been invented to make communities real"(Rose 1999, 189). Rose observes that "boundaries and distinctions have to be emplaced; these spaces have to be visualized, mapped, surveyed and mobilized." For Rose, such work occurs in "cultural space." In Latin America, community building moves from culture to physical space and literal issues of visualizing territories, mobilizing people, and fixing boundaries. This chapter takes up the problem of emplacement. By describing how one group brought a jurisdiction to political life, I show it is at once a practical claim, a material project, and a cultural intervention that assigns meaning and value (Ford 2001). When used to restore justice to a vulnerable people, a successfully asserted jurisdiction can be the crowning achievement of community activism.

Justice and Vulnerability in a Neoliberal Economy

After at least four incident-free years in southern Imbabura province, December 1993 contained two occasions during which peasant communities captured and punished thieves. The most publicized of these occurred just before Christmas in La Compañía, a place of about 4,500 inhabitants that spread out along the northern shores of Lake San Pablo and reached up Mount Imbabura. Reflecting the region's disparities, La Compañía's upper neighborhoods of one-room peasant huts still lacked electricity and piped water. Fields were choked by rocks that had spilled out from the ancient collapse of the mountainside above the community. Most paths were narrow, closed in by bushes and fit only for foot traffic. Meanwhile, the lower community blossomed with the wealth of the handicraft trade. Large two- and three-story homes lined the main road that rimmed the lake. Bothered by traffic, residents had taken to mounding dirt on the tarmac, creating speed bumps to slow the growing number of cars owned by textile entrepreneurs who traveled back and forth to Otavalo.

This main road was the scene of the robbery. The incident began when three men from Ibarra, the provincial capital, held up a local resident at gunpoint and stole the motorcycle he had been riding. The victim screamed for help and nearby residents rushed into the road, caught the thieves, and discovered other stolen goods in their possession. The community council took charge, locking up their prisoners at the school. Tension mounted while current and past officials debated what sort of justice should be served and by whom. Little could be taken for granted. As García (1999, 4) points out, "in no way are the laws of indigenous communities a stable and eternal corpus of norms and judicial rules recognized by the collectivity but instead are in constant transformation in accord with the internal conditions of each community and the wider society."

Without any formal plaza or large community building, La Compañía took care of its business in an irregular grass plaza ringed by the bus road, volleyball courts, an evangelical protestant church, a school, and a one-room health clinic. The foot traffic flowing through this area expanded as residents came by to confirm rumors of the capture. When the police arrived, the crowd converted from curious to militant. People filled the road and forced the police to turn around. At their head, several residents insisted to the officers that it was their community and thus their right to deal with the situation according to their own traditions. While little else had been agreed upon, the community was adamant that the police had no jurisdiction here. Once police left, residents opened the case to local opinion, heard out the elders, activists, and others. They eventually settled on a sequence of punishments involving baths in the icy waters of Lake San Pablo, stinging nettles, and ultimately whips.

If these judicial measures sprang from a local sense of violation, they also tapped into a broader current of social discontent. Indeed, popular justice throughout South America has been fueled by the political losses accompanying "structural adjustments" of the region's new economic order. Weakened by debt and committed to cutting the subsidies for small-hold farmers and urban working classes, states had broken their compact with the poor (Green 1995). Crime increased, yet national and provincial governments lost the will and legitimacy to safeguard the civil order (Huggins 1991). The numbers suggested a stark relationship in Ecuador. In 1980, workers' monthly salary reached $211.51 (1990 dollars). By 1992, after ten years of austerity measures, unemployment stood at 8 percent, underemployment at 46 percent, and monthly wages had declined to $65.87 (Maya Diaz 1995). Meanwhile, over the same period, violent crime had increased 192 percent (Maya Diaz 1995).

The popular press obsessively reported on robberies, assaults, and murder and all segments of society have felt progressively more insecure. Coping with the criminal justice system, either as a victim, potential victim, or as an intimate of an accused criminal, increasingly shaped family obligations and community involvements in Ecuador. Extralegal justice correspondingly mushroomed, spanning forms that included vigilantism backed by conservative elites to spontaneous beatings of pick-pocketing street kids, and "communal lynchings" (Benevides and Fischer-Ferreira 1991, 34). Indeed, Goldstein (2004) has argued that popular justice making in Bolivia has transformed into a political spectacle of vulnerability and rage. In the violence of the lynching, victimized populations put the state on notice, warning it to live up to its "self-proclaimed obligations to its citizens" (Goldstein 2004, 217) .

Yet more than banditry pushes Andean communities to pursue home-grown justice. In the 1980s in Peru, for example, peasants in the northern Andes steadily expanded the responsibilities of anti-rustling patrols until they had created local assemblies capable of quenching residents' thirst for judicial participation (Starn 1999). Why then? While citing the importance of regional and national influences, Starn (1999, 113–14) argues for the decisive impact of local factors. Rural residents urgently needed a system that could deal with the bickering, betrayals, and property conflicts that beset their communities. Such participatory assemblies replaced the disdainful and perfunctory attention that peasants normally got from provincial judges.

For northern Andean peoples, enforcing local moral codes enacts colonial-rooted social truths. Historically, rural communities have exercised a collective self-defense against rival communities, abusive landlords, and authorities (Mayer 1991, 470). While distinct from the traditional, judicially recognized right to customary law, such vigilantism is political action. It has been regarded by both protagonists and the wider society as "the ultimate recourse against exploitation of Indians" (Mayer 1991, 470). These episodes, though, often beget bloody state responses, creating cycles of conflict that divide indigenous peasants from mestizos—and bind that ethnic division to violence (Orlove 1994; Poole 1994a; 1994b; 1994c).[1]

In contrast to many Andean regions, Otavalo stands out for its relative nonviolence. Nevertheless, police incursions and self-defense have stamped interethnic relations here as elsewhere with their imprint of suspicion and hostility. The oral history of Agato and Ariasucu records a deadly encounter between police and local residents in the 1930s. The police had arrived on horseback to arrest residents who had assaulted two tax officials during their trip to the area. Turned back by stone-throwing residents, the police were racing down out of the community, until (as I was pointedly told) a Spanish-speaking Indian informed the police that his neighbors had no guns. Thus betrayed, the residents suffered a renewed attack that ended after the police murdered a woman.[2]

The 1930s event foreshadows elements of 1990s judicial activism. At the time of their attacks on tax assessors, many Agato residents were commercial artisans. This is the community, after all, where the entrepreneur Alfonso Chiza (chapter 2) was raised. Residents were not isolated subsistence farmers. Yet the confrontation cast both weavers and officials in the roles of the unceasing fight between "Indian" and "Hispanic" (Gose 1994). Old narratives came to life: the urban, white-mestizo population fretted about being under siege by Indians, indigenous people despaired of the violation of their territory (cf. Orlove 1998), and the intermediate character—the bilingual native—was capable of betraying either side. For all its connections to neoliberal political and economic circumstances, justice making still unfolds through these narratives of the "primordial encounter" (Gose 1994). Why narratives of defense of native territory should be so compelling, even for those indigenous families who have been making a living in Otavalo, Bogotá, and Los Angeles in recent years, is taken up below.

1. As Poole (1994b) notes, "each (violent or non-violent) negotiation of power is referred back for authorization to the set of utterances or discourses about ethnicity, race, and power which have been generated in the past, by other specific acts of violence."

2. This story was recounted to me by Pedro Vasquez as we toured the boundary that divided Ariasucu from Agato and got to an open patch of grazing ground where these events are said to have taken place.

Crimes, Commodities, and Place

Seemingly a given, the commitment to place is noteworthy given the long-term waning of the economic power of rural regions. As maize fields break up through inheritance, farming in La Compañía has devolved into little more than kitchen gardening and sharecropping. Similarly, independent artisanship yields to temporary piecework. Trading autonomy for a sure sale, weavers take wholesalers' orders for bag straps, woven wall hangings, and other mass-produced commodities. Often, these craftsmen then break the monotony of this bulk manufacture with periodic forays into cities. There they sell small inventories of tourist handicrafts or look for wage work. The paltry weaving wages hardly provide for a household's cash needs let alone desire for advancement, inducing many of La Compañía's daughters and sons to circulate through expatriate communities of peddlers, artisans, laborers, and musicians. They relocate to Quito, Bogotá, Cali, Panama City, Barcelona, Amsterdam, and elsewhere, staying for a few weeks to several years (Lema, Saltos, Barrionuevo, Chimbo, and Garcia 2000). Some do very well, while others never tap a profitable niche and must cut their losses, return home, weave, peddle crafts, save up money, and look for the next opportunity.

In short, La Compañía's work has become deterritorialized in two senses. First, the combination of migration and ephemeral markets has divorced careers from place, as men and women move back and forth across international borders, among cities, and around rural sectors in search of jobs (cf. Kearney 1996). Second, the careers of any one place, even (or perhaps especially) in a rural community, no longer confer a shared habitus related to work. One household might earn income from its looms, making *fajas* (Sp. belts) to be sold in highland weekly markets, their neighbors might live from the sale of used clothes in Otavalo, while another from their neighborhood might work the night shift in the provincial capital as a security guard. Ever narrower specializations and their increasingly disparate rewards have undermined common habits of work.

Yet, the deterritorialization of careers does not mean their dematerialization. Even as residents have moved off to compete in far-flung marketplaces, they return to build their homes and La Compañía is now one of Otavalo's most populated sectors. Consequently, La Compañía becomes defined less through production than consumption. The merchant's showy "trophy" house, the peasant-artisan's new television, and the maid's celebration of a baptism all materialize uneven earnings as tangible, though greatly varying, accomplishments. Through architecture, furnishings, and fiestas, people claim status. But more than that, they use commodities to create the cultural and social continuities that production lacks (Colloredo-Mansfeld 1999; Miller 1995). If the expenditures are personal, the effect is collective. Architecture, even among the most economical cement block homes, encodes a neighborhood's history of high-status styles and shared tastes to achieve an aesthetic tied to place (Colloredo-Mansfeld 1994); fiestas join hosts, compadres, and guests through baskets of cooked chicken, guinea pig and potatoes, cauldrons of soup, and days of amplified music, allowing a reimagining of shared values and accomplishments (Wibbelsman 2005).

Crime itself indexes this newly empowered consumer sphere. When thieves start traveling from the city to the country, not to rustle livestock but to steal motorcycles, radios, and money from residents who earn that same cash down in town, the provincial economic terrain has clearly shifted. In these circumstances, stealing such possessions is an especially grave deed. It strikes at the means of belonging, the symbols that substantiate self-worth as a community member. Small wonder that neighbors instantly and forcefully responded.

From Improvised Justice to Sovereign Territory

With infrequent precedents and no formal training, the challenge for protagonists in matters of community justice lies in fashioning the "vision, symbols, and procedures" of their protest and punishment so as to assert the widest possible relevance of these actions to community life (Starn 1992, 92). Improvising community justice, the protagonists creatively draw upon varied traditions as they interact with often several different audiences (Jackson 1995, 19). The scope of this improvisation is, however, limited. New legal practices that fail to work in "experientially familiar terms" (Watanabe 1992, 14) risk seeming idiosyncratic, or worse, vindictive. In the cases considered here, familiarity came to rest on the locality of events and how these got narrated by community residents and observers alike. Articulated through notions of place, the meaning of events shifted from matters of law and order to a broader struggle for sovereignty over indigenous affairs.

On the second day following the capture, residents followed as the three prisoners were marched down to the lake and scrubbed with stinging nettles. Returned to the schoolyard, the thieves were held amid a crowd of about a hundred adults, scores of school children, and several food vendors who had arrived to cater to the onlookers. My wife Chesca happened to be passing by in a bus at that point and said that she thought it was a festive school gathering, perhaps a Christmas pageant—until they tied the first man to a cement utility pole. Having knotted the rope too loosely, the council member in charge then struggled awkwardly to whip his captive, who flung desperately from side to side to avoid the lash. Moments later the council released the first man and made sure to bind the other two far more tightly.

The police returned later that day with a reporter from a local radio station. Now residents willingly cooperated. Rather than mass at their border and turn the outsiders away, they invited them in and the council handed over the thieves and made declarations to the press. Media coverage of the event soon expanded with both radio and newspaper accounts. The provincial newspaper ran the headline "In an indigenous community: three delinquents tortured" (*Diario del Norte* 26, December 1993). The article pointed out that the thieves were "subjects of the black race," Afro-Ecuadorians from a southern neighborhood of Ibarra, and emphasized the powerlessness of officials against the "fury of the natives." Describing the ultimate police action as a "rescue" not an arrest, the paper implied that the situation stood at the brink of mortal chaos. The reporter reinforced the impression by quoting the president of the community as threatening that "the next people who come here to rob and injure peasants will not be handed over alive."

In a way, La Compañía had it easier than many communities when it asserted its rights within its territory. Named for a long-defunct hacienda, it appears on maps of the Cantón of Otavalo. Cartographers may misalign the borders to include neighboring sectors, but they usually succeed in labeling the sector's core. And yet, to claim the prerogatives of the state, to deny the authority of the national police, and to become the legitimate punishers of thieves, La Compañía required a far more robust jurisdiction than what was printed on local maps. After all, where the state names with specificity it also seeks control. Residents wrested a measure of authority back in the most direct way possible: by assembling on their boundary and turning away the agents of the state. Elsewhere in the Andes, communal patrols of boundaries have roots in the defense of pastures where either landed estates or other communities have encroached on grazing land.

In E. P. Thompson's (1993) analysis of English common rights, this sort of collective physical presence empowered custom law, which was always more "ambiance" than fact. In the last stages of fights against enclosure in England, rural artisans and agricultural laborers would mob surveyors, break fences, and riot in order to eke out concessions from landlords and farmers. Jurisdiction lay in direct action, which in turn was narrated in terms of ancient custom.

Here in Imbabura, if the actions of the community were violent and confrontational, they were also nuanced. They began the event with a show of rejecting the police. Having completed the whipping, though, they then met with authorities and outside witnesses to bring justice to completion. The council formally recognized where community say in the matter terminated and that further action moved to state hands. Residents also moved from shutting out all outsiders to speaking openly with the press, with the president offering colorful quotations. In sum, the community produced its territory by operating along three fronts: physically occupying space, engaging state authorities, and seeking publicity to define the meanings of its actions. With the national rise of the indigenous movement, in fact, local residents can gain the most by projecting a sense of La Compañía as an "organic" jurisdiction that embodies natural rights, despite all the recent economic changes. As the legal scholar Richard Ford (2001, 206) argues, "the rhetorical power of the organic mode encourages any group that wishes to establish a jurisdiction to present itself as an 'organic' social group with distinctive cultural norms and values that demand protection and autonomy that a jurisdiction provides." In La Compañía, the rhetorical strategy was, paradoxically, a racial one—a moment of invoking stereotypes that, in fact, ran counter to both the politics and values of the national movement.

The Cultural Power of Being "Untamed"

With the coverage in general, and the president's threats in particular, the episode took on a racial "clarity" that belied the social ambiguities of Otavaleño life. Given their international experience, suburban work routines, and the increasingly urban standard of living, La Compañíans' appearance as rural, indigenous *insiders* defending themselves against urban *outsiders* is more a consequence of these events than a condition for them. The old trope of "defending ourselves" from the dangers of *mala gente* ("bad people," that is, city residents) sparked collective action among residents and suggested the depth and power of the feelings to others. In this light, both the robbers *and* the police were but the latest manifestation "of invasion" (Orlove 1998, 219). The move to block the roads and physically challenge the outsiders reaffirms an old principle of closing ranks and mutual support among indigenous community members.

The chance for a forceful, mass response also invokes white-mestizos' old stereotypes of unruly Indians. A history of such hostility and factionalism has earned La Compañía, in particular, the reputation of being *brava* (fierce, ferocious), a term otherwise reserved for powerful, untamed animals like bulls (Andrade 1990; cf. Poole 1994c). What was striking in this case was the degree to which urban indígenas invoked these stereotypes. In the week following the capture of the thieves, I received repeated warnings from several indígenas who lived in Otavalo not to go to La Compañía because "ellos no son racionales" (Sp. "they are not rational"). If anything, indígenas were less guarded than white-mestizos in their doubts about La Compañía. "Who knows?" one woman said during the events, "[those in La Compañía] may kill them."

Far from publicly refuting this stereotype, the leaders of the community exploited it. The president of La Compañía would have been aware of how his murderous threat would be interpreted by readers of the *Diario del Norte* and counted on white-mestizo concerns about "the fury of the indígenas" to further safeguard the community's territory from outside meddling. The following year, they celebrated their unruliness further during the fiesta of Yamor. Conceived in the 1950s as a civic fiesta to promote the image of Otavalo, Yamor had been challenged by FICI (The Federation of Indigenous People and Peasants of Imbabura) as discriminatory. FICI leaders secured municipal funds and picked La Compañía as the first host community of an alternative fiesta. La Compañía residents then developed a planting ritual that borrowed costumes from Inti Raymi, the festival of the summer solstice. Leaders also decided to replay the "rooster fight" from the fiesta of San Pedro, a jarring spectacle that featured a melee to tear the head off a rooster suspended above a crush of men. (The event itself belied the message of wildness. Led by FICI and La Compañía, events were so well orchestrated that even the most ferocious dancers were punctual, considerate, and attentive to the mild-mannered crowds [see figure 13].)

In these moments of de facto sovereignty, with indigenous leaders as-suming the prerogatives of the state, activism in the name of customary practices unites people. Political narratives that emphasize resistance to harmful outsiders resonate with those who already feel vulnerable within "outside" worlds of work. Further, connecting those narratives to justice making can work "to communicate the sense of indigenous control to a regional and national audience" as Whitten, Whitten, and Chango (1997, 372) have pointed out in a different but related context. Fixed within the authoritative context of a wider uprising, this "pan-indigenous" commu-nity justice speaks to unifying principles of native self-rule. Yet, in the realities of provincial episodes, community unities can be quite tenuous. Indeed, trial and punishment may help institutionalize the divergences be-tween communities, hardening as political divisions those differences that have their origin in economic disparities, as happened in Ariasucu.

While the theft was random and response improvised, they both had lasting consequences. Most concretely, the police have not entered the community since 1993 without securing the council's permission first (Bar-rionuevo, personal communication). Further, La Compañía's residents disconnected themselves from the provincial judicial apparatus, refusing to bring cases to the *teniente politico* (parish justice of the peace/sheriff), despite the occupation of that position since 1998 by an indigenous lawyer. That is, by aggressively intervening in matters of crime and punishment, indígenas established a practical sovereignty over legal affairs within their territory.

Such a strategy has its costs. In CONAIF publications, native auton-omy is meant to coincide with greater political involvement at the center of national government (CONAIE 1994). Yet, on the ground and couched in racial narratives, autonomy becomes isolation, and the richness of mod-ern Kichwa culture gets lost in stereotypes of violence and irrationality. For the political respect gained, a price of mutual understanding is paid. How people enter, live in, or discuss the countryside shifted them into ra-cial categories, and conversely race was used to defend a place (Bourque 1997; Medina 1998). Such boundary making occurs not only at the edges of indigenous places, but within them, as the next case of justice shows.

FIGURE 14 The Ariasucu cabildo taking care of the mundane administration of a potable-water project, 1994

CHAPTER SEVEN

Class and Councils (Don't Be Lazy)

It was no longer enough for a village leader to only know the ancient customs. Now one had to be versed in the new way of doing things. — Joseph Casagrande and Arthur Piper

Not only does work provide the livelihood of persons, it creates modes of sociality and sustains a vital sense of what it means to coexist and cooperate with others. — Michael Jackson, *Minima Ethnografica*

A week after La Compañía handed their robbers over to the police, the neighboring community council detained and whipped thieves in Ariasucu. Having just moved back to the community for a year of research, I witnessed the proceedings and heard my neighbors out as they explained, "this is the way indígenas do things." One man, a weaver and handicraft vendor, led me back to his house afterward and showed me a poster with the Inka greeting *Ama killa, ama llulla, ama shua* (Don't be lazy, don't lie, don't steal). He explained, "This is the way it was with the Inkas. They punished thieves hard, sometimes throwing them into deep ravines." From this man's point of view, the council had acted, in his word, "rationally." They had dealt with the threat posed by "lazy" men, legitimized his community as an upholder of ancient Andean customs, and challenged corrupt political officers who never prosecuted thieves caught in indigenous sectors.

Yet, others in Ariasucu did not share this man's enthusiasm. Stretched out on the rough cement of a volleyball court in their thin T-shirts and frayed soccer shorts, the thieves waved the poverty of indigenous people under the community's nose. Their mortification could not be shrugged off by those who told me that these men were "of our flesh." Furthermore, rather than a triumph of Andean justice, the flogging struck some as flaunting traditional wisdom that counseled careful deliberations. In short, where some—often the prosperous—reveled in a new era of community empowerment, others—frequently the poor—harbored doubts about the council's swift exercise of power. This episode illustrates a larger paradox of indigenous grassroots politics in the northern Andes: native communities have become more assertive as class divisions among Indians have intensified (Field 1994). The situation has precedent, as elsewhere in Latin America wealthy indigenous people have consolidated their power in the name of upholding "specious traditions" (Nash 1994), and raises a troubling question. To what extent does an emerging indigenous political and economic elite shape grassroots politics to further its own material ends? Put another way, just who does the council serve?

In this middle section of the book, I have been tracing how the political base elements of communities coalesce amid three deeply entangled tasks. I began by discussing how residents substantiate membership. They track the households and individuals whose labor and resources produce the collective base of the community; and similarly, they must name the legitimate beneficiaries of development projects and work parties. Next I described how members remake a place as a "jurisdiction," as a territory with standing in the eyes of both the state and local residents. If jurisdiction requires mapping and registering a physical space, it must also work culturally to become meaningful. A successful jurisdiction, that is, expresses values that a collectivity will make sacrifices to defend. Now I take up what has been implicit in each of the prior explorations. A people need to fashion and accept forms of authority within their ranks if they are to enjoy some sovereignty in their affairs. Effective politics depends on the visibility of leaders who exercise power within a place and who can influence outsiders with interests in that place. This problem of community leadership in the contemporary Ecuadorian highlands usually revolves around the cabildo, or town council.

Initiated in the Toledan reforms of the 1570s, the cabildo, in fact, has more than a four-century-old pedigree. The Spanish crown's push to bring clarity to rural populations—to locate them, enumerate them, and tax them—included rules about who was to lead them. The law envisioned a systematic linking of place, people, and office, with the designation of officers in relation to the number of local families. Council officials carried staffs as signs of their authority, which was not just civic but religious and intimately tied to Catholic evangelization (Orta 2004). From the outset, though, the cabildo meshed awkwardly with homegrown authority and community tasks. In regions with irrigation systems, for example, the cabildo had no clear connection to the complex needs of maintaining canals and allocating water (Guillet 1992).

As communities adapted to the cabildo, its meanings multiplied. In Huaquirca, Peru, for example, a cabildo was a meeting in which residents nominated water judges to maintain the smaller canals of the irrigations system (Gose 1994, 97). In rituals within Huaquirca, though, cabildo was the name given to the highest-ranking mountain spirit. Elsewhere in the Andes, the tradition of staff-holding leaders, known as *varayoq*, continued well into the twentieth century. Mayer (2002, 125) points out how they recruited labor to community work efforts, punished petty crimes, and pushed parents to baptize their children. Undertaken in the spirit of "ceremony, pomp and circumstances and respect," these authorities still blended officialdom with popular Catholicism (Mayer 2002, 125).

Yet by the 1930s their power was slipping. New national laws set out the terms for elected officers related to new functions—president, secretary, and treasurer—which emphasized skills of literacy and numeracy. Where staff holding had interwoven with kinship structures, the new district government was "a creature of national law" (Salomon 2002, 83). Many communities abandoned staff-holding traditions outright; others, such as Tupicoacha, Peru, linked the two systems. Even so, they could not eliminate the tensions intrinsic to leadership tasked with serving two masters, the state and community (Salomon 2002).

Rural Ecuadorian parishes underwent similar modernization in the twentieth century. The colonial legacy had trapped indigenous people within a stifling structure dominated by the hacendado, the priest, and the state appointed teniente politico. The counterpart of these mestizo authorities was the village *apu*, a religious lay leader with civil duties and a general mandate to act as an intermediary on behalf of the indigenous residents of the parish (Casagrande and Piper 1969). By the 1930s, though, non-agrarian work began to undercut the power of the estates and Catholic activists attacked the traditions of saint's day celebrations that anchored the power of the parish priest. The old structure was losing its grip. The national government hastened change by passing the 1937 Ley de Comunas that authorized indigenous peoples to officialize its own cabildo officers. Casagrande and Piper (1969, 1058, my translation) saw here a crucial innovation: "the establishment of the cabildos set the base for a gradual if incomplete transformation of indigenous populations from disorganized settlements of families connected through kinship and proximity to functional units capable of more concentrated action."

Ecuador's cabildos, though, had to find a new footing for their leadership. Traditional leaders availed themselves of ritual power enacted through agricultural rites and family bonds. Further, the old-fashioned investment in saint's day celebrations also endowed leaders with a spiritual authority. And when parish life conformed to a rigid racial hierarchy, an apu's stature rose with the backing of landlords and priests (Lyons 2006, 235). The new councils, though, spurned the power of the church and hacienda. They were secular and elected annually, apparently taking on a mandate issued by the state. Yet, while a government ministry authorized it on paper, the council received neither budget nor any state-backed coercive authority. A cabildo, in other words, was a sign of leadership that had an uncertain referent. Newly elected presidents, secretaries, and treasurers had to demonstrate what the cabildo stood for through their own actions, finding ways to legitimize not just their decisions, but also their formal position. Ariasucu's council is richly instructive in this regard. In 1993, they set for themselves the most contentious of tasks—whipping indigenous men from a neighboring community. And they did so as a body that had long chosen to operate without seeking state authorization as an official council.

Theft and Capture

Ariasucu is located along a gully that once defined the border between the two larger communities of Agato and La Compañía. Its existence as an independent community reflects the deep inequalities of the other two sectors' infrastructure development. Between 1954 and 1980, the people of Ariasucu worked in Agato or La Compañía's mingas, laboring to bring piped water, electricity, and improved roads into their communities. With the exception of the initial bus roads, most improvements stopped short of their own neighborhood, finally prompting the approximately 600 residents to begin setting up their own jurisdiction in the early 1980s. By the

1990s, residents had gained quasi-independence, just as their sector began to intensify its own internal occupational and economic differentiation.

While nearly all families continued to farm in the mid 1990s, direct agricultural production occupied less than 10 percent of people's productive time (Colloredo-Mansfeld, 1999). In the upper reaches of the community stood many of the empty homes of the poor who had gone to Bogotá to peddle crafts or to Quito in search of construction jobs or domestic work. Meanwhile, in the lowest neighborhood, sweater-exporting households were tearing down old adobe homes and building new compounds of cement buildings with broad, tinted windows. Scattered throughout the community were commercial faja weavers. These last wove colorful sashes on treadle looms, hiring local boys and girls to expand production, and thus creating an internal labor market for youths who would either go on to set up their own shops or try to convert their wages into an inventory of tourist handicrafts. When I expanded my research with these artisans, one man in neighboring Agato told me I was wasting my time. "They don't do artisan goods in Ariasucu, only belts," he said, dismissing such nontourist, craft production as an unprofitable holdover from the past.

The Agato resident's contempt did not surprise me. In the region's social geography, Ariasucu stands to Agato (and La Compañía) as La Compañía stands to the prosperous indígenas living in the city of Otavalo. Outsiders denigrate it as a backward sector, overreliant on traditions and lacking the savvy needed for the modern textile economy. Such attitudes shortchange the zone's hidden cosmopolitanism. In Ariasucu, two households lived on earnings of members who worked in the United States. A local folklore music group has toured both Central America and Europe. And dozens of young men and women broke into the handicraft trade by working the streets of Colombia.

Indeed, the existence of Ariasucu as a recognizable, independent sector stemmed from the presence of such ambitious people. The most successful of these adventurers periodically returned to try their hand at political enterprise. In 1982, for example, without seeking formal authorization of their own council, several unofficially elected representatives (who were prolific belt weavers) successfully solicited an electricity development project. Throughout the economically turbulent 1980s, political entrepreneurship increased. Having retreated from broad rural development policies, Ecuador's central governments opened the countryside to other governmental and nongovernmental agencies. Exploiting new openings, leaders in Ariasucu and La Compañía competed for the patronage of at least ten different external organizations (Lema, Saltos, Barrionuevo, Chimbo, and Garcia 2000). Often, such competition led to piecemeal development projects that benefited primarily the neighborhoods of the leaders who secure them. Yet for all these limitations, such activism consolidated the authority of an informal council. It affirmed a tenuous independence and elevated justice makers from rank and file citizens.

The crime happened on Christmas Eve. The victim was a widow whose grown children had recently moved off to Bogotá to sell handicrafts. To earn cash, she ran a small store out of her adobe home in upper Ariasucu. On that December night, several men roused her from her sleep demanding that she sell them trago. She thought she recognized one of their voices and came to the door. Pushing their way into the house, they tied up the woman and then broke into her trunks and storage boxes and stole her skirts, blouses, and blankets. From the small display counter in her store, they took money, pasta, oatmeal, and cooking oil.

The following morning, some neighbors found her struggling in her house. Outraged, a group of men took it upon themselves to hunt for the thieves. They narrowed their search to nearby upper Agato based on the woman's suspicions. Having lost out on development projects over the years, that neighborhood shared Ariasucu's disadvantages—partial electric service, limited access to potable water, overgrown footpaths, and a surplus of *tavernas*, or little stores, that made most of their money selling trago to hardcore neighborhood drinkers. For its limited ties to wider Agato, its drinking, and fighting, residents lower down the mountain warn people away from upper Agato.

The Ariasucu men, though, had little trouble making their way in the sector. They simply drank their way around from taverna to taverna keeping an ear out. They soon caught up with three of the thieves. They jumped them, bound them, and shoved and dragged them back to an abandoned house in Ariasucu where they locked them up. This act in itself guaranteed Ariasucu some local notoriety. To enter upper Agato, accuse three of its residents of theft, and force them back to Ariasucu for punishment confirmed its own reputation for being "bravo."

Councils and Punishment

Thus, in a remarkable coincidence, within a week of La Compañía's punishment of thieves, the council and residents of Ariasucu found themselves deliberating the fate of three perpetrators they had caught. The prior whipping had significantly raised the stakes for this smaller sector. In the past, they would have turned criminals over to the teniente politico, the provincial official in charge of such matters. However, failing to follow La Compañía's example would have signaled the weakness of their community and potentially jeopardized the new autonomy they had achieved. Thus, responding to precedent, Ariasucu's council similarly locked up thieves and rebuffed the attempts of other authorities to assert jurisdiction. Yet, in a crucial difference, this episode lacked outsiders—urban thieves, police, and reporters. Playing out more fully within indigenous society, Ariasucu's case underscored what it means for indígenas to betray each other, seek redress, and make sense of it on their own.

By the time I arrived at 8 a.m., a crowd of about eighty people had gathered around the volleyball court. On the uphill side of the court, the robbers stood tied to a pole. One stood barefoot in threadbare sweatpants and a sweater. The other two of them had had their pants stripped away and stood in their undergarments; the oldest of these shivered uncontrollably, his legs rattling the tattered tails of his shirt. For most of the prior night, the cabildo, the "posse" who captured them, and a past community president interrogated them angrily—abusively at times—trying to find out where the stolen goods and the other thieves were. They learned nothing. They suspected the accomplices had taken the widow's possessions to Quito to be sold.

Now the thieves all bided their time. Agato's council arrived that morning in Ariasucu. Trying to insure that the process would be fair, Agato's vice president insisted to all who gathered that "this punishment must come from the people. Personal meanness is not valid." The comments drew everyone's attention to the intercommunity political risks. Most pressingly, Ariasucu needed to safeguard against the widow's allies exacting personal retribution on the thieves. Mishandled, the whipping would trigger lasting hostility between Agato and Ariasucu (Garcia 1999). Huddled together on the volleyball court, Agato's and Ariasucu's leaders sought a way forward that would not jeopardize harmony among neighborhoods. To do so, Ariasucu made the most of formal state-defined roles of the community council.

When the councils finished their deliberations, the vice president of Agato loudly asked the widow if she wanted to go through with the punishment. She said "yes." Upon her reply, he and most other Agato council members departed, leaving a single representative to observe the event.

Leading a thin robber to the middle of the court, Ariasucu's council had him take off his sweater and kneel down before the president, who held a short whip. Before he delivered the first of his two blows, he made a speech addressed to the thief. Back in the crowd, I caught only brief snatches of talk that returned again and again to the theme of "having to work," of "knowing work." He then cracked the whip once against the man's back. Continuing the speech, he again repeated that stealing was wrong, "not working was not valid." After hitting the man one more time, the president turned the whip over to the vice president.

He continued the routine: speech, a single blow, speech, and one blow. The third council member mumbled something and gave two tentative blows, mostly missing the man on the second one. The fourth council member was much bolder. She took the whip and hit the thief hard across the buttocks, scolded him, then struck again. They then let the man stand up. The oldest man came next. The representative from Agato's council stepped up and asked for leniency. To no avail. He received his eight lashes. After the last man was dealt with, the council made arrangements to turn the thieves over to state officials.

Although Ariasucu's council had long tried to follow the state's regulations that designate community officers and how they should be elected, it had never approached officials for formal recognition. The distance they kept from government ministries fit a larger pattern. As previously mentioned, many Otavalos had treated such state-mandated councils ambivalently. Seen as either an organ of intrusive state power or a vehicle for personal enrichment, councils received little support outside their efforts to coordinate clearly needed development projects (Becker 1999; Villavicencio Rivadeneira 1973). In the flow of these events, though, the council form solved several problems. By rotating the whip among the president, vice president, treasurer, and secretary—and only among them—they tapped into the bureaucratic ideals and minimized the individual personality of the leaders involved. More to the point, the leadership positions mimicked Agato's. Ariasucu matched up, officer to officer, to its parent community and projected political symmetry throughout its face-off with them.

This embracing of council-led, bounded territories shifts the organization of Otavalo's longstanding economic inequality and social diversity. As documented by ethnographers in the 1940s, the area's peasant settlements varied according to craft specialty, income, and cultural skills (Buitrón

1947; Buitrón 1945). Those located near the Otavalo market were already getting ahead in mestizo-dominated institutions. These uneven gradations of wealth and knowledge were accompanied by diffuse overlapping domains of authority. Kinship seniority, for example, elevated leaders within neighborhoods, which often bore the names of the largest extended family of the sector. (Ariasucu, for example, means "inside the family Arias's place.") Meanwhile, saint's day fiesta sponsorship endowed some men status and visibility to serve leadership roles at the wider parish level (Salomon 1981; Walter 1981).

By the 1980s and 1990s, though, this complexity began simplifying into a type of institutional pluralism. Rather than having markets connect households one way, kinship another, and parish obligations a third, separate community jurisdictions became the primary way to affiliate with neighbors. Each sector duplicated the institutions and functions of the others, setting up enclaves where open networks once prevailed. As this case suggests, councils did not spread owing to a state mandate or a spontaneous, democratic urge. At times, residents set up a cabildo to thwart neighboring councils. For Ariasucu, this jockeying was hard, given the larger size, greater wealth, and longer history of the other communities. Making matters worse, Ariasucu's leaders worked under politically adverse conditions. The same tensions that prompted Ariasucu to split from its neighbors simmered within the sector itself. If the antagonisms drew on class differences, they took shape as moral clashes. In working through them, the leaders had to legitimize their choices and gain the respect of even those who did not fully back the punishment that was ultimately pursued.

"Don't be Lazy ... Don't Steal": Punishment and Situated Morality

Once the bedraggled thieves lined up in front of the community, residents could not escape the social issue at hand. The thieves lived among Otavalo's poorest. The leaders who decided their fate were active textile entrepreneurs and some had grown prosperous. In fact, one had been buying parcels of land above Agato and Ariasucu on the slopes of Imbabura. The relative "haves" would mete out the punishment; the "have-nots" would suffer the blows.

This crossover of class and politics sparks the fiercest debates concerning ethnic activism in Latin America. In their overview of Latin America's indigenous peoples and politics, Kearney and Varese (1995) argue that indigenous movements have been fostered by conditions of "post-development" (Escobar 1992) and that new ethnic consciousness downplays internal class conflicts (Nagengast and Kearney 1990). CONAIE, for instance, has described economic differences in terms of occupation and geography, not class: "We indígenas are immersed in the structure of Ecuadorian society and for that reason we are *campesinos* [peasants], workers, business people, artisans, etc.; some of us work in the country, others in the city, some of us receive salaries, others do not." (CONAIE 1989, 261, cited in Meisch 1997, 13, her translation). Such heterogeneity, in the analysis of CONAIE, offers opportunities for allying with other popular sectors and strengthens the movement (Radcliffe 1997).

Writers, however, have pointed to the eclectic and impoverished rural economy in order to dispute the supposed importance of ethnic movements. The challenges proceed along two fronts. First, pushing aside cultural explanations, some argue that the real issues of rural unrest are enduring structures of exploitation (Arizpe 1996; Paz 1996; Powelson 1996, 6; Rus 1995). In the Mexican case, for example, analysts show that economic hardships unite peoples across cultural divides (Collier 1999; Cook and Joo 1995; Veltmeyer 1997). Similarly, in Ecuador, many insist that the failure of land reform, not cultural resurgence, acts as the primary cause of the 1990s indigenous uprising (Korovkin 1997).

Second, along with championing the *economic* struggle of the poor, writers criticize the *cultural* fight of indigenous professionals who work for such causes as bilingual education, an issue which may be leave many rural people indifferent (Zamosc 1994). A few scholars have probed such activism as a potential ploy that secures middle-class indígenas a privileged position vis-à-vis both rural groups and the nonindigenous middle class. In her analysis of indigenous politics in Guatemala, Warren (1998a, 182) takes up this critique and provocatively asks, "is Pan-Mayanism a social movement or is it instead an emerging class-ethnicity seeking to consolidate its power and privilege?"

Critiques that focus on economic differences within indigenous society provoke several responses from defenders of ethnic movements. For example, Warren resolves the difficult issues she raises by emphasizing the shared vulnerability of all Mayas; she and others affirm the idea of the movement as fundamentally multiclass, antiracist, and inclusive (Grandin 1997; Warren 1998a). Taking another tack, some writers insist that Mexican and Ecuadorian movements offer "new ways of being indigenous" that supersede fading, peasant-centered politics and transcend the divisions besetting indigenous groups (Mattiace 1997; Meisch 1994; Nash 1997; Selverston 1994, 141). While challenging materialist critiques of ethnic politics, these arguments nonetheless reinforce the assumptions underlying such critiques: internal economic differences are antithetical to an effective indigenous politics (cf. Tilly 1998).

Councils, though, have extended their power at a time when class differences have grown. Furthermore, by invoking the Inka, punishing thieves, and defending community territory, leaders do not transcend wealth differences or value conflicts. They draw attention to them and the moral antagonisms that come as leaders push their communities in new directions. Indeed, an active council cannot place unity above all ideals. Even the effort to bring electricity, piped water, and "houses with floors," as the leaders in Tigua put it, can require picking sides. In Quiloa in the late 1980s, commercial craftwork trumped peasant initiatives. In this robbery, the protagonists had already ruptured the ideal of solidarity. Having risked their safety in the tavernas, torn the criminals from their neighbors, and lined them up for a flogging, men in Ariasucu declared "justice" as paramount. To serve justice, the council could not appeal to generic community brother- and sisterhood. They had to morally frame such a provocative act as fitting, even in the face of the social bonds it would break.

If Ariasucu's council held its own against its neighbors by borrowing its form from the state, it sought to legitimize its actions among witnesses through "words that were given." The emphasis on moral lecturing in the course of the whipping reflected a key practice of rural Andean authority. In personal terms, people grow up with the expectation that elders, parents, and other responsible figures must offer strong guidance to their charges, to advise or "to give words" (dar palabras) that reinforce rightful behavior (Lyons 2006). And "knowing work" is clearly rightful behavior. A team of anthropologists and indigenous lawyers that researched community justice in Kichwa communities (including La Compañía) in three different provinces reported that the Inka injunction—"ama killa (do not be lazy), ama llulla (do not lie), y ama shua (do not steal)"—were the "three basic principles of Kichwa justice and culture" (Lema et al. 2000, 29). Nationally, in an analysis of CONAIE's rise to power, the newspaper El Comercio reported: "In fact, with a monk-like mysticism, the leaders assume the three principles of CONAIE and the keystone of its philosophy: do not be lazy, do not lie, do not steal" (*El Comercio*, June 4, 2000, B4–5).

Such a hardworking, straight-laced ethos would seem to have no better representatives than the Otavalos. Documenting the industriousness of 1940s weavers, local anthropologist Aníbal Buitrón (1947, 52) remarks that among Otavalos, "relaxation . . . consists in switching one task for another." Decades later, in his detailed analysis of Otavalos' sense of self, Chavez (1982, 127) records how weavers and merchants insist that their advancement came through being "rational." Years after these ethnographic accounts came out, the council's lectures apparently confirmed their words: hard work built an honest life. However, in Ariasucu after the punishment, common sense notions of "hard work," both as a practical matter and ideological issue, gave way to contradictory interpretations. These disputes, in turn, cast a shadow on the council's new stature.

In the wake of the flogging, prosperous indígenas of the sector appropriated the idea of rationality, sounding very much like Alfonso Chiza. They used their belief in their own successful hard work to distance themselves from the thieves and the neighborhoods that they lived in—and robbed. Galo Ajala, the man who quoted the Inka greeting to me in his justification of the event, was one of these. He blamed the thieves and their neighbors in upper Agato and Ariasucu for their own poverty: "they play too much—too much soccer, too much volleyball. They also drink too much. They're not rational people." For Galo and like-minded people, the speeches exhorting thieves to work hard meant specifically to work *rationally*—to spend hours, days, and years at the loom or a trade, make money, save against the inevitable setbacks, and to "advance little by little." Rationality (again for him) was clearly materialized in his and others' rising standard of living, the cement block homes, elegant outfits, and elaborate fiestas; and irrationality was equally apparent in the eroded adobe huts and concrete block lean-tos on the slopes above the volleyball court.

That is, even within this small community, discourse divided a progressing neighborhood from a stagnating one. Here again, the region's new consumer culture channeled relations. Commodities, and the lack of them, put in play the respect owed, the dignity achieved and ties of mutual support. In talking about the thieves, the crime, and the hunting down of the perpetrators, women and men identified neighborhoods by their *chozas*, or run-down houses, the patios littered with shot glasses and empty bottles, and by the worn-out garments of the residents. Put another way, the uneven spread of new architecture, cars, and consumer goods from Otavalo to the periphery achieved meaning not just for its absolute monetary value—which was quite modest—but for the way it related people to each other, strengthening or attenuating their feelings of connection. More and more, neighbors turned to the material world for tangible signs of each other's moral fitness.

Residents of marginal neighborhoods knew of this contempt and understandably had another take on the "rationality" of the council. Santo Conejo was one of them. He had been president of the community the previous year, and, though no longer in office, had been present when the council interrogated the three thieves as to the whereabouts of the stolen goods. The intensity, and ultimately the physical brutality, of the questioning upset him. He told me that among indigenous people, it is said that if you accuse someone of stealing, you will become a thief yourself in two to three years. He paused and then stated, "Soy como racional" (Sp. I am like a rational person), as if he did not agree with the irrational "superstitions" of tradition. Yet, he could not fully associate himself with those advocating rationality. He paused again and added that he was reluctant to accuse the thieves because he had daughters—leaving unsaid his fear that he may become a thief through false accusations and jeopardize the girls' futures through his moral corruption.

Beyond his ambivalence about guilt, innocence, and the appropriateness of making strong accusations, though, another aspect of the whole event troubled Santo. He said that the thieves were of the "same flesh as me; they lived poorly." Thus, the meaning of the ragged clothes worn by the thieves had shifted. What Galo saw as signs of irrationality, Santo took to be a shared humanity. He recognized a common fate of a *yanga kawsay* (humble/fruitless life)—a lifelong struggle that yields little more than some exhausted possessions and broken-down bodies (Colloredo-Mansfeld 1999).

Ultimately, though, Santo, like Galo, backed the council. He too faulted the thieves for what they had done and left undone. He said, "They did not know how to work properly." However, in his case, he seemed to refer to the work not of advancement but of "defending oneself"—providing for one's needs and the means to participate in community life (Isbell 1978).

At the outset of this chapter, I sketched these events in Ariasucu and the different perspectives that surfaced in my interviews in order to ask, is this the polarizing politics of the rising indigenous middle class? The short

answer is no. There was community-wide support of the council in their
negotiations with Agato and a general moral consensus that the thieves
deserved their punishment for "being lazy" and stealing. Yet despite these
unities, the event also highlighted an intracommunity "us vs. them" atti-
tude, a difference that foreshadowed potential political division. Defined
physically by whether people were located in upper or lower Ariasucu, the
opposition was marked culturally through "rationality."

In the light of Ariasucu's deep differences, we therefore need to recognize how situated the moral consensus was. In contrast to the newspaper's
description of monk-like devotion to moral rules, Ariasuqueños' agreement represented ama killa, ama llulla, ama shua more "for today at least"
rather than in enduring principle. On that day, the latent factions' coming
together reflected tense intercommunity relations with powerful neighboring sectors, widespread empathy with a particularly vulnerable victim,
and indisputable evidence of the thieves' guilt. Such conditions sufficed
for a durable collective commitment. Another time, though, and absent
some of these factors and one faction's punishment for alleged stealing,
might be seen by another as misapplied justice. Arguments would flare
about a council bent on extending their own values throughout the community, and many would find grounds for yet another break and episode
of community formation.

Councils, Rivalry, and Autonomy

An invention of the colonial state, the cabildo, began its Andean life in
a scheme to tax, convert, and control rural populations. In some areas
of the Andes, the word entered into the language conveying notions of
authority, primacy, and civic order. In others, communities preserved elements of staff-holding authority well into the twentieth century. In Ecuador, though, councils withered, squeezed by the power of landlords and
priests. The post-colonial state revamped the cabildo in the 1930s, inspired
by visions of modern, cooperative peasant comunas with direct ties to the
state. Transformative where parishes embraced it, this new secular, democratic order caught on slowly. Gradually, beginning in the 1960s, residents
appropriated the council, elevating its authority in ways never anticipated
in the original legislation.

Indeed two trends converged in the 1980s to spur the near hyperactivity
of councils. Two decades of rural activism consolidated in the national in-

digenous movement, which skillfully built its organization by working with communities. This stepped-up political activism coincided with promarket ideologies emphasizing decentralization, freedom from state control, and an expanded role of nongovernmental organizations (Schild 1998). Across Latin America, the devolution of power to local communities was the sweetener that made cutting state programs in rural areas democratically palatable (Demmers, Fernandez Jilberto, and Hogenboom 2001). In Bolivia, for example, the second generation of neoliberal reforms during the administration of Gonzalo Sánchez de Lozada linked market-oriented initiatives with decentralization and recognition of plural cultures (Healy and Paulson 2000). As Albo notes (1994, 70), it is in the context of decentralization where the "Kataristas (Bolivia's indigenous movement) and neoliberals find so much common ground."

And as both the state and social movement touted local control, national and international NGOs rolled out resources to support projects that exhibited local leadership. Indeed, growing numbers of organizations targeted indigenous communities in particular for funding. In his analysis of NGO investment, Victor Breton (2003) shows that donors went looking for Indians rather than just the poor. A single, rural canton (township) in Chimborazo, for example, attracted 20 percent of all Andean NGO activity in the late 1990s, despite accounting for less than 4 percent of the region's poverty. Breton concludes that "Indianness is the primordial element that has induced—and induces—external agents of development to converge in their interventions" (Breton 2003, 243). Leaders who could formalize councils and promote the Kichwa identity of a sector stood first in line for development assistance. Breton insists that in seeking NGO support, communities sacrifice their political potential and spread rivalries among themselves.

Throughout the 1990s, the Otavalo hinterland consolidated into mutually exclusive jurisdictions—the separate incarnations of La Compañía, Ariasucu, and Agato, for example—fitting this broader competitive pattern. However, this episode of community justice reveals how much more people staked on their councils than an NGO handout. Justice, respect for one's neighborhood and kin, advocacy, and fealty have all driven people to petition their council for action. And like lists and jurisdictions, councils emerge as a particular kind of technique to advance community goals. People uphold their council officers in order to approach a sense of bureaucratic neutrality. President, vice president, secretary, treasurer stand as a secular and broad-based alternative to narrower leadership rooted in

church, ritual, and kin and thus may be the only means to transcend interpersonal conflict—especially when all officers work together. Tactically,
the council offers a uniformity that allows communities to connect across
scales and ambitions. Ariasucu, thus, can hold its own against sectors ten
times its size, both for the presence of its officers and for the chutzpah of
its residents.

As they assembled communities to match and oppose their neighbors,
and as communities tackled more state-like functions by meting out justice, negotiating with foreign donors and the like, the provinces have taken
on the air of a "segmentary society." Stripping away the idea of kinship
connotations, Gellner (1983, 30) describes such a society as one in which
"a 'segment' is simply a smaller variant of the larger society of which it is
a part, and can do on a smaller scale everything done by the larger unit."
New Otavaleño communities have not yet achieved such self-sufficiency.
However, with the passing of time, more and more sectors independently
regulate local life. Councils organize soccer tournaments, call out community mingas, confront abusive husbands, and mobilize residents to blockade highways during protests. When possible, they will hustle NGOs for
projects. Much work continues, though, when donors are absent.

As residents partition provincial society through community-based activism they produce a disturbing pattern. New councils and jurisdictions
overlay landscapes formed through decades of unbalanced development
and private accumulation. Indeed, residents in places such as Ariasucu
back councils precisely to redress the inequalities. Yet, the deprivations
live on in relations among communities. Rather than conform to the equal
and opposed nature of segments proposed by Evans Pritchard (1940) in
the classic formulation of segmentary society, Andean communities line
up against each other in an invidious ranking. A core wealthier community
looms over the politics of a poorer neighbor, positioning itself as rational,
the other as backward. In turn, the disadvantaged community emulates
the tactics of the powerful sector and distances itself from the more impoverished settlement on its periphery. Thus Otavaleño indigenous residents
warn others away from La Compañía and La Compañía scorns Ariasucu.
A council accomplishes much when it challenges this logic, stands up to
superior sectors, and claims new respect for its own citizens. Ariasucu's
leaders acquitted themselves well on that score in December 1993.

Yet the invidiousness percolates within Ariasucu, too. The tension between economically advantaged and disadvantaged arises at the political
launch of the community. In fact, an ironic condition of seeking autonomy

from overweening councils at core neighborhoods is the consolidation of elites within the community on the periphery. In Ariasucu prosperous artisans took the lead first in pioneering new handicraft markets for belts and later in activating a local council. If the wider community had supported the council's development initiatives, they balked at the extension of its power. Indeed, this hesitancy inhibited achieving official state jurisdiction throughout the 1980s and 1990s. Consequently, the council never moved beyond having to justify its actions; the community never arrived at a place of spontaneous compliance with its authorities. And activism, even within such an intimate collectivity was not predicated on an enduring, unified agreement in outlook. Rather, politics charted its progress more in practical solutions and moral calls made for the moment.

In the next section of the book, I describe three different encounters between native peoples and the state. Such practicality and pluralism marked each one, whether the target was the judge in a provincial traffic court or the executive of the national government. People used councils, jurisdictions, and formal community or trade association membership in widely varying ways (or not at all). Their achievements take the measure of community power in the age of indigenous activism.

PART III

Statecraft

FIGURE 15 Selling Tiguan paintings in El Ejido Park, 1999

CHAPTER EIGHT

Markets and Parks (Don't Sell Out)

"And I think, whether we know it or not, that we are united," the Body Shop and Pipe Queen operator said gently. "I mean, how in God's name can a bunch of sorry types like us live together in the same damn valley for three hundred years without being united?"—John Nichols, *The Milagro Beanfield War*

In 1999, sixteen years after securing the rights to sell in the El Ejido Park, Tiguans again had to fight city hall to keep control of their sales posts. But now the stakes were raised. Up to forty Tiguan households living in Quito came to sell on Sundays. National and foreign clients in turn came to seek out painters and discuss large orders or possible exhibitions. And rural Tiguans themselves still arrived to sell their paintings, either directly to tourists or to a contact from home. All this activity, however, struck the Mayor Rocafuerte as misplaced. His new municipal policies sought to restore civic order by removing vendors from parks and streets. Green space regained, however, would mean community lost—and the end of the commercial visibility Tiguans had created and controlled.

The ensuing fight for the market posts tested the statecraft of Tigua's leaders. Most immediately, they faced their own organizational mess, with multiple trade associations and cooperatives stepping up to speak for Tigua's painters, while individual painters enrolled opportunistically in several groups. City authorities put this diffuse apparatus of jurisdictions, membership rolls, and council leadership under great pressure. More fundamentally, though, the fight posed dilemmas about indigenous self-determination, both in relation to the state and to the marketplace.

Indeed, Kichwa peoples such as the Tiguans strikingly reveal the contradiction of self-determination in the "global cultural economy" (Appadurai 1990). On the one hand, the ideal of "autonomy" has become paramount. In indigenous movements throughout Latin America, in fact, the demand for autonomy is foundational, the one through which calls for land rights, bilingual education, and sovereignty over cultural remains and property rights are articulated (Díaz Polanco 1998). On the other hand, market expansion and failing subsistence resources eliminate the last independent elements of peasant economies (Nash 2001). As Kearney (1996, 145) has noted, agro-industry, mass migration, occupational change, and the consumption of global popular culture all promote degrees of dependence. Peasants no longer seem native to any one place; native people no longer live as "simple" peasants. Autonomy projects thus appear as daring political architecture being built on economic quicksand.

In arguing that such projects are nonetheless feasible, anthropologists and political scientists have pushed two points. The first holds that power is bound up in place: the greater the congruence among political control, indigenous culture, and physical territory (as both heritage and subsistence base), the more robust the autonomy (Nash 2001; Van Cott 2001). The second turns from spatial issues to ideological ones: autonomy succeeds where nationalism gives way to multiple histories that connect different groups in different ways to a single country. People exercise new creativity in joining the fabric of ethnic identity to the cloth of the nation. In the long run, multicultural frameworks for new unified identities finally emerge to hold plural nations together (Stephen 1997). While distinctive lines of analysis, these discussions of place and multicultural ideologies often blend in current writings to a model of "nested nationalism"—sovereign democratic realms within sovereign democratic realms (Colloredo-Mansfeld 2002).

And yet, sized up in territorial terms, autonomy is drained of its potential. Native peoples have made their mark through a surprisingly mobile politics—asserting indigenous power in ever-wider settings. Ecuador's Kichwa peoples operate across locales and alliances, here with the World Bank, there with the Communist party, and in the next place with the army. Issue by issue, from seeking bilingual education to fighting for the preservation of the national currency, autonomy materializes more in strategic connections than in the zonal separation. Warren (1998a, 18) makes a similar point about the Pan-Mayan movement, writing that the "social relationships through which Mayas assert their cultural gains are integral aspects of self-determination." Indeed, new occupations and urban homes have forced peasant councils and cooperatives to press agendas *without* retreating to a delimited territory.

Working without the certainties of territorial sovereignty, Kichwa leaders are learning to promote self-determination on the spot, wherever decisions are being taken that affect their lives. Once again, this leads people to creatively use (and abuse) council, trade association, jurisdiction, and membership. Further, they couple these primary forms of community praxis with secondary elements. Autonomy happens in setting up meetings, timing negotiations, choosing languages, scaling up group involvement, and restricting contacts with allies and adversaries alike. It is highly situational—flowing from the attentiveness and responsiveness of indigenous organizers. In Tigua in 1999, such dynamism reflected more than the tactical struggle with the city. It sprang from a schism within the culture of painting itself.

Following the differing visions of Julio Toaquiza and José Vega, the painting profession had developed a dual personality early on. The founding Toaquiza family infused many other painters from their community with a commitment to live and work in rural Cotopaxi province. At the same time, the migrant community had not only expanded in number but in artistic talent and earnings As time passed, younger men had stepped up to defend each lifeway—and voice opposition to the other.

Julio's son Alfredo, for example, had created an association of Chimbacucho's painters and forcefully articulated a vision that bound community, place, and art. He insisted that real Tigua paintings only came from Tigua and his community in particular. Even in the late 1990s, he still painted in Tigua and made the long trip to Quito on weekends to sell. In early June 1999, I caught up with him on one of his sales trips to talk to him about the future of Tigua painting. He was dressed in a spotless white shirt, open at the neck to reveal a leather necklace with a silver pendent of a Plains Indian headdress. He had on pressed pants whose crease had just managed to survive the bus ride, a vest, brown wingtip shoes, and a carefully kept indigenous man's fedora. Sitting in a folding chair he had arranged next to him on an easel a limited set of detailed paintings of shamans. On a small table by his side, he had three publications about Tigua art, all mentioning his father and some him.

Meanwhile, on this Sunday, Alfredo's neighbors in the park were Ti-guan residents of Quito. Among their leading lights were the couple Juan Luis Cuyo and his wife Puri Cuyo. Similar to their brother-in-law José Vega, Juan Luis and Puri had historic ties to Quiloa. And like José, they identified with the commerce of painting, helping to open up a new mar-ket for Tigua art in Otavalo's Plaza de Ponchos. Most importantly, Juan Luis and Puri professionalized the occupation of Tigua art selling. They fully stocked a proper market stall with numerous paintings and other Ti-guan crafts such as boxes, mirrors, and wooden bowls. While the painted wares and Puri's indigenous outfits (with thick, pleated skirts and cro-cheted shawls) bespoke native authenticity, Juan Luis's appearance sig-naled prosperity. He eschewed country garb and presided over his wares bareheaded (without his countrymen's distinctive hat) and in bright white shirts, pressed slacks, and polished shoes. Not simply a comerciante, Juan Luis also painted ambitiously. His cuadros were often twice the size of his rivals' and sold for somewhere between $120 and $400.

Tiguans from several different peasant sectors have emulated Juan Luis. They have developed extensive commercial networks, cultivated foreign clients, and purchased homes in Quito. Even so, Juan Luis was considered by many as the most securely established of the Tiguans in Quito. Conse-quently, the split between migrants and nonmigrants expressed itself as a community division: Tigua Chimbacucho (home of the Toaquizas) stood for country artists; Quiloa symbolized urban painters.

Beginning in the early 1990s a more bitter antagonism surfaced among the artists. Painting was producing a few clear economic winners among many anonymous toilers. Class divisions had opened up. With data gath-ered from interviews with twenty-six artists and an analysis of more than 1,200 paintings in Quito's six main folklore galleries on display in 1999, 2000, and 2001, I ranked the artists in four groups. At the base were ap-proximately 300 Tiguans who had sufficient talent and interest to main-tain their memberships in the artists' associations. Most of them, however, painted only part time. About eighty households, though, made their liv-ing from their art, half of whom earned somewhere between $30 and $120 per month, similar to the Ecuadorian minimum wage.[1]

---

1. At these wages, journeymen and -women painters deemed painting comparable to, and substitutable with, other employment (working on commercial potato farms, apprenticing in mechanics shops, loading cargo at the bus terminal, etc.) in the summer of 1999. In other words, they saw no economic advantage to painting per se, but rather chose to paint because

The other forty households consistently earned higher incomes of about $200 a month or more—a rate that allows for some material advancement. This group subdivided into two overlapping parts. The first included "first rank" artists—a term painters used among themselves to identify those whom they particularly respected. The second group was that of men and women like Juan Luis and Puri, *intermediarios* (Sp. intermediaries) or *comerciantes*, who sell others' works as well as their own. In 1994, Humberto Vega[2] bought a small, used blue pickup truck with his reseller's profits, becoming the first Quiloan to own a car. Since then his earnings have been eclipsed by Juan Luis and Puri, and a few others who have invested much of what they have made in their homes.

These resellers inspired resentment. The goods and practices that gained Juan Luis and Puri market share—large inventories, multiplying sales posts, and an urbane, nonindigenous fashion—cost them goodwill among painters. Disliking their success, a few artists who once worked with them refused to continue to sell to Juan Luis and Puri. Anger reached a collective level around 1997, when a faction of artists forced the issue within Quiloa's artist association. With the backing of Quiloa's association president, they tried to outlaw reselling of art among members. The effort backfired though. The intermediaries denounced the idea, claiming that reselling among community members insured work for many more painters. Their indigenous clients who painted for them backed them. After a rancorous debate, no steps were taken. Worse, the association stopped meeting regularly and its leadership gave up pursuing projects. The officers were angered that the intermediaries would still capture much of the value of the association's effort to promote Tigua painting.

Envy, exploitation, political paralysis, factions, embittered leaders: Latin American peasant communities have long had a fame for such divisiveness and anthropology a history of exploring it. Foster (1965), for example, tried to unpack the enviousness of the smallhold farmer with his discussion the Image of the Limited Good. Others have sought to explain the frequent conflict in communities that also often cooperated (Whyte 1976). However, as social movements have moved to the center of anthropological inquiry, the investigation of disunity has been neglected, if not explicitly discouraged.

---

it was "much softer" work, because it allowed them to work in their homes, or because they took cultural pride in it, seeing it as "our own" indigenous work.

2. A pseudonym.

The debate surrounding David Stoll's (1999) research into the discrepancies of Rigoberta Menchú's autobiography is instructive in this regard. In laying out the gaps in Menchú's account and other sources on the events in her life, Stoll intended to widen the debate on the problems facing Mayan peasants. He explained that the testimony in *I, Rigoberta Menchú* (Burgos-Debray 1984) excluded all but a single cause of rural misery: the oppression authored by Ladino landowners. Decentering Menchú's account, Stoll wanted to raise other urgent issues, including land conflicts among peasant communities, population pressure, and ecological degradation.

For other scholars, however, Stoll's efforts clearly underscore reasons not to play up the feuds and flaws of impoverished groups.[3] In particular, a number of researchers saw his study as violating two principles of ethical scholarship among vulnerable communities. The first might be called "Do no harm" (Fox 2005). The *New York Times'* front page article "Nobel Winner Accused of Stretching Truth" (Rohter 1998) and similar stories in the popular press that were inspired by Stoll's book have done permanent damage to Menchú's reputation. Many anthropologists find this unacceptable. Research that destroys the basis for constructive, collective action or tears down leaders with indisputable records of promoting their people's well-being fails basic ethics of benefice (Hale 1996).

The second ethical principle could be labeled "Eyes on the prize." The challenge in researching local fights is not to allow "the crushing weight of oppression and structural inequity to fade from view" (Hale 1996, 54). Scholars who would seek a just society must frankly acknowledge the root causes of suffering, stay vigilant of the rich and powerful, and must not dodge the deep changes that must occur. In contrast, Stoll's targeting of Menchú seems to shift blame from Guatemala's elite to the struggling Mayan communities. Or, for that matter, my discussion of Tiguan internal resentments ignores Ecuador's politicians and business owners who have supported the austerity policies that pushed people into the informal economy and ad hoc marketplaces like the art sales in El Ejido Park.

And yet, as compelling as these principles of ethical research are, turning a blind eye to internal fights will not do. In a recent book on Ecuador's

---

3. For examples of the intensity and bitterness of the debate among North American anthropologists sparked by Stoll's work, see the special issue of *Latin American Perspectives* 26, no. 6 (1999).

Amazonian indigenous movement and the Organization of Indigenous Peoples of Pastaza (OPIP), for example, Sawyer (2004) keeps the focus on how activists challenge both neoliberal policy makers and multinational corporate executives. Sawyer takes pains to show the ideological divides in all these encounters and the analytical acumen of indigenous leaders. Indeed, the account of OPIP leaders is so positive that it comes as a shock when, in the final pages of the book, we learn in passing that OPIP tore itself apart in a corruption scandal and its articulate leader was impeached by followers.

Clearly, a political story has been missed, one essential for the long-term prospects of indigenous activism. Furthermore, this story is important to account not only for the collapse of unity, but also for its emergence. Indeed, native groups can also unpredictably come together, as happened in the 2006 protest against the free trade agreement with the U.S. (see chapter 10). Given the significance of such political turbulence, Warren and Jackson (2005) have recently argued that anthropologists must find constructive ways to examine internal conflicts. Rappaport's *Intercultural Utopias* (2005) offers one starting point. By examining an overlooked field of relations in native politics—the negotiations among indigenous leaders and leftist activists—she traces how actors worked across differences *inside* Colombia's indigenous movement. The exchanges among indigenous people and outside collaborators functioned as "incubators for the generation of pluralist demands in the national arena" (Rappaport 2005, 59). This logic could be extended. The negotiations among indigenous people themselves built habits of wider political engagement.

This chapter documents an intense two-week period of community politicking. In this event, Tiguans explicitly spelled out the fundamental differences they had with one another's way of work and related issues of relocating to live in the city. The bitterness was palpable and in retelling the event, I stay close to the animosity. In the pages that follow, I detail four critical meetings that led to the partially successful defense of the Tiguans' marketplace. Amid the arguing and airing of grievances, the flow of action in 1999 revealed a new political asset, a coordinator with ties to the national indigenous movement. It also underscored the power of an old political practice, sustained dialogue. More than anything, though, Tiguans demonstrated that unlike anthropologists' recent ducking of internal feuding, for Kichwa men and women, the path to unity is very often directly through conflict, not around it.

Meeting #1: The Engineer Sets the Terms

The meeting with the city engineer to establish a list of Tiguans who could continue to sell in the park had been set up by six resellers who had had some contact with city hall. The vendors were also in touch with a mestizo-led artist association, Asociación de Artes Plasticos, which was close to striking a deal to save their posts. The engineer agreed to meet with the six Tiguan vendors on a Friday in mid-June at 10 a.m. At 9 a.m., around a dozen Tiguans and I had gathered outside the municipal building in Quito's famous Plaza Grande, the heart of the old colonial city. Puri and one of her sisters chatted together on a bench. Several men were having their shoes shined. Alfredo Toaquiza then arrived.

People drew close to him as he started to talk about the upcoming meeting. Right off the bat, he raised the issue of the resellers. He said, "Let's be clear about this. Those of us here are *negociantes* [Sp. business people]. We are here as negociantes, not painters." He needled the others, saying that many could no longer sell directly in the park because they could not compete against the resellers' stalls. "We have to find a solution so that all can sell."

No one directly replied to Alfredo. After him, Francisco Chugchillan spoke. He was the president of Tigua-Chami's artist association, but he began by downplaying that role and seeking wider unity in a shared heritage. He said, "We are not here as Pichincha [Quito's province and home to one of the new official painters' associations], as Chami, as Quiloa. But we are here with this art that we have from Julio Toaquiza."

The third and final speaker was a stranger invited by Chugchillan. He was a young, lean man named José Atupaña who wore an expensive leather jacket and spoke in a formal Kichwa that spanned dialects. After thanking people for the opportunity to speak, he urged them to think tactically. He was very explicit about the goals of this meeting, enumerating them and ticking them off on his fingers: "First, we have come to learn. We have come to find out the policies of this administration. Second, we come as one group, *mingashpa* (K. collectively; literally, "making a minga"). Third, we have not come to say yes or no to anything. We have just come to find out and afterwards we will meet and discuss things and then meet again with the city government."

Atupaña was a new kind of activist. In the wider gambit of his organizing of Kichwa organizations in Quito, the Quito-Pichincha Tiguan artist association counted loosely within Atupaña's constituency (Atupaña

2001). Yet, he had no personal stake in the issue beyond the politics itself. Versed in confrontations with authority, he sought mostly to guide the migrants and strengthen their position. After he spoke, he accompanied the Tiguans to the office of the engineer. He was not there. An assistant, overwhelmed by the size of the group, arranged to have a municipal auditorium for the meeting and led everyone there. Over the next hour, the numbers swelled to over forty. Still the engineer did not show.

Finally, with the clock approaching noon, the engineer strode onto the stage. He was a tall man and balding, with his remaining hair worn long and swept back. He did not bother apologizing for keeping people waiting two hours, but took a seat alone at a table on the dais. Calling out, "Senores Pintores who participate in the project of El Ejido," he went on to welcome them to city hall for a discussion of their selling activity.

José Atupaña jumped up after the engineer spoke. He said that the posts were a central issue, yes, but more importantly, he wanted to know about the policies of this administration.

The engineer did not even look at Atupaña. He slowly leafed through the notebook he had opened on his table as Atupaña spoke. When the activist stopped, the engineer asked, "What is your name?"

"José Atupaña of the movement of indigenous associations."

The engineer wrote it down and then asked for his telephone number. In a very quiet voice, one that barely carried the six rows back to where I sat, the engineer said he did not want to talk about general policy. He stared at Atupaña and added, "A lot of people want to take advantage of the small business person. I want to work with him.

"We are here for the first time, to initiate something. I am here to speak individually with people. I do not want polarization." The engineer said, "This is not the first time I have worked with indígenas. I just had a meeting with 400 Otavalos with much happiness."

And having brought up this invidious comparison with the Otavalos (large numbers, eagerness to work), he indicated that already he was not happy. He observed, "If you have a dinner at your house and you invite me, then I do not have the right to bring along others who are not invited." Clearly Tiguans' numbers and the presence of an independent indigenous organizer upset his plan to quietly cut a deal with a small number of painters and be done with this particular group of park users.

Puri Cuyo challenged even his first remarks. "This is not the first time we have met," she called out. Several others agreed. José Atupaña stood again and complained about the lack of respect shown and the two hour delay.

Amid general murmuring, the engineer sat there looking down at his notebook, flicking through the list of names that pertained to the mestizo-dominated Asociación de Artes Plasticos. He said that there was not one Tigua artist here on his list. "Why aren't you organized with the other artists who work in the park? I do not want a confrontation here, but why aren't you part of the associations that we run in the park?

"Do you know how many people worked in the parks? [pause] 2,000." He picked up a thick gate-folded printout, presumably of these 2,000, and waved it for effect. "I am responsible for the welfare of all these people." He stood up, took out a marker and turned to the whiteboard behind him, drawing a long, narrow oval representing Quito.

Then, in the most simplistic terms possible he talked about the growth of Quito. "Centuries ago, there was one small place to buy and sell, and it was the Plaza Grande, [He drew a small square representing the plaza] and now there are over 300 markets. But, what else does a city need? Streets? [He squiggled in some streets] Churches? Schools? Parks?" He punctuated each question by adding little boxes to his diagram.

Then he drew a house and said that it stood for the city government. "We have rules that we live by. When you come from the country you cannot bring your horse on the trolley, can you? Like that we have rules and we have rights, so we can all live in the city. The city government is the one who determines our obligations to build a harmonious city.

"Who are the constituents of the city government? First, those who were born in Quito. Then those who move here, the Manabitos [from Manabi on the coast], the Otavalos [He drew dashes down to the bottom of the board where he wrote "gringos"], all the way to the gringos who need their hotels and restaurants." Finally above the gringos, he wrote in "Tigua" a dash and the number 30. "Here is the community of Tigua," he announced.

"What would happen if I asked the other 2,000 whether the Tiguans should have a special place? They would answer, 'They should go back to their land.' This is where the city government comes in: to work things out, because it is clear Tiguans have a special work." The engineer then got out his original list of Tiguans and called out a name.

José Atupaña had had enough. He stood and said, "Those born in Quito are one thing, but we have 500 years of being born here." And having alluded to the anti-Columbus protests that launched the indigenous movements to prominence, he thanked the engineer and the Tiguans for their time and left.

Francisco Chugchillan then stood and addressed the crowd, this time in Kichwa. If the engineer assumed Francisco was translating, he was wrong. Rather, Francisco voiced what most were thinking. So far the engineer had been wasting their time, he said. Yet Francisco asked for people to stay so that they could all get on the list. The use of Kichwa was symbolic, reinforcing Atupaña's point about the authority and authenticity of their indigenousness (Graham 2002). The language confirmed that they did come from their "own land" with its own cultural heritage and now with its own movement, represented in this meeting by Atupaña.

But the language did more than represent indigenousness. It was an instrument in managing the situation. After an hour of the engineer's hectoring and intimidation, the Tiguans could use their language to open up a restricted political space for themselves. They excluded the engineer from their deliberations, affirmed their own impressions, and arrived at their next move. Still, they preserved the frame of the meeting. The official had suddenly been denied access to the flow of events but was technically presiding, consecrating and officializing the actions even as he stared mutely at the audience.

The engineer simply ignored both Atupaña's exit and the Kichwa interlude and went on to read his list after Francisco sat back down. He then looked up and asked about the rest. Some asked why they were not already on the list. Others said that they had claims for posts. He gave in to reality and went along row by row asking for names. He finished writing and asked, "Why isn't there one organization that can speak for the Tiguans?"

Francisco spoke up and said that there were three organizations. Another added the group that Alfredo Toaquiza ran. The engineer shook his head in disbelief and rephrased his question. "Why are there four associations for such a small group of painters?

Francisco said, "We are different communities, each with its own regulation. There are twenty-five communities in Tigua."

"Why didn't you just make a single group?" the engineer repeated.

"I completely agree that we need one," Francisco said

"Well, I appreciate your thoughtful assessment of the situation," the engineer said and then moved on to the crux of the matter. He said far too many people in Quito wanted to sell in the park. Thus they have to come up with some alternatives. He suggested having a space in the park that was representative of Tigua but did not contain posts for everyone, a "site for the sale of Tigua Art." He noted that the artists would have to find some fair allocation of the space in these sites. "I'm thinking collectively, not individually," he affirmed and then moved to wrap up. Saying that the meeting was only for informational purposes, he would tour the park the following Sunday to confirm who was occupying which posts in the park. He then opened the floor to questions.

Alfredo Toaquiza got up with two sheets of notebook paper on which he had written down the points he wanted to make. He introduced his remarks by saying that he spoke both for himself and for his cooperative in Chimbacucho and admitted that "the reality is that we [Tiguans] are divided," but he pointed out that among the different organizations there were 175 *socios* (Sp. members) challenging the number 30 that the engineer had been using. He went on to raise a number of resources that he felt Tiguans were entitled to.

The engineer thanked him for his words, got up, shook hands with a couple of people, and left without waiting to hear what any of the other artists had to say. The Tiguans got up and filed out, reconvening in the Plaza Grande. On the whole, the Tiguans were not upbeat. Although the engineer had augmented his list and shown he was willing to work with the Tiguans, he had implied that they had only two choices: either throw their lot in with the Artes Plasticos group run by mestizos or form a single organization of their own. The first meant activating the moribund memberships that many actually already had in the Artes Plasticos organization to become minority block—both numerically and ethnically. The second meant opening up and trying to resolve old problems among themselves.

As they talked over the options, José Atupaña returned. Counseling patience, he urged people to hold off making any decision and set up to meet Monday morning at 10. He reminded them of their tactical success. They had thwarted the ready-made maneuver of a quick, private act of patronage. In essence, policy making became more two-sided, with indígenas creating scope for offering counter proposals that reflected their interests.

Meeting #2: Making Hard Choices

Unable to use any conference room at city hall, José Atupaña had turned to his network of indigenous activists for space. A young gynecologist, an indigenous Otavaleña woman who had done her training in Cuba, offered her office. She ran a low-cost health project for migrant indígenas. Ushering everyone into her waiting room in an old building a few blocks off the main plaza, she chatted in Spanish with the visitors about the services she provided. Several Tiguans asked a lot of questions, apparently worried about the health of a family member. The doctor then left to attend to her own business and conversations reverted to Kichwa.

Alfredo Toaquiza arrived last, but spoke first. He began by apologizing for his lateness, saying that it is hard to get down here from Tigua, in a not-too-subtle allusion to his exclusive status as someone who still lived in the valley. He then went on to chastise people for "sleeping these past fourteen years." They had worked in the park but never got the prime space or official rights. Next he observed that those gathered in the room were the "business people" of their communities. To José Atupaña he said, "These people buy from others. Properly, each should have his own work, not represent others."

He went on, however, to say that these complaints are "internal things." His real problem was with the Artes Plasticos association. He did not want to unite with a mestizo organization in order to keep their rights to sell in the park. "Runapura! [K. Only indigenous people!] With one thought, one heart, one hand." He repeated this several times, borrowing the motto of the sierra's regional indigenous organization.

After Alfredo finished, José Atupaña asked who else wanted to speak. Francisco Cuyo, as president of Quiloa's association, spoke right up. He pointed out that *mishus* (K. mestizos—the leaders of the Artes Plasticos association in this case) came to deceive and that they cannot always be believed. However, he did not blame current problems of the division among runa on the mishus. Instead he turned and looked hard at Teodoro Ugsha,[4] one of the richest resellers from Chami, and said, "It is because of you all that we are divided, from the sales posts, from individualism. One person can't just work with the mishus for his own posts. I want to work to unite the four organizations to make it happen, to make things advance. Clearly some *compañeros* [Sp. comrades, meaning again Teodoro] are getting ahead, the rest are not."

José Atupaña stepped back in and emphasized that people need to talk things through. He then asked who wanted to speak next. Juan Luis Cuyo and several others pointed to or nodded to Teodoro, recognizing the right to respond. Teodoro stared at Francisco. "I am not working with the mishus," he said.

4. A pseudonym.

After the interchange between Francisco and Teodoro, Atupaña spoke up again. In a smooth, calm voice, he laid out two ground rules. He said, "The sad things, the bad things stay in this room. People can say what they want. It is like filling up a balloon." With his hands he showed a balloon getting bigger and bigger and bigger with the bad things that people had to say. "In the end . . . [he clapped his hands] they disappear." The second rule was that people had to listen to each other all the way through.

An older man, another reseller from Chami, spoke up to defend the value of reselling, especially the importance of not selling to the galleries who he said merely exploited the painters. Atupaña tried to summarize things to move the conversation along; he listed three main ideas. "First, whatever differences we have we are all painters of Tigua. Second, we need to make one organization out of the four. Third, we need to get above the problems of the smaller organizations."

Alfredo agreed that he wanted to make an overall Tigua painters organization, but he laid down two conditions. First, he did not want it to be in Quito. Second, alluding to the failed effort to eliminate reselling, he said, "I do not want to put in my hand and build this block by block and only to have it break down when it is half made. To build this group, Lucho [he sat forward on his chair and pointed to Juan Luis Cuyo] has responsibility for bringing along the resellers. For organization, Francisco [Quiloa's president] has responsibility. For Chami, Teodoro. For Pichincha, Francisco Chugchillan."

Then Teodoro spoke up, directly confronting Alfredo with a rumor that was clearly at the base of a lot of this day's ill feelings. Interestingly, he switched to Spanish. It was the first time the language had been used and reflected, in part, how Teodoro had moved from Chami when he was a young teenager and had come of age in Quito and was more comfortable speaking in Spanish. He reported that he had talked to a mestizo artist who said that Alfredo said, "They [all other Tiguans in the park] are resellers." This was a damning accusation since the Artes Plasticos group was working with the engineer to exclude intermediaries of any ethnicity from the park. Worse, according to Teodoro's source, Alfredo had named names. Because of this sort of backbiting, Teodoro said the people of Chami did not want to join an organization.

Alfredo denied saying it. He added, though, that anyone could tell when a person was selling others' paintings. An argument broke out as to whether this was true. Eventually, the topic switched back to creating a single Tiguan organization, but the confrontation between Teodoro and

Alfredo continued. Alfredo asked Teodoro what his personal concerns were about a single organization. "I have no worries about joining a single organization," he said. Alfredo paused, then repeated his question. Teodoro looked at him and repeated the answer.

Teodoro went on, though, to support the importance of indigenous resellers. "In the beginning it was just three people selling: me, Lucho, and Humberto. We had to defend ourselves against the galleries. Other Tiguans came for a week, for two weeks, and could not sell. Olga Fisch would buy some, but the galleries would not buy. They said no to the painters. We started to buy to protect ourselves from the exploitation of the galleries."

There was a lot of vocal agreement with what he said, a lot of nodding of heads.

Teodoro added, "I am also a painter. I am a good painter. My paintings have been shown in Canada at a university."

After Teodoro spoke, Alfredo backed down a bit and brought up an issue in which there was common ground. He reminded people that "the engineer said that there would be shared park space. That just won't work." In fact, people just started to laugh at the idea. Here was the old fantasy of peasant communities as cooperative production units. It bore no relation to the entrepreneurial, kin-ordered, petty capitalism of Tigua artisans.

Moving toward a conclusion, José Atupaña then tried to get people to think about some concrete steps. First, they would have to deal with the city government. The general idea was to delay things, bypass the engineer, and to deal with more senior administrators. Toward that end they should draft a letter that pointed out that they were from indigenous communities with "great quantities of problems and great quantities of things in which they are involved, including paintings." Further, they should say that in light of these problems, they would not be able to attend the next meeting scheduled by the engineer.

Working on another front, he said they would need to play with public opinion, get on TV and on the radio to talk about their paintings. José launched into a long pep talk on the virtues of indigenous culture of which the paintings were a part. He spoke of the power of their grandparents' grains, their barley and quinoa and potatoes. He reminded them that these gave them force to work all day, not like the rice and candies of the city. Finally, Atupaña forced the issue of whether they would work through the Artes Plasticos association and use their membership in that group to get a portion of the posts the engineer had promised them. He asked Teodoro, "If the city government says yes to the Artes Plasticos and no to Tigua, what are you going to do?" Teodoro smiled and said that he had to go to the meeting with the mestizos to find out what was happening. Atupaña then went around and asked every single person the same question. Everyone said they would resign from Artes Plasticos and work with Tigua. The president of Quiloa's group was asked last. "Shoot, I'll enter that mestizo group," he joked. Everyone laughed.

As they broke up, Atupaña added, "We are not fighting for sales posts. We are fighting for our life. There is a great quantity of things that we are as a people, among them are these paintings." They all promised to gather in a week to report on things and keep trying to unite the four organizations.

Meeting #3: Sharpening Lines of Conflict

In a week's time, Tiguans again gathered in the Plaza Grande and then headed to the gynecologist's office. They were locked out, so they went down the street to a little plaza by a trolley stop and had their meeting sitting on the edge of an empty fountain that stank of urine. A group from Chami ended up missing the gathering when they could not find the alternative location.

José Atupaña again started things off. He began by saying everyone had to commit to uniting, especially the resellers. However, he also brought Alfredo to task. Addressing him directly he insisted, "You have to make it clear, are you speaking for yourself or for your association?" Either was legitimate, he said, but to keep claiming to speak on others' behalf when you had not actually consulted them was wrong.

Next, someone reported back on their meeting with the Artes Plasticos association. Several of the Artes Plasticos board members believed the Tiguans to be craft sellers, not artists themselves, and suggested a test of painting ability. The indígenas were outraged. For all the problems they had with their own middlemen, they bristled at the arrogance of the mestizos who presumed to judge their compositions and techniques.

In the ensuing discussion, several Tiguans who were members of the mestizo group suggested a procedural way to defend their art. They would demand that the meetings of the Artes Plasticos association must henceforth be in both Spanish and Kichwa. To be sure, translating into Kichwa would slow meetings down and would be unnecessary for Tiguan members, all of whom spoke Spanish fluently. Yet the use of Kichwa would

underscore the differing cultural worlds and aesthetic standards of indigenous and mestizo members. While the gathered Tiguans all liked this idea,
they also concluded that just the suggestion of a painting test showed that
the Artes Plasticos option would be unworkable. "That is the situation;
let's form our organization," Atupaña concluded to general affirmation.

For Atupaña, though, organizational work had to be connected to
creating a public position of strength. He underscored, "The issue of the
posts remains open. . . . Now we work with public opinion and connect
with the indigenous movement that is taking place here in Quito. Not only
are we more than the 30, but closer to 13,000, [members of Quito-based
indigenous associations] and we are not sitting around but are organized.
They will be brought along with this matter of Tiguans in the Ejido." Concretely, he thought they could work up a media campaign for fifteen days,
especially working with the radio, but also with a newspaper.

The idea of such outreach, though, met with a cool reception. Others
at the meeting turned their attention to the pragmatics of bringing themselves together. Alfredo, for example, spoke after Atupaña but ignored his
comments. Taking a confrontational tone, he called out the names of the
associations. What he was making clear was the weak representation from
Chami and the absence of Teodoro.

Juan Luis Cuyo said that Teodoro told him he would not come to the
meeting and he did not plan to follow the new organization. He quoted
Teodoro, saying, "I do not agree. People are not united." Juan Luis added
that Teodoro had been divisive for a long time, that he always worked
"one person, alone."

José Vega then spoke up, broadening the meaning of Teodoro's lack of
cooperation. José began by recapping the story of his fight for the posts
in 1983. In this version he was very explicit about the fact that it was first
Quiloa's association that got them, and Chami came after. He had been
fighting Chami for fifteen years, he said, and as far as José was concerned,
Teodoro was one more sign of the trouble with Chami.

Alfredo spoke up, his words coming out loud and fast. He said that if
one person alone did not want to do it, that it should not stop them. "Just
leave Teodoro alone," he said. "Teodoro deserves whatever punishment
that is coming from the council of his community—the big council. They
are the main leaders. . . . Teodoro is like a rotten potato, the potato with
worms in the middle of a big sack. If you do not reach in with your hand
and take out that potato, the whole sack is ruined. Let's not wait another
sixteen years to unite because of Teodoro."

Atupaña then shifted the topic from Teodoro to the pragmatics of moving forward. He said that they must create a commission for the new organization they wanted to form. The Tiguans agreed and quickly came up with members of such a commission and charged it with visiting each individual association.

Alfredo, who was becoming increasingly vociferous, called out, "The people of Tigua need a house, a floor, their land in Quito. We are fighting for land, compañeros, not water or electricity. We are 200 painters, forty or so are in the park, we need space. We will not advance within the Artes Plasticos group. The government says that there is only one nation, one education, one language. This is a lie. We are not one nation, we are many. And we are not one art. We must have our own space. The time of these patrons is over."

While Alfredo borrowed from the discourse of the indigenous movement, his and others' actions, in fact, shrank back from the politics the movement engaged. Atupaña's vision of a public relations campaign, for example, was ignored. For most Tiguans, there was little in this fight beyond the crucial need of preserving the posts. They did not intend to make this a matter of citywide politics. At the same time, many Tiguans consistently elevated the fight from personal disputes to community politics. To be sure, they targeted Teodoro for his individualism. However, in Teodoro, the president of Quiloa had selected a focus for his anger that lay outside his community. Indeed, Quiloa's Juan Luis Cuyo was both wealthier and more directly living from the artists of Quiloa. Rather than confront Juan Luis, though, Francisco and José Vega converted economic conflict into a dispute between two neighboring sectors, Quiloa and Chami. The next meeting among Tiguans directly addressed this confrontation.

Meeting #4: Unity (After a Fashion)

Quiloa called the first of the individual association meetings intended to poll members about joining a new combined group. Humberto Vega, the intermediary who had bought the pickup truck, agreed to host it. Humberto, in fact, had stopped selling paintings and instead worked as a potato middleman and had recently bought a second truck. His house in the southern Quiteño neighborhood of Guamani, though, stood a block back from the Pan-American Highway and was easy to get to. The meeting took place out front on the patio, which had begun to crumble under the weight of the two vehicles he kept parked there.

From the beginning of the gathering, it was clear that it was going to be about more than the whether Quiloans wanted to join up with a unified association or not. For one thing, about twenty people from Chami came, roughly matching the number of Quiloan painters who had gathered. For another, the "rotten potato" himself, Teodoro, was among them. The Chami painters stood along a brick wall, while Quiloans sat in a line of chairs at a right angle to the wall. They appeared as two opposing camps that could not even face each other.

Francisco, the president of the Quiloa organization, started the meeting by recapping the sentiment of the last meeting and the need to form one group of Tigua painters.

Teodoro then spoke up and in Kichwa this time. He said that he did not come to the last meeting because he thought it would be in vain, that it had not been clear what the meeting would accomplish. "If we make a larger group, whatever we say, whatever we hope to gain must be very clear. What solutions are we going to look for? Where are we going with Quiloa people, the big organization? All of this must be very clear."

Another man from Chami, one who had attended the last meeting, followed Teodoro: "I respect José Atupaña, Alfredo, but the unification and the plan must come from us. They are advanced [that is, politically experienced], but we are not children. And José does not know about art, about the posts in the Ejido. I have not seen José in the Ejido."

José Vega then spoke up. He agreed that Atupaña did not know about their art and the park. He then went on to speak, once again, about founding the artist association and the first fight to sell in the park. He said, though, that now he would be in favor of one single association.

A third man from Chami then spoke, saying that one single association would be good. He added his voice to those seeking to distance themselves from the two men who saw a broader struggle in this, "Alfredo is a very hard man. José wants the Tiguans to work with other organizations, to work with peasant groups. But we have our ideas, our art."

Teodoro spoke again, this time to defend the mestizos and the Artes Plasticos association. Teodoro said that it was a misunderstanding that the mestizos are intent on testing Tiguans to kick them out. He said that at a recent meeting, the Artes Plasticos directors told him, "We will not leave the Tiguans out to die." More than that, they had concrete proposals on the table with the city government. "Things are very clear with them."

Quiloa president Francisco spoke again, talking more directly about what worried him. He said, "My work is with all the people or with no one." He did not want to secure sales posts so that only intermediaries could continue their work. He also refuted Teodoro, saying,"We have clear proposals. We will go directly to the city government and leave the Artes Plasticos people, but the problem is all this competition among ourselves. It is not for nothing that we have divisions."

The next twenty minutes was spent disputing what happened two years ago when they tried to end reselling. Teodoro refuted Quiloans' (particularly José's) assertions that it was because of Chami that there was no agreement. Another man from Chami then asked rhetorically, "Who reported Tiguans to be businesspeople?" He implied that Alfredo was at the cause of the split among Tiguans. "I have to respect him as a founder and a good painter, but if one causes problems, you have to remove him. If you have a wormy potato in your sack you must find it and throw it away."

Yet even as the rotten potato status was being transferred from Teodoro to Alfredo, Quiloan president Francisco spoke in defense of Alfredo and of his critique of reselling. Francisco's comments elicited more lengthy defenses of intermediaries. Teodoro was most explicit about the economic service intermediaries offered. He said, "I once went with my cousins to sell clothes in Colombia; we worked for days and sold nothing, not one thing. For weeks we walked, we suffered. This painting work is tranquil; with it a Tiguan can live with one's wife, peacefully with one's family. If we do not do this (buying from each other), what do we have?" He went on to point out how hard it was to be a reseller. "We do not have capital like someone selling stock, who can buy and store and buy and store paintings. We have to get out and sell them or else we cannot buy."

Francisco responded by saying that he was not speaking against the businesspeople out of envy, but as a good director of the association. He worried about the lack of creativity of painters who produce in quantity for resellers and who no longer have direct contact with tourists or collectors. He said that Teodoro, Luis, himself, and others used to come out to the park and compete against each other and got better. But, the art had become "totally paralyzed. It will be dead in five years. You yourselves are killing it."

Another man from Chami claimed signs of renewed creativity and the debate continued. Having started the meeting at 2:30 p.m., they were still hashing it out three hours later. In the course of the lengthy discussions, many Quiloans got up, stretched, and walked around. Some Chami men went and found some crates to sit on. Others sought out shade near the Quiloans. As time passed, the rigidity of two communities that were right-angled in stiff lines against each other broke down and the men formed a wide circle that mixed people from the communities. People were smiling and joking. Finally, at about 6 p.m., having cleared the air with Chami, Quiloans said they still wanted to talk among themselves about whether they would join a single organization. Even so, it had become clear that they would go into the discussion with an open mind and willingness to make it work.

Conclusion

At the outset of the mayor's campaign to clean up El Ejido, the circum-stances were rigged for a Tiguan political sellout. Rural-based painters disparaged the migrants. Quiloa disliked Chami. Chami envied Quiloa. Young painters and association officers fought the resellers. Wealthy in-termediaries had factionalized the associations. A small group of Tiguan merchants already had an inside line to city hall. Finally, a rival organiza-tion, Artes Plasticos, offered a backdoor to the sales posts for those who would walk out on the Tiguan groups.

The Tiguans, though, held it together long enough to create some op-tions. Even if the city government thought little of Tiguans' artist organi-zations, they could no longer ignore them. *Why* the Tiguans would stick together was more or less clear. For some it was a matter of a shared heri-tage. They all lived from "this art we have from Julio Toaquiza." Others joined together in their distrust of mestizos, whether the city engineer or the artists of the Artes Plasticos group. And many wanted to defend the economic autonomy they had achieved—their own work in their own home, free of patrons. Indeed, both those who attacked the reselling and those who defended it made their case in the same terms: insuring the survival of Tigua art. All immediately agreed that the posts were clearly central to the art's survival. *How* they overcame their divisions, though, needs more explaining.

The trade associations themselves offered a starting point. They grouped the painters, offered leaders, and defined a forum in which people could debate and legitimize courses of action. Yet the city government, not the associations, was the final keeper of the lists of project beneficiaries. Even the officers of the different organizations did not have clear authority within their own groups as each meeting involved naming officers and nonofficers to commissions to take care of specific tasks. And the associations were homeless, shifting their gatherings among public plazas, borrowed offices, and private houses.

In the event, the key to moving forward was as simple as it was contentious: talking it out. The discussions, though, had their own logic, shaped by a mediator, by the expectations of dialogue, and by choice of language. Intervening as a neutral outsider, Atupaña was nonetheless clearly committed to the same ideals as the Tiguans, especially keeping their economic fate in indigenous hands. Throughout the meetings, he kept people focused on what they needed to accomplish. Without cutting off arguments, he reminded people that they could not be content with a factionalized status quo. He urged people to work it out and move ahead.

Tiguans were more than willing to raise the issues that needed to be worked out. Nothing was hidden, nothing ducked. From the first speaker at the first Tiguan meeting, people accused others, repeated slanderous rumors, brought up old fights, underscored old divisions, and raised new ones. They named names, stared each other down, skipped a meeting when they were needed, and showed up at another when they were not. In sum, no Tiguan showed signs of buying into a new, unified group for its own sake. All seemed willing to let the fight for unification fail unless grievances were redressed.

And in seeking solutions, dialogue in its most basic form was key. Not guided by formal agendas, or rules of order, or motions and votes, political debate took its structure from the turn taking of conversation. Mannheim and Tedlock's (1995, 2) larger claim about culture has a special relevance for the narrower domain considered here: community politics "are continuously produced, reproduced and revised in dialogues among members." Put another way, the particular strength of debate is not that all have a say, but that "sayings" have "respondings." When Chami residents pushed to get their way, José Vega answered (twice) with the story about the Quiloa artisan association and its original defense of the posts. Francisco and Teodoro also played out their argument about reselling twice over, neither persuading the other one iota. When someone present was named as the source of trouble, others wanted that person to respond. In the end, the consequence was not unanimity among Tiguans but a restoration of damaged relations—a willingness to listen and reciprocate with one's own thoughts (Macas 2001).

Throughout the crisis, language itself served as a powerful instrument of solidarity and organizing. Teodoro's failure to use Kichwa early in the fight contributed to his isolation; his return to Kichwa was part of his reconciliation. The use of Kichwa during meetings diverted authority away from monolingual Spanish speakers. Out in the streets, gatherings of Tiguans drew curious eavesdroppers who would insert themselves into the edge of the group only to turn away again when they heard Kichwa. In city hall, speakers could shift into Kichwa while still accepting and affirming the conventions of meetings. Relations with authority could be simultaneously preserved and restricted. No surprise, then, that they insisted on Kichwa translation to cut the Artes Plasticos leaders down to size. A modest, practical autonomy could be achieved with their language without resorting to spatial separation. In some ways, such language-driven autonomy comes closest to the ideals of self-determination *and* engagement enunciated by CONAIE.

In the end, the results were mixed. They never formed a single association. Instead, a commission negotiated a block of eighteen posts exclusively for Tiguans, allocating them among current sellers on the basis of seniority, family connections, and community membership. City hall kept the list for the posts, offered identification cards, and collected fees for the use of the posts. From time to time, the posts changed hands, but only from one Tiguan to another according to prices set between the two parties. When this happened, the engineer was (and still is) informed after the fact.

For José Atupaña and his defense of 13,000 members of indigenous associations in Quito, the El Ejido struggle was a lost opportunity. The Tiguans could have been his Rosa Parks. They were worthy, hardworking men and women done wrong. Their paintings, Sunday sales posts, well-dressed intermediaries, and articulate officers could have been the public face of other struggles. With them, Atupaña could take the fight citywide. He was all set to use the media to defend Tiguans and others who are pushed around, reminded that "they should go back to their land," that Quiteño-born have a higher claim. Alone among the Tiguans, Alfredo Toaquiza saw the value of placing the fight in wider terms. Others understood Atupaña's goals, talked them over, and quickly put them aside. The political invisibility of urban, indigenous organizations would remain a problem at both a personal and collective level for Kichwa peoples, as the remaining chapters show.

FIGURE 16 A Guamani tenement where many Tiguans started life in the city in the 1990s, Quito, 1999

Cities and Kin (Don't Lie)

Whenever you see a man who gives someone else's corruption, someone else's prejudice, as a reason for not taking action himself, you see a cog in The Machine that governs us. —John Jay Chapman

For Evans-Pritchard (1940), the feud was a political institution that helped constitute lineages and defined tribal insiders: "Inter-community fighting and the feuds that result from it are part of the political relations that exist between segments of a common tribal organization" (Evans-Pritchard 1940, 152). Victor Turner (1957) likewise found that a social breach and crisis, followed by acts of redress and repair—sequences he labeled "social dramas"—were integral to the formation of communities. Regulated antagonism, that is, went hand-in-hand with enduring political structure. These authors made their points about acephelous political systems, but their insights matter for contemporary activism. In similar terms, the prior chapters could be read as showing the ways crisis and community come to depend on each other for form and consistency.

Indigenous communities and trade associations cohere when a dispute takes on a narrow set of characteristics. Generally, for a clash to trigger productive political activity, it must accomplish three things: affect a group of people with social bonds exceeding any single household, reveal the shortcomings of state action, and set up a trial of effectiveness among organizations from different communities or trade groups. Such trials can be outright rivalries, such as Ariasucu's challenge to defend its jurisdiction against Agato. Conversely, they can be indirect, such as when the Quiloan council tried to measure up to Chimbacucho's leaders during its minga to build a bridge. Whether a crisis takes on these three attributes depends on the decisions and rhetoric of the protagonists. In the small ruptures, personal problems, and accidents that recur in life, people may see neither a communal crisis nor the relevance of their councils or association officers.

Indeed, most encounters between indigenous people and the state are not mediated by community institutions. Even so, they often entail a type of collective mobilization. Registering for school, titling lands, documenting births and marriages, getting services at government clinics, and coping with the court system all pit individuals against bureaucracies. As the problem gets more complicated, concerned parties enlist greater numbers of family members. Tiguans in Quito, in fact, had a long history of working with family networks. At first, kin contacts helped organize migration to the city and the spread of painting skill. Later, wealthy intermediaries reinforced extended families by contracting among relatives for the purchase of paintings. They formed bonds of *compadrazgo* (Sp. coparenthood) with cousins, nephews, and nieces who had been prolific suppliers. As families fell into internal patterns of patrons and clients, they wound up elevating a few wealthy households as both economic hubs and social authorities.

Yet the power of such networks in the marketplace did not translate into clout in bureaucratic or judicial settings. Humberto Vega's[1] misfortunes in 1999 and 2001 illustrate the different tactics that emerged when legal problems struck Tiguans. His arrest for drunk driving in 1999 illustrated both impressive solidarity and the resources people can summon when facing trouble. Unfortunately, the episode also showed that indigenous wealth does not buy much. Legal process strips indigenous people down in ways that their money and their family cannot build them back up. Indigenous clout beyond collective responses of community and association remained elusive. The second episode, in contrast, shows how individual legal troubles can become officialized as a community problem. Yet this second incident, one of urban gangs and assault, replayed old Tiguan rivalries. Together they offer something of a negative case study. Reveal-

1. A pseudonym, like all names used in this story.

ing again the state in its dreary, plodding process, the first arrest shows the vulnerabilities of indigenous people stripped of their statecraft.

* * *

One of a few Tiguans to get into commercial trucking, Humberto has long had a high profile in the Tiguan migrant community. He succeeded in the Tigua art trade by leaving Quito to open a new market in Otavalo and then leaving Otavalo to sell in Guayaquil. In 1999 he set himself up as a potato broker, staking his success on taking out large loans and striking risky deals.

Comradely drinking greatly facilitated his deal making. I got a taste of this at Corpus Christi that year, when he spotted me at a bus stop in Zumbagua waiting for a ride up and out of the valley and back over to Quindicilli. He beckoned me over to a roadside tavern, where we downed four big bottles of Pilsner beer in half an hour and reminisced about the FUNHABIT housing project in Quiloa. He then offered me a ride, which I declined. When, a few weeks later, my host in Quito told me that Humberto had been arrested for drunk driving, I was not surprised. The police had picked him up in Cotopaxi province at a routine checkpoint as he traveled the Pan-American Highway home to Quito from Ambato.

They locked him up in the municipal jail in Latacunga. Here his troubles began. In the 1990 uprising, these same jailers were the subject of protestors' street theater, when indigenous leaders acted out the police's abuse of their impoverished prisoners and deference to rich landowners' sons (see chapter 4). Worried that little had changed, the family responded quickly. Early on the day following his arrest, a small group of people traveled to Latacunga to secure his release. They returned to Quito that afternoon with bad news. Although officials rarely held motorists for more than a day, the police planned to lock up Humberto for twenty-one, the maximum allowed by law. Because Humberto's wife, Mercedes Cayo, and her four sisters comprised a pivotal node among the network of migrants from Quiloa, the response to this setback was forceful and well coordinated.

Mercedes fretted over how to get food to her husband, earn money for the family, take care of Humberto's loans, and work things out with the traffic court. She found a lawyer and worked closely with two of her brothers-in-law to comply with his instructions. By the end of the week, they had arranged for testimony from a third brother-in-law who lived just south of Quito and from a compadre who had moved to a town near

Latacunga. I accompanied family members down to the court on the day of the testimony. We arrived too early to see Humberto, so we sat down to a bowl of soup in Latacunga's quiet market. Two Tiguans at an adjacent table moved over to our bench and later accompanied us back to the jail.

Humberto was in a large free-standing cell that stood in the middle of an old courtyard. He had a broom in one hand and some disposable soup containers in the other, all of which he was trying to hand back to the guard. We in turn handed him another bowl of soup and he joked that he was getting fat. After the visit, we went down to the lawyer's office. One of the witnesses was waiting in a doorway across the street, stepping out of the shadows when he saw us appear. Forty-five minutes later, the second witness and his brother arrived. The Tiguans entered the lawyer's office, a storefront operation that opened fully onto the street the way a dry goods shop would.

From the outset, the Tiguans (and I) had difficulty following the lawyer's plan. He had before him a set of typed documents. At first, I thought they were some kind of police report of the incident. The lawyer started to review drunken driving laws and the possible penalties. He then turned to the pages laid out on his desk. Here was the gist of what then transpired, as I recorded in my field notes that day:

> Having driven home the severity of the problem, [the lawyer] pulled out several light-blue, long, wispy sheets of paper and said that these were the statements of the witnesses. There were some lies here, he admitted. "Sometimes it is necessary to tell some little lies," he said.
>
> He started to read the major points. At first I thought he was going through and clarifying things. For example, he said, point one, [Humberto] is not a relative, or a compadre, or an employer, just an acquaintance. And they agreed. Then he went on to point two and asked them if they knew Raul Orgullo. They said no, they did not know Raul.
>
> "No!" shouted the lawyer. "You *do* know him. He is a driver from Ambato. You've known him for five years.
>
> "Look," he pleaded. "These are all lies," he said, shaking the blue papers. "You are here for a lesson in lying. If you do not get this right, then the whole thing falls apart, the whole thing is screwed."
>
> Then he returned to the subject of Raul Orgullo, saying that they had known him for five years. "He is an imaginary man," he said. If they are asked, they say that he is of medium build, *moreno* [dark complexion], not too fat, not too thin, his black hair combed back. (An utterly unfalsifiable description since it

covered every man in the room, with the exception of the lawyer himself who was portly with thin, gray hair.)

After conjuring Raul Orgullo into existence, the lawyer went on with the rest of the statement. It was one long, boldface lie. I had thought the witnesses were there as character witnesses. No, they were characters in a fictional tale. . . .

Once the lawyer told the witnesses the specifics, he urged them not to talk too much. "The worst witnesses are those who go on and on. The best just shut up." It's clear that this was pretty routine for him.

The story fabricated by the lawyer bewildered everyone. In brief, this Raul Orgullo had supposedly been driving the truck with Humberto sleeping at his side in the cab. The witnesses, according to the lawyer's sheets, had been picked up on the way out of Ambato. At the checkpoint, Raul got down from the cab and told the police he needed to check his tires. The lawyer had the witnesses peering over the top of the truck panels, observing Raul check the left rear tire, then walk around to the right rear tire, then race off like a rabbit across the fields never to be seen again. Frightened, the two witnesses then climbed out and snuck off themselves. Poor Humberto then woke up alone in the cab staring into a policeman's light. Rotten luck.

After drilling the men in their parts in this story, the lawyer packed up his notes on the case and led us down to the courthouse. Several more painters separated from a group of men loitering in the median of the road by the court building and came over to join us. At the doorway to traffic court number two we met Mercedes and her oldest son. Now almost a dozen strong, Humberto's support group had arrived from three different cities and materialized in the streets of Latacunga like a network of clandestine agents bent on a special mission. We all crowded into the judge's waiting room as a secretary cranked a sheet of paper into the typewriter, anticipating the first witness.

The oldest in the group, one of Humberto's brothers-in-law, a former officer of the painters' association and skilled artist, stepped forward. He had been a vocal participant in the ongoing meetings about the El Ejido posts and had long worked with both state agencies and NGOs. Now, he made no eloquent speeches. Suitably taciturn, he sat in the chair next to the secretary's desk and stared into the middle distance as the woman re-typed text from the lawyer's blue stationary into the court proceedings. She checked with the witness to confirm each element.

"Are you a relative of Humberto Vega?" she asked.

"No," the witness murmured.

"Raul Orgullo was driving?" she asked.

"Yes," he quietly said.

"You got on the truck in Ambato?" she asked.

"Yes."

Finally, the obligatory question: "Why have you come forward?" asked the secretary.

"Because we want the truth to be known," said the witness, repeating a line drummed into him by the lawyer.

The second witness took the chair to verify the account of a runaway driver in monosyllables and mumbled responses. The secretary rolled the sheets out of the typewriter, tapped the carbon paper back into place and set them on her desk top. They both signed the forms and went in the hall to wait for the lawyer. After a private conversation with the secretary, the advocate bustled out of the office and beckoned everyone to follow him. Upon returning to his office, he praised everyone, saying that it went "*super bueno*."

The Tiguans had their doubts. I heard one of the witnesses talking it over with his comrades. They rationalized the lies, saying that there had not been an accident. No one had been hurt. Even so, all recognized this for what it was. "Do you have corruption like this in the U.S.?" one man asked me. I said that our court system works differently. "This is why Ecuador goes back, back, back," he went on. "The lawyers are corrupt, the judges are corrupt, the politicians are corrupt." In the end, the ploy achieved mixed results: Humberto served five more days after the hearing, eleven in all. While he escaped the full sentence, most Tiguans suspected no one else in Latacunga had ever served such time for drunk driving. Many of Humberto's relatives grumbled that hundreds of dollars spent on lawyer's fees went in vain.

The Tiguans seemed to sell out that day. They made no effort to mobilize community authority or Cotopaxi's provincial indigenous movement, which had a strong presence in Latacunga. Of course, in the logic of social movements, Humberto's wealth and likely guilt undermined his worthiness as a political cause. Fighting the unfairness of Ecuador's legal machinery, activists strengthen their hand by defending those who combine vulnerability with righteousness. Such weakness in a victim, in fact, strengthens a movement's ability "to emphasize the unjust treatment" of a whole category of people (Tilly 1998, 212). Accused perpetrators such as Humberto fall short of this purity. Their chance of allies beyond family diminishes. In contrast to social movements, though, community leaders will take up the cause of the corrupt or criminal in their ranks. Yet, even their involvement requires wider stakes than one person's misfortune, as the subsequent incident shows.

Other Arrests, Other Fights

Tiguans' trouble with the law, in fact, takes a variety of forms and provokes diverse responses. A month after Humberto's problems had been worked out, a Tiguan youth was found with a stolen stereo and television, arrested, and taken to Quito's main jail. Inconsolable, his mother came in the company of her brother and a compadre to call upon Juan Luis Cuyo to ask for a loan to hire a lawyer. He did not hesitate in granting her request. Another young man from Tigua was badly mugged in Guamani when returning from a wedding of two Tiguans being celebrated in that barrio. The youth was knocked out and robbed of his money, watch, pants, and shoes. The police ignored both the crime and his injuries, despite the victim's clear suspicions about the perpetrators.

Amid the paranoia that now prevails in many Quiteño barrios, the Tiguans' artistic occupation alone suffices to put some migrants at risk. Spending day after day indoors at their painting tables, they give neighbors little clue how they earn their living, despite sometimes living in intimate proximity with others in an urban tenement (see figure 16). The officer from one neighborhood council, for example, confronted a painter in 1999. He said that others on the block believed the Tiguan and his relatives were thieves who slept all day and left to rob at night. While my informant laughed when he repeated this accusation, I know of another painter who was falsely denounced as a thief and spent a harrowing week in jail.

A more troublesome case occurred in October 2001. In the barrio Chillogallo, two sons of an older Tiguan migrant named Segundo Millangalle had joined a street gang. Segundo himself counted among the first generation of migrants, helping to found an artisan association with migrants from the Chami. He also had been elected an officer of the mestizo-led artist organization of El Ejido Park. In sad contrast, his sons had made little headway in Quito, encountering exclusion where their father had found opportunity. Instead of being an open marketplace for their art, El Ejido was dominated by rich Tiguan intermediaries who set low prices for young artists' work and dictated the types of scenes they wanted painted.

Socially, in school they had always been indigenous "migrants," outsiders who were not properly Quiteño. Politically, their neighborhood had been run for decades by a tight clique of mestizo families that shut out people such as the Tiguans.

The boys joined a gang and here they made a mark. In fact, their violence raised the stature of the whole gang. Residents of Chillogallo began to ignore the old barrio officers and instead complied with the gang's leaders. Feeling their authority threatened, the neighborhood council aligned with thugs who went after the gang and especially the new indigenous members.[2] The council's hooligans missed their mark. They beat up the father Segundo and not his sons. When the neighborhood council heard about the assault, they washed their hands of it. They went further and lied to the police, denouncing Segundo himself as complicit in gang activities. The police then arrested Segundo, who was gravely injured from the assault, and took him to the Comisariat Nacional.

The day after the attack and arrest, Segundo's family, members of Chami's painters' association, and a number of Quiloans showed up at the Comisariat to demand Segundo's release. In a savage and bizarre turn, Segundo's sons led an attack on the Tigua-Quiloan migrants right in front of Comisariat. They assaulted none other than Humberto Vega for supposedly meddling, injuring him so severely that he had to be taken to a medical clinic.

The following day approximately forty Tiguans gathered on the sidewalks in front of the Comisariat. Unlike Humberto's past problem, this conflict drew both present and past officers of the Quiloa artist association. Some came from as far away as Latacunga. Given the complexity of the episode, the group lobbied first for the gang members' father's release, for his access to medical care, and for action against those who had harmed him, including the neighborhood council. Second, they were going to hold Segundo responsible for redressing Humberto's injuries.

While angered, several past association officers from Quiloa were surprisingly positive as they shuttled among the dozens of people clustered on the sidewalks outside the Comisariat. "I want to get more involved in the association again," a former officer told me. He saw this as a turning point for the group, a sign that it was getting back on its feet. Tiguans were speaking with authorities, mobilizing their community. They seemed

2. One man told me that the neighborhood bosses had actually hired this rival group of youths and contracted with them to drive the gang out.

beyond some of the past divisions of the association, and they were act-ing—not sitting around an office with some old-time lawyer and his les-sons in lying.

Of course, the reasons for the community response in this double as-sault case were not hard to find. Here they had two worthy victims. For his part, Segundo had long served his community and Tigua painters more generally. Indeed, honoring Segundo's efforts, Humberto had arrived in a show of support only to be shockingly attacked. This second assault then injected old intercommunity hostilities into the action. Thus, those with collective authority sought to achieve reparation while keeping the anger from spilling over to create more lasting problems between Quiloa and Chami. Finally, the perfidy of neighborhood officials festered at the base of the troubles. The mestizo-led barrio council had long excluded na-tive residents, conspired in Segundo's assault, and lied to the police. They crossed the line from ignorable neglect to unacceptable abuse.

Such experiences with authorities underscore why "Don't lie" has been one of the trilogy of values professed by the indigenous movement. This is not just high moralizing. "Don't lie," along with "Don't steal" and "Don't be lazy," is a code of political conduct that represented a break, not just from false promises of national politicians but from the backhanded treat-ment Tiguans and other indigenous people have received from local au-thorities. If schemes of corruption are complicated—tall tales spun by lawyers, underhanded deals struck by neighborhood authorities—their enactment is often all too simple: bearing false witness.

Indeed, it was for all the suffering they have endured through the lies of others that Tiguans' behavior that morning in 1999 in traffic court was so depressing. Without the associations they had built, ignoring the values held up by the movement, and lying through their teeth, Tiguans found themselves right back where they did not want to be: powerless and in cahoots with an untrustworthy mestizo. It would be a mistake, however, to read the Tiguans as being duped. They were neither ignorant nor for that matter lacking morals in all this. Humberto's extended family had rapidly come together to stand by one of their own. On this day, "Don't forsake" had trumped "Don't lie." They were accompanying a relative through his troubles, taking a calculated risk to try to minimize the burden his arrest would cause his wife and children. The gathered men and woman had sacrificed their work, bought bus fares to Latacunga, and contributed to the lawyer's fees. Once again, they threw their lot in with the system. Once again, it let them down.

FIGURE 17 Anti-TLC protest march organized by urban artisan association, Otavalo, 2006

CHAPTER TEN

Uprising, 2006

1. With the TLC [free trade agreement], indigenous peoples and peasants will be obligated to mono-culture, to use seeds treated in the laboratories of the United States (transgenetic), and use, in an indiscriminate manner, chemicals that damage the soil, poison the water, and propagate diseases such as cancer.—Reason #1 from "15 Reasons to say NO to the TLC," a pamphlet distributed during the anti-TLC protests by CHIJALLTA-FICI (The Federation of the Kichwa Peoples of the Northern Ecuadorian Highlands)

The Anti–Free Trade Strike, from the Windows of Our Pickup

On Wednesday, March 14, 2006, Chesca and I and our three children along with friends of ours from Iowa City and their son crowded into the double cab of our pickup truck. Driving toward Otavalo, we were trying once again to find an open road over the pass that connected the provinces of Imbabura and Pichincha. On the previous Monday, CONAIE had called a *paro*, or general strike, to try to force a national referendum on the free trade treaty between Ecuador and the United States. The protest far surpassed expectations. Indigenous communities had occupied the Pan-American Highway (known locally as the Pana) throughout the highlands. Interprovincial travel was at standstill.

Our friends needed to pick up their belongings and get back to their jobs and school in the states. I needed to start teaching a course back in Quito. And our three-year-old daughter, who was feverish and coughing at night, needed medicine from our house. After spending two nights at an empty conference center twenty kilometers short of our destination, we were anxious to find some way through. We had seen military trucks moving down the highway the evening before, leading a convoy of commercial buses and private cars. If we left early enough, we thought we might still get through.

When we got to the Pana, though, it was empty and quiet. Within half a kilometer, we arrived at the first blockade. A small eucalyptus tree had been dragged out, covering little more than half the road. A few soccer ball–size stones stood in the remaining gap. Two boys watched us from a grassy knoll next to the barrier. The younger one, about twelve years old, paced around. At our approach, he threw a couple of small rocks down into the barrier. I stopped the truck and got out to speak to them.

"Strike," said the twelve-year-old. "No hay paso. [There is no way through.]"

"I have my family. We need to get back to Otavalo," I tried.

"No hay paso. There are other strikers, close by. They have dug a big ditch." A month earlier, this stretch of the Pana had been stripped of asphalt for repaving. Taking advantage, strikers had cut deep trenches across the highway.

The older boy lay on the grass, eyes half open, looking at his cell phone screen, which glowed a bright blue. He smiled and looked like he might doze off. While I sized things up, the twelve-year-old wandered up behind the barricade, kicking at a stone in the dirt of the Pana, laughing to himself, muttering, "I need some rocks."

A still younger boy, no more than ten years old, came up the steep embankment at the side of the road.

"What have you got?" The twelve-year-old demanded.

"Wire," the boy answered, tugging along a thick tangle of rusted barbwire. The other one's face lit up. He jumped up the embankment, grabbed the wire and dragged it into the gap between the tips of the eucalyptus leaves and the gutter. He paced behind his improved barrier, and said to no one in particular, "Que viva el paro! [Long live the strike!]" And when the other boys ignored him, he answered himself, "Viva!"

I looked again at the cell phone, imagining the ditch down the highway, the men and women sitting around it, and the cell phones there whose numbers had been programmed into the speed dial on the phone here. "Hasta luego," I said and went back to the car, annoyed at the way strikes endowed kids with the purpose of a revolutionary and the power of a petty border officer, lording over some forgotten frontier outpost.

Insiders and Outsiders in the Time of the Neoliberal State

While always fighting *for* a distinctive cultural vision, Ecuador's indigenous movement nonetheless maintained its national profile owing to what it was *against*: neoliberalism (Garcia Serrano 2003; Guerrero Cazar and Ospina Peralta 2003). They had plenty of opportunity to attract attention with this cause. Government after government stayed the promarket course. From the orthodox conservatism of Sixto Ballen to the neopopulism of Bucarem to the patriotic nationalism of Gutierrez, men came to office under different banners. Once elected, though, they followed the same path: they cut back state-led development and pinned hopes of improved social welfare on economic growth (Guerrero Cazar and Ospina Peralta 2003, 12).

This philosophy found expression in a series of laws. The 1994 agricultural development law pushed to privatize land and water rights and end the state's commitment to land reform. The 2000 dollarization killed the Ecuadorian sucre and ended the use of currency devaluations to aid Ecuadorian business. The 2001 proposal to reduce fuel subsidies sought to bring basic household budgets in line with international commodity prices. Finally in 2006, the push to sign the Tratado de Comercio Libre (TLC or Free Trade Treaty) with the United States aimed to bring about a new competitiveness of Ecuadorian industry. These initiatives reflected none of the indigenous movement's ideals. CONAIE's platform of locally directed development rooted in community property and supported by state-sponsored credit and technical know-how had no more impact on state policy than an indigenous folktale.

If unchanging neoliberalism undermined indigenous goals within government, it elevated the indigenous movement outside of it. Indeed, leaders had become adept at using "the different measures of structural adjustment adopted by the governments as a rallying point of struggle and opposition" (Garcia Serrano 2003, 199). The most radicalized indigenous levantamientos occurred in response to the policies mentioned above. In 1994, the Second National Indigenous Uprising against the land development law lasted twenty days and paralyzed commerce in most of the nation.

In 2000, mobilizations against the dollar brought down the government of Mahuad. In 2001, strikes against the government's raising of fuel prices lasted fifteen days and resulted in negotiations that stretched out more than eight months.

As with the dollarization, if ever an issue seemed to call for a national effort, the fight against a free trade agreement between Ecuador and the United States was it. Imports of subsidized U.S. grain and tons of mass-produced chicken parts threatened the small earnings still available to peasants. The potential for U.S. "bio-prospectors" to patent medicines derived from plants identified by indigenous healers angered both highland and lowland people. Further, as an international negotiation, the treaty also seemed beyond the scope of local community activism. Indeed, what role could there be for communities in the politics of international trade?

Reviewing the two weeks of anti-TLC protests, I argue the role is in fact a significant one. Where national organizations offer coordination and visibility, communities deliver the practical punch. Indeed, community efforts in March 2006 led to surprisingly strong mobilizations. They effectively suspended state authority in Imbabura province, and they did so even as CONAIE faltered in its efforts to negotiate with President Palacio or make its case to the nation. While the steps undertaken by community leaders complement the work of the national movement, they also permit an alternative logic of protest, one that is far more decentralized.

Popular protests have long been recognized to grow through their own "aggregation process" (Glance and Huberman 1994; Granovetter 1978). In classic sociological analysis this surge relates to an individual willingness to jump in once the size of a crowd crosses a threshold that minimizes the political risks of any one participant. Rheingold (2002) has argued, though, that recent protests around the world reveal enhanced power of street activism. The protagonists in such events—be they the antiglobalization protestors in Seattle in 1999 or the millions of Filipinos who mobilized to remove President Joséph Estrada from office in 2001—are independent agents. Made up of individuals and autonomous subunits, they nonetheless have high connectivity among their constituents. The technology of these connections, especially cell phones and wireless Internet, facilitates educated decisions, confirms others' dependability, and amplifies cooperation among people.

At one level, protests in Ecuador share key characteristics of contemporary protests. Decentralized, with many-to-many connections, and equipped with mobile communications, indigenous street politics grows ever more agile. Yet, indigenous protests differ in an important respect. While Seattle and Manila might show off the new technology of strikes, they adhere to an old-fashioned, liberal model of politics. The individual stands at the center of the action. In Ecuador's indigenous politics, though, the community lies at the heart of mobilizations. Thus, the crucial public sphere for personal opinions and individual decisions is not the street scenes filmed for the evening news, but one step removed, in the forums of community debate. Power, in turn, develops and flows through bonds among communities.

This cooperation within and between communities challenges liberal ideals of what popular participation in politics means. Further it also calls into question social movement terminology that would see community as "base" and national organization as "leadership." The hierarchy implicit in these words is not only inaccurate but destructive for the ways opponents use it to discredit the indigenous movement. In the reality of uprisings, organizational know-how and political consciousness are widely distributed. Local organizations and national groups work in parallel as sites of authority, decision making, and information. Function, not power, differentiates them. In this chapter, I chronicle events at the blockade set up outside Peguche, Imbabura, to illustrate how community power has consequences well beyond the jurisdictions of local councils.

Launching the Strike in the Shadow of National Elections

Negotiations for the Tratado de Comercio Libre began in May 2004. The treaty was, in effect, the United States' plan b to reduce barriers to trade, pursued after the more ambitious Free Trade Area of the Americas stalled. The final round of negotiation was scheduled for late March in Washington, D.C., when Ecuadorian representatives were to arrive and hammer out the details: setting timetables for the reduction of tariffs on rice and corn, defining the tonnage of U.S. chicken wings and drumsticks that could come in each year, and working out the length of time for copyright protection, among other matters.

CONAIE had pledged its opposition to the TLC from the moment the country entered into negotiations. When asked what the TLC had to do with CONAIE, the sierra Kichwa leader Humberto Cholango said (*El Comercio* 2006d):

The signing of the agreement will affect directly or indirectly eight million people who depend on agriculture. We have more than 1.6 million producer communities. Also the small retailers and consumers will be negatively affected. If one imports rice and corn or imposes patents and appropriates biodiversity, they will affect the development of the people.

When Luis Macas was again elected president of CONAIE in 2005, mass protest became a certainty. Returning to the organization he left in 1996 to serve in congress and later as the Minister of Agriculture, Macas declared that the fight against the TLC and the defense of Ecuador's natural resources, such as petroleum, were the two pillars of his agenda. The recapturing of national resources for social development would begin with the expulsion of Occidental Petroleum Corporation (OXY), which had a multiyear, multibillion-dollar contract with the government to exploit Amazonian reserves. After a fruitless meeting in November 2005 with Ecuador's new president, Palacio,[1] Macas and the leadership set a timetable for the strike.

On February 2, Macas announced that the mobilization was imminent and its targets were both the TLC and the contract with OXY. Coming in the wake of several years of CONAIE's inactivity and ineffectiveness, few paid attention to his threat (*El Comercio* 2006b). Ultimately launched on Monday, March 12, the mobilization of 2006 had some of the hybrid characteristics of the 1990 levantamiento. To begin with, CONAIE arranged the strike to coincide with separate, mass civic protests scheduled in the central highland provinces of Chimborazo and Tungurahua. Down in the Amazonian province of Pastaza, a different group of indigenous activists and labor leaders had set off on a grueling march up into the Andes and on to Quito to protest both budget cuts and the TLC. Meanwhile in Quito, nearly thirty members of CONAIE and Seguro Campesino (a peasant organization) declared a hunger strike and occupied the Metropolitan Cathedral in the heart of colonial Quito.

1. Palacio had come to power in April 2005 after residents of Quito forced Lucio Gutierrez from office in a week of massive demonstrations. Indigenous groups who had backed Gutierrez's campaign and were rewarded with significant political appointments had fallen out with Gutierrez when he too pursued a neoliberal line. Most Pachakutik officials had left Gutierrez's government by the time of the protests against him. Even so, indigenous people were conspicuously absent from the marches that brought him down.

TABLE 1 **The political work of national organizations**

Constituencies	Action
Communities	Coordinate
	Inform, advise, listen, relay
Indigenous men and women	Represent
	Express demands to outsiders
	Create discourses, symbols for selves
State Authorities	Negotiate

In this new mobilization, CONAIE once again tried to fulfill three functions that local indigenous organizing could not (see table 1). Each task in turn engaged a distinct constituency. First, for the thousands of indigenous peasant communities, CONAIE had to coordinate action across provinces. Working out the timing of events, conveying information among local groups, hosting assemblies, and relaying decisions counted among the tasks necessary to mobilize on a grand scale.

Second, for the hundreds of thousands of indigenous men and women drawn into a national protest, CONAIE provided the kind of self-representation discussed by Warren and Jackson (2002, 12). Such an effort was twofold. On one hand, CONAIE and other organizations spoke on behalf of indigenous individuals, conveying their political agenda within governmental arenas. On the other hand, the national groups portrayed the lives of native peoples both "for their own consumption" and for distant audiences (Warren and Jackson 2002, 12). In the course of protests, leaders enacted panindigenous values for all to see. They spoke in Kichwa, made decisions in assemblies, insisted on community property, fought to subsidize the poor, and rejected the economic and military power of the United States. Such actions define indigenous identity as a set of positive claims: smallhold farming is a cultural way of being, not just a class position, autonomy is both political and economic, political action is participatory, and economic justice is a core condition of life and thus a state responsibility (cf. Pallares 2002).

Third, in their engagement with state officials, the national indigenous organizations promised to undertake the tedious task of negotiation with the government. In practical terms, their role was unavoidable. State agencies could not enter into dialogue with each community; communities could not spend the weeks and months in discussion of legislative minutiae.

The negotiating role, however, has also been strategic. The national organizations were intermediaries that protected communities from direct intervention and cooption by the state. They created a space that allowed proposals to be removed from the settings of the state and discussed on native turf. The shift from national movement to community assemblies erected barriers of time and space to top-down state action.

From the beginning of the TLC strike, though, CONAIE only partially succeeded in its tasks. It struggled, in particular, with representing indigenous worries about free trade. In fact, both the media and the government rejected the motives put forward by strike leaders. Politicians and journalists insisted the real reason that CONAIE forced the issue had to do with electoral politics. The movement, in the view of commentators, wanted to show that it would again be a powerful player in the upcoming presidential election. They were using the TLC as a "political pretext" for mobilizing, as the national newspaper, *El Comercio* (2006a), opined in an editorial. For its part, the government declared the anti-TLC position "irrational," driven by ignorance of the treaty. Neither officials nor the press credited CONAIE and indigenous people with having a wider concern with the how U.S. agricultural imports would affect Ecuadorian farming livelihoods.

In the coming days indigenous leaders would be repeatedly accused of "stage-managing" the base, playing on its ignorance. For many urban Ecuadorians, a photograph in the newspaper of an indigenous woman sitting at a barrier on the highway juxtaposed with the words free trade agreement sufficed to make the argument. The woman stood for simple, backward country folk. "TLC" meant complex trade relations with an economic superpower. The rocks and tree trunks in the street represented a primitive fight against the unknown. In the racism of the Andes, the meaning of such an image was as clear as the phrases being used by the government to characterize the opposition as "irrational," "ignorant," "manipulated." Indians were too dumb to get it.

Yet, as CONAIE struggled to refute these arguments, the communities showed their own leadership in expanding the strike during its first week. Indigenous people had set up twenty major roadblocks on principal roads in eleven highland and Amazonian provinces (see map 3). And as the strike's magnitude grew, more people joined in to shut down back roads. In the northern Andes, this dynamic stole the initiative from the movement's leadership, radicalizing the strike. Some of the first people to pay a price for this intensity were found in indigenous communities

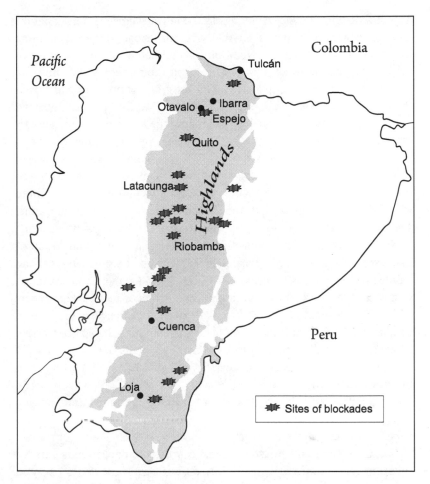

MAP 3 Location of primary strike blockades during first week of anti-TLC strike, 2006 (Source: *El Comercio*, March 15, 2006)

themselves, as I saw when we tried to complete our trip home during the first week of the strike.

Getting Home

After our failed attempt to make it down the highway on our own, we bided our time until the military came back through. This time, we merged with a convoy of heavy trucks that had just been released to resume their northbound trip. We moved along slowly, at times inching across planks laid over newly dug trenches. At one point, the whole caravan again came to a stop. A police vehicle swung out of line behind us and sped down the left side of the road. Trucks turned off their engines. Ten minutes later, though, we started up again, whatever group of protestors had been there had been driven back, their rocks shoved to the side. In stops and starts we progressed, eventually abandoning the highway and arriving by dirt tracks and lucky timing at a country inn, twelve kilometers shy of home.

The next morning, I set off again with my neighbor from Iowa City to try to get his family's travel documents and some ibuprofen for our three year old. In La Compañía, we abandoned our truck at a small blockade. The strikers promised to look after it and we set off for Peguche on foot.

We stopped in Ariasucu, visiting our compadres Galo and Monica.[2] Their son José was deeply worried. His own son, a stout, one-year-old toddler was very sick. The boy had a high fever, a cough, and had been vomiting in the night. José had neither medicine nor money. He desperately wanted to get to the southern Andean city of Cuenca where he sold handicrafts. I said that I would return with something. José asked where the truck was. I said that I had to leave it in La Compañía.

"You left it well?" he asked, meaning well guarded.

"Yes," I assured him.

"In the strike in La Compañía, people will slash the tires."

I shrugged. Years pass, but La Compañía has kept its reputation for being *bravo*, dangerous and wild.

We walked on to the house in Peguche. We got our gear, the last of our children's ibuprofen, and caught a ride back to Ariasucu. There I poured out some medicine into the measuring cap, left it with José, and we carried on through La Compañía. The truck was fine. Since we had left, a pile of dirt had been dumped next to it and our vehicle itself completed the barricade. The woman who led the strikers asked for some cash for looking after the car, and my phone number, in case anyone from her family ever got to the United States. I handed over the change and patted my pockets, looking for my pen. The leader spotted my pen behind my ear, reached up, took it, and wrote my cell number on her palm, but asked me to write

---

2. Pseudonyms, the same as used in my book *The Native Leisure Class* (Colloredo-Mansfeld 1999).

my name. I held her hand in my left hand, and wrote "Rodolfo" across the smooth skin below her thumb. We drove back to the hotel.

The following day Chesca and I decided to try to get our family home. Stopping in Ariasucu we picked up José. His son had another bad night and we brought José with us to see what other medicine we could find. On this trip, our luck ran out. Five minutes from home, a patrol of about a dozen young men chased down our truck. One man with a piece of sharpened rebar went straight for our front tire, jabbing his weapon into the sidewall. As air hissed out of the tire, Chesca, the kids, and our friends evacuated the truck and walked off through the crowd and down to the house. José lost his temper with the men, yelling that we were not forcing our way through a blockade and there was no cause to go after our tires. The young men backed off, leaving the other three tires intact, and carried on up the road behind us. José stuck with me as we reversed the car, picked a different fork in the road, and sped back to his house before the tire went totally flat.

While we changed the tire, José blamed the attack on the disrespectful people from La Compañía. While I tightened the bolts, he complained bitterly:

> They do not know what the strike is about. They leave their community because they are told. They do not understand the TLC, this treaty. If they do not go out and join the strike, they are fined, ten dollars, twenty dollars. I was there in Peguche in 2000 for the strike where they got rid of the president and that is the way it was.

Later that afternoon, José and I made it down to Peguche without incident. The next day, indigenous communities declared a partial truce for the weekend, allowing some circulation on secondary roads. Our Iowa City friends were able to hire a pickup driver and eventually made it to Quito and their rebooked flights. José did not leave, though, deciding it was better to stick with his wife and son. We found some painkillers for his boy and antibiotics for our daughter, whose fevers had been getting worse.

Among other lessons, a week crossing strike barriers taught me that solidarity does not come easy when one's child is sick. In José's case, in fact, I learned that for many indigenous people any strike is a hunger strike. Although Indian leaders boast of homegrown grains that can sustain strikes, most rural residents earn their daily bread in cities. Certainly, José's family could have been fed by his parents throughout a long strike.

But José's son needed medicine and the family had a loan to pay back. Lost earnings owing to the uprising meant unavoidable financial sacrifices ahead. And here a crucial political issue stands out. Such sacrifices are not always offered. They are imposed. In allocating the burden of a political mobilization, community leaders reveal the true test of their own statecraft.

The Making of a Strike Blockade

The blockade in Peguche went from nonexistent to one of the four most militant in the country in the space of a week (see map 4). In the pages below, I describe what it takes to set up and radicalize a blockade. At the heart of the steps taken to fight the state's free trade policy are the habits of community administration honed over years of coping with development projects and local conflicts. Mingas, list keeping, assertion of community jurisdiction, the interplay among independent councils, and even interventions from nonterritorial, urban trade associations enabled indigenous people to hold the line.

*   *   *

Mingas and Lists

After a week with no blockade on the northern edge of Otavalo, people from Agato came down to set up the first barricade at the *entrada* (Sp. entrance) to Peguche on Sunday afternoon. Like any other minga, it began with council members walking the paths of Agato with a battery-powered bullhorn, calling people out to work. They informed people of the location of the block and the fine for not participating. Between eighty and one hundred men and women heeded the call. They walked down the two kilometers or so to the Pana, searched the gully and some uncultivated fields near the highway for materials, and set out a line of rocks and tree stumps. An Agato council member then distributed chits of participation, small squares of paper stamped with the Agato seal on one side and signed by the council member on the other. These were the proof needed later to avoid paying a fine.

Opponents of the strike sharply criticized this use of fines and minga lists to mobilize community members. Enrique Castañeda, for example, led an Otavalo indigenous group called Ruminahui that did not agree with

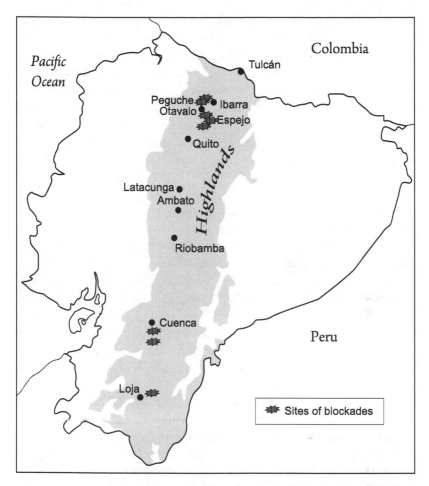

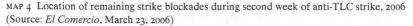

MAP 4 Location of remaining strike blockades during second week of anti-TLC strike, 2006 (Source: *El Comercio*, March 23, 2006)

CONAIE's and FICI's actions. His words echoed of José's dismay with the strike. In a newspaper report (*El Norte* 2006), he declared that "indigenous people are being manipulated." He was quoted as saying, "The councils take the water away from them in an arbitrary and illegal act; everyone is participating because of this imposition." He went on, "They treat the people like sheep and protest against the TLC is without a basis for their actions."

The complaints about council pressure to participate relate to a specific and deeply held notion of democracy. In the liberal tradition, political progress appears as human institutions shift to protect the individual and legitimacy grows when individuals choose to back those institutions (Niezen 2003). Indeed, this personal volition in and of itself expresses a moral good—freedom. With freedom to participate in, or abstain from, demonstrations, individuals can endow large turnouts in protests with an electoral authenticity. They become an honest voting with feet. The riskier the protest, the more citizen participation seems the very enactment of democracy. In contrast, denying water to a resident who does not agree with the TLC strike, who in fact might want a free trade agreement, coerces where freedom ought to prevail. At best such tactics seem to bully, at worst they smack of grass roots tyranny.

The community politics developed in the Andes, however, blends participation with the trade-offs of representation. Leaders, authorized through elections, make decisions based on their best judgment. They then use the resources and administrative rules at hand to carry out policy. This is a politics rooted in a separate good—consent. Very few projects have unanimous support. Some, like the house-building project in Quiloa, only benefit a minority. Others, like the bridge-building project, benefit most, but never quite equally. Turning to fines and sanctions, councils bring noncooperating individuals into line. When local institutions work well, these leaders are then later held accountable by residents when council elections are held.

Outsiders tend to celebrate mingas when they build water systems, widen roads, and fill in where the state falls short. Turn the tools of community administration to national politics, though, and complaints follow. And yet, community concerns do not stop at their borders. Amid debate and dissent, leaders push for programs at provincial, national, and even international levels, linking residents' interests to wider political projects. To insist on either unanimity of support or individual freedom to opt out of any projects at will is to hold indigenous groups to a higher standard than other democracies.

*   *   *

Boundaries and Jurisdictions

Using mingas to turn out individuals for strike duty was only one administrative task among many. Strike leaders had to maintain a strong, round-the-clock presence at the barriers and coordinate actions with other provincial blocks. To distribute the required sacrifices as fairly as possible, they sought to set up a rotation among Peguche and its neighboring communities La Bolsa, Quinchuqui, Agato, Ariasucu, and Yacu Pata (see map 5). Indeed, during the first twenty-four hours of the Peguche blockade, residents of Quinchuqui and Agato did all the work.

I visited the Quinchuqui strikers during their first night shift at the barrier. The young men questioned why I was there. I answered that I was seeking information on the causes of the strike. Since I lived in Peguche at the moment and we were speaking in Kichwa and they were bored, they soon opened up their circle to me. Conversation turned to how Peguche residents have not come out in numbers. One of the strikers observed, "Some do not see the suffering of the people. They do not do their part."

Headlights then approached the barrier from the north. The whole group started whistling loudly and the littlest guy took off running at the car. The lights came to a stop then started to back up, swinging wildly from side to side in retreat. The man jogged back to the group, laughing. He had no weapon of any kind. Hours at the block had made him giddy. An older man next to me said with pride that this car-chasing youth was studying engineering in Quito. "He is from Quinchuqui," he added.

Class and occupational differences seemed to recruit people into the action in contradictory ways. From within the communities, younger, wealthier people volunteered for longer hours. Along with the engineering student, I met several other university students, most of whom studied in the provincial capital. Far wealthier individuals had also turned up at the entrada once the barrier was in place. A factory owner from Otavalo, a man with fifty employees and a large retail store, used his truck to get strikers to and from the barricade. A hotel owner from Peguche spent hour after hour trying to coordinate strike shifts, and an indigenous restaurateur from Otavalo brought up food.

Between communities, however, the old pecking order reasserted itself. Poorer communities from higher up put in the longer shifts. It was as if poorer, more agrarian communities were quicker to organize and cooperate, yet across all communities it was the elites with resources to spare who took the initiative both to participate and organize others' involvement.

On Tuesday, the third day of Peguche's blockade, a challenge from the army and the newly mobile convoy of northbound trucks unified the communities occupying the intersection. The movement of the trucks and soldiers also revealed a wider jurisdictional divide that had developed between two blockades.

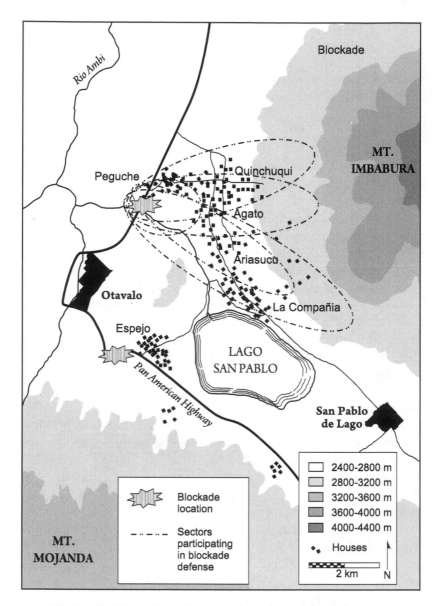

Blockade

Rio Ambi

MT.
IMBABURA

Peguche

Quinchuqui

Agato

Ariasucu

Otavalo

La Compañia

Espejo

LAGO
SAN PABLO

Pan American Highway

San Pablo
de Lago

☐	2400-2800 m
☐	2800-3200 m
▨	3200-3600 m
▨	3600-4000 m
▨	4000-4400 m

MT.
MOJANDA

Blockade
location

Sectors
participating
in blockade
defense

Houses

2 km   N

MAP 5 Blockade "jurisdictions" near Octavalo during anti-TLC strike, 2006

Earlier that day, the government had declared a state of emergency in eight highland provinces where strikers had dug in. Thousands more soldiers had been called up and a curfew declared. Meanwhile, within Imbabura a humanitarian crisis had developed among a stranded convoy of about one hundred heavy trucks, the same convoy that facilitated our move through the pass a week earlier. Outside of Espejo on the south side of Otavalo, the drivers had spent more than a week sleeping in their rigs, scrounging food from roadside stalls, and using nearby fields as a latrine. Several drivers now needed medical attention. For their part, Espejo residents worried about a leaking gas tanker and rotting food on board a number of trucks.

Local strike leaders called in Benjamin Inuca, president of FICI, while the drivers recruited the military commanders to speak for them. Soldiers, community leaders, and peasant federation representatives worked out a deal. Espejo would let the trucks pass. With troops accompanying them, the trucks moved down the Pana, around Otavalo, and on toward the provincial capital of Ibarra. A kilometer north of Otavalo, however, the Peguche strikers stopped them.

Negotiations started anew. Soldiers stood around the trucks while police armed with tear gas and padded in riot gear dispersed among the strikers. Military commanders talked with Peguche strike leaders and soon a fundamental difference became apparent. The military, the media, and residents of Otavalo and Ibarra felt the humanitarian crisis was much broader than the truckers. Gas stations in cities had started to run out of petrol, food prices were escalating, and hospitals were cutting back on services for lack of medicine. The military and the drivers argued that the truce agreed to in Espejo meant free passage to Ibarra where crucial supplies could be delivered. During the negotiations in Peguche, a radio station in Otavalo sought to reassure the truckers. As soldiers and protestors talked in the intersection, other participants listened to two broadcasters on a local radio station who spoke in reassuring terms:

> This afternoon FICI, Sr. Benjamin Inuca, met with the barrio presidents and formed a truce to let these trucks through. The leaders of Iluman and Peguche were there. If you are listening, Mr. Drivers, be patient a little longer; representatives from FICI have not yet arrived to clarify the situation.

FICI, however, had not built and defended Peguche's blockade. It was not theirs to negotiate away. Further, if leaders from Iluman and Peguche had attended the meeting they did so to contribute their own opinions and to learn what was happening. They, too, did not have the authority to decide the fate of the Peguche or Iluman blocks. Only a debate at the blockade could decide that. In short, mestizos and the military assumed decisions came from the top down, from FICI officers through community leaders to residents (see figure 18).

The "top," though, was at the bottom; leadership was diffuse (see figure 19). When two representatives of FICI finally arrived in Peguche, they backed Peguche's autonomy. They stood in the middle of the crowd, soldiers and policemen on all sides, and urged Peguche strikers to do what they thought best.

Once again, linguistic choice created political room to maneuver. All the strikers spoke in Kichwa, denying mestizos access to indigenous political deliberations. At times strikers spoke defiantly. "We must deny these savage mestizo soldiers [K. Awka mishucuna]," one woman exhorted. Others cautioned about the new powers the government had due to the state of emergency. The first man from FICI explained that it was the condition of the drivers and not the state of emergency that led to Espejo's decision. He then added, "What happens in other communities will happen. Espejo does not make the decision for you."

Not too concerned with directing Peguche's decision, the FICI leaders then changed topics. The first man urged people to continue supporting

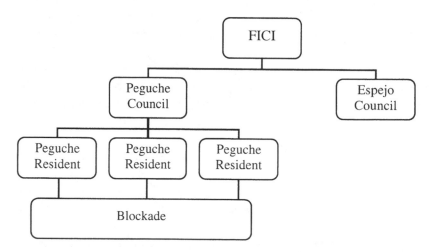

FIGURE 18 Strike hierarchy assumed in media accounts

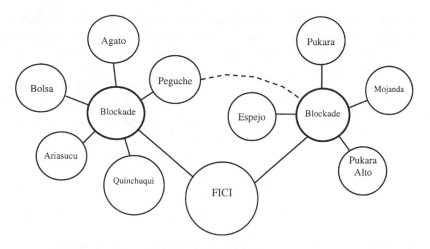

FIGURE 19 Strike hierarchy exhibited during decisions

the strike, saying, "Our grandparents in earlier times lived on the mountain. They raised their grains. When they came to town they were called
'Indian, dirty Indian, Indian thief.' Now we are fighting back." The second speaker spoke about the wide lack of support for the TLC process.
He pointed out that only 19 percent of the country supported President
Palacio and that congress had support from only 5 percent of the elector-
ate. "If Palacio signs it and the congress approves it, who really supports
the TLC?" he asked. After they left, strikers remained firm. Confronted
by hundreds of men and women occupying the highway, the military did
not force the issue. The trucks turned around and parked in Otavalo.

*   *   *

Councils and Leaders

Not only was authority distributed across communities, but leadership
was frequently spread beyond the councils who organized strike mingas.
Unelected community members took an active role in debate and made
decisions about the course of action. Indeed, Peguche itself lacked a single council that represented all its neighborhoods. Consequently, leaders
from the potable-water board stepped in to keep lists of participants. If
the right to take charge hinged on anything, it was identity as a community

member. When strikers had to develop a plan to cope with the curfew or the continuing charges of indigenous ignorance about the TLC, they solicited input by finding someone to speak up from each of the communities responsible for the block.

On the fourth day of the barrier, for example, two radio stations came to interview protestors. A young man from the parish council spoke up and defended the strike. He insisted the strikers knew what they were protesting, observing that imports of subsidized grains would hurt indigenous peasants and insisting that U.S. corporations would steal indigenous plant knowledge. Some, though, were not reassured. After the microphones were turned off, the Peguche hotel owner who had set up the shifts among communities took the bullhorn and said, "Indigenous people must understand the treaty. Some people are mistaken in what they say. The radio says we do not know. We need to form a commission to inform the people about the treaty."

He started reeling off the names of the communities. "Agato?"

"Here," someone answered.

"Peguche?"

"Here."

"Bolsa?"

"Here."

"Ariasucu?"

[no answer]

"Yacupata?"

[no answer. Someone pointed out that these smaller communities were down below blocking a side road off the Pana.]

Together they named a representative from each community to a commission and charged it with going by the FICI office to get more information about the TLC. The commission would then report back to each community. A similar roll call was used to solicit input about how to deal with the curfew. Speakers introduced their remarks, calling out a greeting and naming their community ("Hello fathers and mothers, I am from Agato. . . ."). Discussion went on; the bullhorn was passed around. Consensus built to defend the barricade throughout the day but not risk violence after the curfew.

As each person spoke up, I finally understood the meaning of CONAIE leader Blanca Chancozo's eulogy for the woman who died in the 1990 uprising (quoted in chapter 4). When interviewed by Jorge Leon, she said, "It was not that one could say she was the primary one or a leader, just one more member of the community and was, in that, the equal of all" (Leon 1993, 135). In managing the strike, commissions were needed, but titles did not matter. Each person had a right to advocate a course of action. If one wanted to find liberal democratic ideals, these tactical sessions were the place to look. Respect for individual rights, open debate, and active political participation were the order of the day. When all was said, however, it was the community's will to be done. The position taken was enforced as a collective one.

*   *   *

Trade Associations

The Peguche blockade received support from one organization that lay outside of the half-dozen communities with territorial jurisdiction. UNAIMCO (Union de Artesanos Indígenas del Mercado Centenario de Otavalo or Union of Indigenous Artisans of the Centenario Market of Otavalo) represented the artisans and vendors who sold handicrafts in the Plaza de Ponchos. Even before the Peguche blockade went up, the union had acted. They shut down the famous craft market on Saturday, carried the organization's white boards down from the office, and held a teaching session on the TLC. Afterward, with musicians from some of Otavalo's most popular folklore bands leading they way, they sponsored an anti-TLC march through Otavalo (see figure 17).

UNAIMCO leaders continued their support for the mobilization by bringing food out to the blockade. When the state of emergency went into effect, UNAIMCO organized a march of solidarity to come out from Otavalo to Peguche. Though a minor contributor to the strength of the block, UNAIMCO was the only urban group involved, the only one to create a forum of protest, information, and debate in the city. FICI, although headquartered only a block away in the heart of Otavalo, abandoned the urban zone throughout the strike, shuttling constantly among the major blockades and organizing assemblies in rural locations. The lack of coordination with urban social movements became, in fact, one of the greatest weaknesses of the strike.

Urban residents felt unfairly besieged by the indigenous protest. Radio station call-in programs became forums of discontent. Expressing a common theme, one woman phoned in saying that she needed to work, that she had no fixed salary and lived from what she earned each day. She empathized with the indígenas but saw the strike as punishing people like her. Repeating the charges of the press and politicians, she complained that the strikers were "manipulated." A short letter published in *El Comercio* similarly declared (*El Comercio* 2006c),

> We are being held hostage by a miniscule group of indígenas that do not represent anyone but themselves. We cannot buy food, we cannot move, we cannot work in peace because the leaders of the strike are blocking the country without knowing the meaning of what they are asking for.

In Ibarra, industry groups ran ads asking for a lift of the blockades. A counterprotest, not for the TLC but against the indigenous strike, drew thousands into the streets. Had the strike continued another day in Otavalo, a counterprotest would have occurred there as well, with much graver consequences. A provincial councilman predicted that such a march would have caused a race riot. With no coordinated outreach to urban market vendors, school teachers, or other potential allies, FICI and CONAIE had left indigenous protestors exposed to a bitter backlash.

Finally, in its fifth day, Thursday, March 23, the eleventh of the mobilization, Peguche's blockade ended with both a bang and a whimper. Using the curfew, the military had taken over the intersection the night before. In the morning, they waved a thin stream of traffic through. Residents from all six of the strike communities began to arrive. Some gathered small, fist-size stones. A few stayed out of sight and collected bottles, rags, and gasoline to make Molotov cocktails. Around 9:30, soldiers grew anxious and started to fire tear gas and the residents counterattacked. Two hours later, the supply of tear gas exhausted, the soldiers gave up the intersection. Short of lethal force, they had no way to keep the community out. Tires burned in the intersection throughout the afternoon while groups of adrenaline-charged young men took pickaxes to the asphalt of the Pana and tried to put in a trench.

Then it was over. As the protestors agreed, they once again gave up the intersection at curfew. The next morning, they did not return.

The wider mobilization had already wound down in most parts of the country. Taking stock, the national organization declared a truce. They wanted to meet and evaluate other options. FICI relayed the message to the strikers and they decided to go along. On Friday, March 24, a few soldiers stood near the ashy remains of the previous day's confrontation, watching a normal flow of intercity traffic racing back and forth.

FIGURE 20 Events at the Peguche roadblock coming to a head, 2006

Conclusions

In its immediate aftermath, the TLC strike seemed to have gained nothing and cost a lot. Free trade negotiations were going ahead. The contract with Occidental remained in effect. Vilifying CONAIE and disparaging indigenous people, the government refused to dignify the protest with a public dialogue. The press was full of racist accusations about Indian ignorance and a place that prided itself on intercultural understanding, the province of Imbabura, seemed on the verge of an ethnic confrontation.

And then, in an unpredictable turn of events, by the end of May the primary demands of the strikers had been met. The government used a technicality to cancel OXY's contract, forcing the oil company to forfeit its massive investment in the Ecuadorian Amazon. The U.S. negotiators had already stalled the talks because of their concerns about higher tax payments on petroleum earnings. The OXY dispute caused an indefinite delay in the U.S. response to Ecuador's free trade proposals. The TLC was all but dead. Given the government's early hard line, these actions ostensibly happened independently of the mobilization. Commentators attributed the change of heart to a populist streak in Palacio's administration. In Peguche, though, they had a different view. "At the time, it looked like a failure," one woman said to me. "Now it looks like we got what we wanted." Having seen how she and others went about it, I came to a number of conclusions about the anti-TLC strike in particular and the role of communities in indigenous uprisings more generally:

1. Anthropologists often mention that indigenous movements have led to new ways of being indigenous in a postagrarian world (Korovkin 1997; Selverston 1994). The strike, however, offered a very old starting point for defining identity. The days of protest were ones of a pure and simple us vs. them mentality. Even mestizos sympathetic to indigenous strikers spoke easily of "los indígenas" as a monolithic, separate, and unknowable group of people. Likewise, for those occupying the roads, the blockades clarified who was literally on their side.

2. In a similar, old-fashioned vein, the Kichwa language itself was a powerful political instrument. Ideologically, speakers reinforced their solidarity through their native tongue. Practically, leaders got things done in their own language regardless of the police circulating among protestors or media intruding on their deliberations. Kichwa offered a zone of organizing that resisted meddling or misinterpretation on the part of outsiders.

3. The most common reason strikers gave for their participation in the levantamiento was a rejection of the government's handling of the treaty. People argued that the government was rushing the treaty through at the last minute, that Palacio did not have the support of the majority of Ecuadorians, that a trade agreement that affected so much of the economy should be put to a vote, and that only a few powerful business interests had participated in the process. Beyond their anger at the government, strikers also felt they were fighting against the economic and political power of the United States. While for some strikers this meant defending their grains from the threat posed by U.S. imports, more people talked about protecting the knowledge and use of medicinal plants from being exploited by U.S. companies. Most strikers, however, also wanted more information about the advantages and disadvantages of free trade with the United States.

4. The blockades were zones of intense political action, not simple lines of confrontation. Indeed, the images in the newspaper of a few strikers standing defiantly in front of a tree trunk miss the point. Over the course of a strike, blockades develop into literal multicommunity "parliaments"—forums for talking and making decisions. In Peguche, the occupied Pan-American Highway was in fact a "jurisdiction," a political space involving six communities and established procedures for taking action. Neither FICI nor Peguche established this blockade, and neither could decide its policies. Some activities at blockades depend on individual community cabildos and are organized as mingas. Minga lists, in fact, give strikers a means to "finance" the strike through enforced contributions of time and occasionally food. In Peguche, though, no cabildo had final say over the fate of the blockade.

5. The communities that come together to run a blockade cooperate with other blockades but maintain their autonomy. The provincial organization FICI plays a crucial role in developing this cooperation by organizing assemblies for discussion, communicating decisions taken at one blockade to others, and offering advice. However, strikers at one blockade also maintain direct contact with strikers at others through visits and cell phones. Informed about what others are doing, strikers act according to their own judgment. Espejo, for example, erected their barrier during the first week of the strike; Peguche did not. Peguche did not allow special passage for the convoy of heavy trucks, Espejo did.

6. Blockades are active nodes in information networks. Strikers do not simply wait for instructions from the national movement. They seek information, disseminate it to the wider communities, and offer interviews to

TABLE 2 **The division of political labor**

Constituencies	Action	
	National Organizations	Communities

Communities	Coordinate
	  Inform, advise, listen, relay
		Cooperate
		  Divide tasks, implement

Indigenous men
and women
	Represent
	  Express demands to outsiders
	  Create discourses, symbols
		Debate
		  Enable discussion

State Authorities	Negotiate	Stop

the press to give their perspective. At the blockade in Peguche, people had access to radios to hear the news and many had cell phones to get direct reports. Indeed, I found that in the uncertainty of the mobilization, the zone of occupation on the Pana was the best place to stay informed.

7. The division of political labor between communities and the organizations of the indigenous movement was more about specialization than hierarchy (see table 2). Concretely, communities pushed forward in three areas that complemented the work of the national movement. First, the zones of occupation and protest were places where people went beyond the tasks of coordinating among groups and found the means to cooperate to put decisions into effect. Where coordination entailed communicating, informing, and giving advice, cooperation meant defining each share of a task, assuming the cost, and doing it. Second, strikers and their leaders spent more time in discussion than in trying to represent their goals to outsiders. In fact, most refused to speak for others, limiting their comments with the phrase "From my point of view, I think . . ." Third, face to face with the state, their task was one dimensional—to stop policies thought to be harmful. When successful, they set up the negotiations that were central to the work of the national organizations. Schematically, the division can be represented by the table above.

So, how much power do indigenous communities have in a national movement that has organized to fight economic globalization? Quite a lot. Communities can in fact strengthen themselves independently of national organizations; their potential does not rest on, or derive from, a distant hierarchy of leaders. In creating zones of blockades, indigenous people illustrate the reach of decentralized, interconnected, and information-rich protest that has become a part of antiglobalization and prodemocracy movements around the world.

This power, however, comes at a cost. The political activists within communities coerce others into giving up time and resources to make blockades work. The political outreach of the blockade stops short of urban areas, leaving other social movements cut off. In short, when communities flex their political will, tensions grow among local residents and between ethnic groups. Consequently, even if communities do not depend on national leaders for direction, they cannot succeed without them. The core tasks of the national groups—coordinating, representing, and negotiating—complement the direct action of communities and vice versa. In Imbabura in March 2006, the communities showed that although they may challenge those who would write the rules of economic life, they cannot by themselves create an alternative future amid the barriers erected on the Pana.

FIGURE 21 Corpus Christi Fiesta sponsors from Quindicilli arrive at the bull ring in Zumbagua, 1999

Fighting Like a Community

The history of political thought has, to a large degree, consisted in a duel between these two great rival conceptions of society. On one side stand the advocates of pluralism and variety and an open market for ideas, an order of things that involves clashes and the constant need for conciliation, adjustment, balance, an order that is always in a condition of imperfect equilibrium, which is required to be maintained by conscious effort. On the other side are to be found those who believe that this precarious condition is a form of chronic social and personal disease, since health consists in unity, peace and the elimination of the very possibility of disagreement. . . . — Isaiah Berlin, "Marxism and the International in the Nineteenth Century"

The BBC and the *Washington Post* covered the anti-TLC strike, seeing in yet one more corner of the world a story of anti-Americanism and antiglobalization. Most Ecuadorian strikes, though, do not make international headlines; many do not even make the national news. In 2000, the bus I was riding from Quito to Otavalo came to a stop behind other vehicles on the Pana outside of Espejo. An army truck passed, stopped, and released troops who rushed off into the cornfields. In a few moments, some indigenous men and women jogged out from another field with a eucalyptus pole. Small explosions were heard. Tear gas then filtered in through the bus windows. Babies started to cry. Passengers lit cigarettes and blew smoke into children's eyes to stop the stinging. With no end to the skirmishing in sight, I disembarked, put on my backpack, picked up my duffel bag, and walked to my compadres in Ariasucu. Certain that something big was unfolding, I watched the news that night and searched the papers the next day. No mention of it. Eventually I interviewed a woman from Espejo who explained that they had been protesting in order to secure more funds for a potable-water project.

In Ecuador, everyone seems to strike these days. The causes are routine—public works, school budgets, city hall administrative policy, and road tolls—and the protagonists diverse. Indigenous communities, though, are among the fiercest combatants. As a taxi driver said to me, "it used to be that we transportation strikers were the most hard-core. Now it is the indigenous people." These protests can be read as a sign of the times in two ways. First, the state's anemic defense of the security, health, and education of its citizens has spawned civic unrest. Second, in an era where the government orthodoxy lies in decentralization and private initiative, communities have stepped up politically, consolidating what power they can. To be sure, they still work in terms set by the state—electing officers, maintaining membership rolls, creating territorial boundaries in the countryside, and seeking formal jurisdiction for trade associations in the city. Yet with each step toward official life, they have found ways to bypass or displace the state. Communities have pursued justice, sometimes brutally, breaking the state's Weberian prerogative of legitimate violence. They have worked with representatives of foreign governments and NGOs to build infrastructure. When new state policies interfered with their trades, they mobilized to maintain control over the marketplaces they made.

The primary cases of this book, Tigua and Otavalo, stand apart from other indigenous communities in a key respect. Each has opened up a distinctive niche in the tourist economy. Other important changes have followed. Tiguans now have a distinctive art tradition, and for those who know anything about the western parishes of Cotopaxi province, Tiguans are also known for their infighting. In Otavalo, indigenous capital has materialized on a scale and in cultural practices unseen elsewhere in Ecuador. Their cultural economies, however, make their political organizing that much more notable. For all their differences, Tiguans and Otavalos have worked hard to create themselves in the same political image as other native communities. A structural conformity prevails where occupation has divided. More to the point, Otavaleño and Tiguan councils and trade associations fight for the resources and recognition that most highland communities seek and have long sought.

Indeed, their agenda is not new. Justice making, collaborating with foreign technicians or missionaries, and occupying urban spaces to market goods have been hallmarks of indigenous community practice since the early twentieth century. Novelty lay in the political meaning indigenous people have given their acts. These were not merely local protests, nor were they steps toward integration with the government. People took justifications from the national indigenous movement and heart from the protests of other communities. Council officers began to see the work of communities as a legitimate alternative to the state—governance that was *runapura* (indigenous only), to use Alfredo Toaquiza's words—not merely the state's extension to the local level.

Latin America has other pockets of community radicals. In Nicaragua and Honduras, some of the wiliest land claimants are blocks that mix black and indigenous communities in new coalitions. More powerful than individual communities and more decentralized than bounded native territories, they offer a new model of local self-determination (Hale 2005). In Mexico, the lasting legacy of the Zapatista rebellion, with its telegenic, ski-masked rebels and native peoples' credibility, has been a tenuous zone of autonomous communities in the Lacandon forest. Unlike the highlands of Chiapas, where Maya communities have come to stand for deep cultural continuity, the settlements of the Zapatista heartland mix colonists from different highland and lowland regions (Harvey 2001; Nash 2001).

Thus, a puzzle. In these struggles that pit residents of rural backwaters against the authorities of the central government, neither the localness nor the diversity of the community protagonists defeated them. The threat (or use) of force has not brought them to heel. Nor can the state, whether Ecuadorian, Honduran, Nicaraguan, or Mexican, contain these plaintiffs with simple administrative formulas. There is more to community power than meets the eye.

From Seeing to Massing

As Scott pointed out in his book *Seeing Like a State* (1998), the modern state has invested heavily in the legibility of its domain in revealing aspects of community life for its inspection. It has made a science out of specifying individuals, defining populations, demarcating political communities, recording property, and tracking natural resources. The state's power inheres in its lists and maps; its force, though, has been felt when it has used its records to embark on massive projects to improve nature and society—and to extract the gains of its improvements. An ideology of "high modernism" has held the efforts together. A strong faith in technology, in the rational order of nature, and in the unity of human needs has oriented actions and justified the costs.

Scott's argument sets up a series of dualisms. The large-scale and orderly state takes on the small-scale and idiosyncratic community. The highly trained planner champions the first; the highly experienced local tracker navigates the second. Universal laws of science prevail in state actions, *metis* or practical skills, common sense, and intuition outside them. Industry on the one hand, craft on the other. Such dualisms have been cast as modes of power in others' work. The state, for example, enables an "imperializing power," a top-down power seeking to control the daily minutiae of others' lives (Fiske 1993, 19). In response, people manage a "localizing power," a bottom-up attempt to control the immediate condition of one's own life. Foucault and his notion of "governmentality" are just a step away. That is, the final consecration of state power occurs as the rationality of the state gets taken up by its subjects and used in "the regulation of everyday conduct" (Ong 2006, 4).

Scott, though does not take the step. Rather than pursue the way citizens enact the logic of the state in their own relations and careers, he keeps his account grounded in the activities of the state—especially the disastrous ones. The power of the state stems from its technologies, is projected by its vision, and is cemented by the requisites and rewards of industrial capitalism. In this scenario, community reservoirs of knowledge and production must ceaselessly parry the force of the state's intrusions.

The problem with this whole binary scheme, though, is that Andean communities do not exist outside the state to be intruded upon by it. Far from being the antithesis of state rationality, indigenous communities are the synthesis of state principles and local political aspiration. Indeed, if the provinces were partly organized by a state that once encouraged modern, cooperative units of production, they were largely self-organized by residents who aspired to the progress the state never delivered. Decentralized rivalry with other sectors pushed people to establish boundaries, regularize councils, and list residents. As mentioned above, by 1990, the Ministry of Agriculture had registered over 2,250 comunas and more than 3,000 other base organizations (Deere and Leon 2001, 52n40).

Foreign NGOs drove this process onward (Breton 2003). Favoring indigenous communities in their development agendas, they reinforced the formation of a civil society that prided itself on its native Andean heritage. José Vega was one of many Kichwa political entrepreneurs to capitalize on outsiders' pro-Indian bias when he secured the money for the FUNHABIT housing project. It is hard to conceive of any other circumstances in which a foreign government would build private homes for forty families unless they had their threefold worthiness of being indigenous and impoverished and self-made artisans.

Provincial and municipal governments added still more incentives to standardize local authority. Both basic services and commercial resources could be best claimed through a simple, sanctioned association. The indigenous movement did its part, as well, to reinforce an orderly civil society. In fact the community identity is so important to the work of national organizations that small sectors such as Ariasucu have a far clearer place in indigenous mobilizations and ad hoc assemblies than well-established, indigenous trade associations that may have a larger membership and more resources to contribute.

For Scott, this successful, widespread blend of local action and state administrative procedure is the point. Practical knowledge fills in and makes a go of an abstract formula that the state used to define a community. This is the metis-friendly arrangement he comes to favor after his review of failed development schemes. But Andean communities reverse Scott's view. The state's universal rules, not local knowledge, have been the crucial supplement. The universalizing schemes regularize politics and make one rural political unit similar to another. Because of the long shadow of the 1937 Ley de Comunas, local politics is again and again led by councils and continually restricted to particular sorts of territories.

Urban indigenous peoples fit awkwardly into this scheme. At times they create associations that reproduce rural community affiliations—such as the Tiguan artist groups. Yet these may be ill-suited for the problem at hand. At other times, they develop and grow in direct relation to urban markets, trades, resources, and issues, forming groups such as UNAIMCO. Yet this larger group did not match up well with its rural counterparts, largely owing to its lack of a mutually exclusive territorial identity. In contrast, rural sectors have been strengthened by becoming simplified, readable, and place-based, for in this uniformity lies the power of segmentation.

If the classical anthropological accounts of segmentary politics from the 1940s and 1950s immerse today's reader in the theoretical confines of functionalism and the political baggage of colonial anthropology, they also offer a sustained look into how local groups can scale up politics without centralized control. The Bohannans (1958a; 1958b), Evans Pritchard

(1940), and others (Sahlins 1961) began by spelling out the workings of lineages as local political units. Their ethnographies then explored the instrumentalities of connection of these groups: the kinship narratives that specified common ancestors, the age sets and religious societies that cross-cut immediate family and neighborhood ties, and the feuds that triggered alliances. Assessing this work, Sahlins argues that the power of highly developed segmentary systems lay in its "massing effect," the situational ways that multiple units could be tapped to confront a common enemy. Contemporary anthropologists have returned to segmentary analysis to explain such different issues as the politics of L.A. gangs (Phillips 1999) and the authority of Somali clans (Simons 1995; Simons 1997). Yet for all the differences in cases, authors have found a useful framework for explaining political affiliation and the pragmatics of mobilization. As Anna Simons (1997, 277) points out, when the state fails to protect individuals and respect their political participation, "they seem far likelier to engage in conflict at the level in which they do have fair representation from their perspective."

As Kichwa society self-organizes in the Andes, it has formed sectors whose very alikeness allows new levels of cooperation. As in classical accounts, the identity of the opposition creates order within a hierarchy of affiliations. Aligned against the president's free trade policy, for instance, a resident of Agato is an Ecuadorian "indígena," in common cause nationally with Amazonian shamans, regionally with sierra peasant farmers, and locally with Peguche's sweater exporters. Up against city hall, Quiloans reach parish-wide unity with Chami and Chimbacucho to become "Tiguan." They do not, however, seek an enemy, stakes, or set of allies at the provincial level, despite the best efforts of José Atupaña to bring the Tiguans into the fold of the "pueblos indígenas de Quito."

And in Ariasucu's punishment of the blanket-and-oatmeal thieves, the protagonists were neither generically "indígena," nor were they "Otavalo," but very specifically Ariasuqueños, in opposition to residents of Agato and La Compañía. Ariasucu's ability to pull off the whipping, just as its capacity to take a shift defending the strike blockade, illustrates the authority of form. Having achieved the requisites of council, boundary, and listed residents, the undersized sector thus enjoyed the prerogatives of self-determination. Much smaller than its neighbors, it nonetheless cannot be overly bullied by them. Its sovereignty is vouched for in the moment of acting during a shared crisis.

If community organization "packages" provincial residents for mobilizations of different sizes and intensities, the instrumentalities that link one segment to another lie outside of those packets. Here, among its other roles, the national movement plays a crucial part. Where idioms of shared ancestors unite lineages in the classic kin models, the movement connects people through narratives of indigenousness. Sometimes these stories are heard face-to-face such as with the words of José Atupaña, sitting in a gynecologist's office and reminding Tiguans of the strength of their grandparents' barley gruels. Sometimes they arrive as newspaper quotations from leaders about farming communities and what they need and what threatens them. Creating a shared consciousness through such discourse is only the start, though. CONAIE long invested a lot of human effort in assemblies, face-to-face contact, and community-based consultation to open up communication not only between national and local groups but among the communities themselves.

The national indigenous organization, though, is not reducible to the rise of this new "segmentary system." CONAIE builds coalitions with other social movements, develops policy, and intervenes in electoral politics, among other functions. Its service to communities, however, helps to distinguish the indigenous movement from other social movements. By the same token, community activism cannot be reduced to the movement's efforts. Communities move into wider politics at times with minimal attention from national indigenous leaders. Yet the sustained presence of the national movement has made multilateral bonds among communities not only conceivable, but, in certain conflicts, compelling.

So, what does it mean to fight like a community? It means replicating a limited political repertoire across dozens or hundreds of localities. Operating without central control from an overarching leadership, decisions are made and enforced in parallel, with power growing as separate collectivities reinforce each other. Widespread community action is decentralized, protecting the ideal of self-determination in its debates, assemblies, and intercommunity division of labor. The more communities become readable to each other in their leadership practices, fixed membership, bounded territories, and manner of politics, the easier it is for them to come together. Scott's account of the state has been critiqued for making too much of the rationality of the state and underplaying the practical knowledge of its agents and the irregularities of its day-to-day program (Herzfeld 2005). The untapped value of Scott's work, though, is how it points the way to the opposite issue: the rationalization of local politics, its shedding of irregularities, and the growth of forms that make both community autonomy and mass protest possible.

This type of uniformity, which joins politics, territory, and indigenous culture in a state-sanctioned form, worries some scholars. Hale (2005), for example, argues that neoliberal states recognize cultural differences and cede domains of civil society to tidy up political dissent. Officials combine multiculturalism with corporatism, granting favors to clearly defined social units within the national population. The state thus creates a new "grid of intelligibility" that contains the possibilities for radical economic and political change (Hale 2005, 13). Such fears, though, beg two questions, one practical the other theoretical. First, since the Ecuadorian state began passing community reform measures in the nineteenth century, has it ever offered enough resources to indigenous communities to defuse dissent? The short answer is no. Second, does formal legibility, the ability to read which groups are out there in the political landscape, deliver situational legibility, the knowledge of what they will do in a moment of crisis? The difference between these two types of legibility returns us to a core issue of this book: the radical pluralism of indigenous society.

Fights of Another Stripe

Anyone who has grown up in a small community or lived for long enough in one knows that "fighting like a community" has two meanings: taking on outsiders and fighting each other. I did not have to go to the Andes to discover small town conflicts, especially ones involving land or faith. Just before I entered kindergarten, my family moved back to the town in Massachusetts where my mother grew up. Dismayed by a new and haphazard sprawl of houses, she joined the conservation commission. Over the next ten years, she worked with others to create a master plan for the town, a struggle in which long time residents, people whose last names were on the town's street signs, were pitted against each other. After college, I drove to visit my aunt and uncle in West Virginia. I told them how impressed I was by all the little churches I saw on the drive out to their place. My uncle replied they were less a sign of religiosity than hostility; each house of worship spoke of a bitter argument and fission. In general, it seems the older the community the greater the reserve of alternative values, old wounds, personal jealousies, sunk costs, and fixed investments.

Such assets and liabilities engender opposing interests that are not easily smoothed over with appeals to community spirit.

To work for years among Otavalos and Tiguans is to be reminded about all the ways that wealth differences, in particular, can perpetuate antagonisms. At a personal level, enough households have gotten ahead through their artisanship or hard work or timing or exploitation of others to keep the fires of envy burning. When economic entrepreneurship crosses over to community activism, the personal becomes political. The relatively prosperous ally themselves with foreign NGOs or some government agency, finding ways to pad advantages by securing electricity, water, or bus service for their neighborhoods. Resentment on the neglected edges of a community grows. At times the tension flares into naked class conflict as when Tiguan painters went after the merchants in their community. Often, though, it transfers to fights among other deeply held values. Rationality and advancement, for instance, faced off against a poverty-born, indigenous solidarity in Ariasucu's moment of community justice.

Fission between wealthier and poorer neighborhoods offers the excluded a way to fight back. As places like Ariasucu seek a boundary between themselves and domineering sectors, they put the brakes on overbearing councils. Such organizational moves, though, do not erase inequality. Instead they can make the growth of formal sectors an exercise in invidious segmentation, with new communities born in a defensive position relative to established ones, with fewer resources to call on to remedy their problems. Furthermore, the very creation of a daughter sector speaks to the emergence of elites within—a group of relatively prosperous people who may be especially frustrated by wealthier households at the core of the original community. They likewise need the trappings of a council to perpetuate their ambitions for themselves as well as their neighborhood. The community, that is, creates itself with the seeds of the same arguments that it is trying to escape.

The value differences put in play by post–land reform livelihoods, however, are not reducible to class positions. People, for instance, do not see eye-to-eye on the importance of farming. Nor do they agree on whether the move to the city requires one to fully immerse oneself in urban culture or to give up speaking Kichwa with one's children or to stop spending savings on fiestas back home. Where some see unconscionable abandoning of family and land, others see a praiseworthy effort to do the best for the next generation. And even when most would agree on shared community values, the cost may be too high. When a relative has been arrested for drunk driving or gang violence, others may shelve publicly minded virtues to accompany family during hardship and try to find the quickest way out of trouble without seeking a political fight. Don't forsake, don't be backward, and don't suffer are all lofty ideals, but they can be hard to square and harder to uphold.

A short walk through Agato in 2006 revealed to me once again how irreconcilable lives can be. In a crude, cinderblock house along the upper bus route, neighbors had set up a Pentecostal church and gathered there regularly for Bible study. Across the road stood one of Agato's first successful mechanized poncho operations. Setting out from this little corner of faith and industry and down a dirt track, one quickly arrived at the lower bus road and an elegant two-story adobe home. A yachac owned the house, a man famed for his ability to reverse the curses of others. His cool, shadowed waiting room doubled as a taverna and reeked of spilled trago (sugar cane alcohol). On most weekends, one could find inside a handful of middle-aged men forcing drinks on each other until none of them could stand. Church builders and workshop owner, taverna customers and yachac. In a stripped down sense, pluralism shows up in these Agato residents. They live by different rules to create different lives, yet all build their future through the same community.

What is true for the national vision of a pluricultural society, then, is also true for these localities. The very idea of pluralism is that value systems *need not* be unified as a condition for shared political action (Cook 1994). Rather, pluralism depends on a commitment to working together precisely in the absence of a broad consensus of what is right and good and worthy. Indigenous self-determination has depended, in large part, on building attentive and responsive relations among groups who disagree about some, perhaps many, things.

Group interactions thus are contingent and changeable, grounded in immediate interests, resources, and problems, not objective, universal principles (Smith 1997, 22). Politics emerge from the situation and as the situation changes so does the politics. During Tigua's fight for its marketplace, a few forceful orators pushed the importance of a runapura (indigenous only) solution. Teodoro thus became the "rotten potato" for his conversations with the mestizos. At a subsequent meeting, people worried most about defending the widest possible selling opportunities in El Ejido Park. Alfredo then became the rotten potato for internally dividing Quiloans with his runapura discourse. During the anti-TLC strike, the residents who created and defended blockades near Peguche reversed their first position in order to shut down local traffic. Meanwhile, those at Espejo reversed their hard line and released some traffic.

Absent a unifying value system—national, multicultural, or indigenous—people must make do with the judgments of those present and work with the circumstances at hand. And making things work is one of the core tasks of vernacular statecraft. The day-to-day practices of councils, community, and trade organizations move projects forward by forcing some arguments and dodging others. The minga, or community work party, illustrates most clearly how this works. At the outset, the council and sufficient numbers of community residents must get behind a project, usually after long and meandering discussions. Once committed, the council persuades through idioms of state regulations and kinship authority. Councils also coerce through the use of fines and the withholding of services. Community politics can thus present peculiar blends of direct and representative democracy. Residents have opportunity to actively determine policy yet can also find themselves submitting to the authority of the council, giving up time and effort to a project or protest in which they see little value.

Vernacular statecraft is thus the hinge between internal politics and external mobilizations. Tailored for self management, the organizational work of communities underpins a wider, collaborative self-determination. While I have used the word "self-organizing" several times in this chapter, I mean it in the narrow sense of a political structuring of provincial life through the repetitive acts of local groups, not the state. To paraphrase Wolf (1999), a community has no inner drive to organize; rather, local groups drive on such organizing for distinctive purposes and with uneven consequences for the residents involved.

Some Updates

I have followed the fortunes of Julio, Alfonso, and José since those interviews some eight years ago. Julio's paintings are once again finding their way to market. I came across one canvas in 2006. It was a detailed rendering of Zumbagua's annual Corpus Christi fiesta, celebrating the kind of drunken revelry that Alfonso Chiza so scorns. In the scene, a woman brandishes a shot glass and yells at the bullfighters in the ring below her; men charge into the ring or stumble as they try to flee it; a pair of men ply each other with alcohol on the path home; still another urinates in the street, squinting at the wobbly stream he has unleashed. A Tigua intermediary bought the painting for $800, hoping he could get almost twice that, but acknowledging that he paid such a premium because Julio needed the cash to help a relative of his who had recently been arrested.

Alfonso can still be found most mornings at his desk in his showroom. Business, though, has slowed considerably and he has tried to sell some of his big knitting machines. On one of my visits, he told me to follow him out of his shop. Without another word, we got into his pickup and drove in silence out to a gas station at the edge of town. He pointed to a large, three-axle flatbed truck. "That belongs to my son," he finally said, with great pride. Times are hard, but the young man has some capital to protect him.

José had come close to quitting painting during the summer they fought to retain the sales posts in El Ejido Park. He was disheartened by low sales and constant fighting among the painters and told me that he was thinking about moving down to Guayaquil where an associate had a lead on some work. A few years later, I met up with him in Otavalo's Saturday market, where he manned a sales post. His smile was back, but not because he was selling paintings again. Rather he and his wife Mercedes had formed a new trade association, this time dedicated to apparel making. He was once again looking for support, seeking funds for twenty industrial sewing machines.

And I continue to meet up with indigenous men and women who act for their communities and who grant interviews because they want their story on the record. Most recently an Otavalo businesswoman living in the mestizo apparel-making town of Atuntaqui wanted to explain her organizing efforts. Elvia Maigua owned a sock-making factory that employed around seven workers. She also served as the treasurer of the newly formed Atuntaqui Chamber of Commerce. Her work for the Chamber of Commerce, though, is not why she invited me to her house. Rather, in 2006, she wanted to talk about the Corporación Atahualpa, a group that she founded the previous year to help preserve indigenous culture in the city and to undertake literacy projects in nearby rural communities.

She explained to me, "We are very few. We are worried that we will lose our culture. There is a lot of mixing here; we indígenas have mixed with the mestizos, married, losing our culture, such as clothing, long hair, our language, many customs." Thus one of the first tasks the new group embarked on was a multiday celebration of Inti Raymi, the annual solstice festival. The fiesta was popular across the township and her group grew to eighty members, both indigenous people and mestizos, and mestizos married to indigenous people. Most lived in the urban center and many were professionals like her: town employees, teachers, shop owners, and the like.

I asked if her group was officially recognized. She smiled ruefully. "It is in process," she answered. "Look, the problem is that they will not let us register as a community [meaning a peasant comuna] because you need to be rural. So after this rejection, we had to change to a corporation, but the bottom line is that we are founded as the community Atahualpa, because community is having something in common, it is unity. We are all united as indigenous people; this is what community refers to, no? There is the European community, the community of . . . well, whatever. We are Otavalos, strongly indigenous, but here in Atuntaqui."

Of the different paths indigenous people are moving on toward their future, I found particular hope in Elvia's project. Dedicated to strengthening indigenous culture and actively including mestizos, Corporación Atahualpa seemed prepared to make something of its urban roots. Even as I have concentrated on community action amid differences, Elvia reminds me of what a powerful cultural symbol "community" is. She insists on it as a political consciousness, as an orientation that sets the stage for engagement. Her pursuit of recognition as a community underscores for her the basic fact that Otavalos can and must act together. Sometimes the connection seems to be only a fight, sometimes a celebration. As Elvia reminded me though, communities remain central to indigenous self-determination.

References

Newspaper sources on anti-TLC strike, March 2006

El Comercio. 2006a. El desafío político de la Conaie. El Comercio, March 15.
———. 2006b. El personaje de la semana: El líder saraguro que resucito a una CONAIE moribunda. El Comercio, March 18.
———. 2006c. No al Paro. El Comercio, March 27.
———.2006d Si no hay respuesta, habra levantamiento. El Comercio, March 15.
El Norte 2006 Segun coordinador de movimiento "Ruminahui": Indigenas estan manipulados. El Norte, March 18.

Scholarly Sources

Abercrombie, Thomas. 1998. *Pathways of Memory and Power: Ethnography and History among an Andean People.* Madison: University of Wisconsin Press.
Albo, Xavier. 1994. And from Kataristas to MNRistas? The Surprising and Bold Alliance between Aymaras and Neoliberals in Bolivia. In *Indigenous Peoples and Democracy in Latin America*, ed. D. L. Van Cott, 55–81. New York: St. Martin's Press.
Allen, Chadwick. 2002. *Blood Narrative: Indigenous Identity in American Indian and Maori Literary and Activist Texts.* Durham, NC: Duke University Press.
Alvarez, Sonia E., Evelina Dagnino, and Arturo Escobar. 1998. Introduction: The Cultural and the Political in Latin American Social Movements. In *Cultures of Politics, Politics of Cultures*, ed. S. E. Alvarez, E. Dagnino, and A. Escobar, 1–29. Boulder, CO: Westview Press.
Anderson, Benedict. 1991. *Imagined Communities.* Revised edition. New York: Verso.
Andrade, Susana. 1990. *Vision Mundial: Entre el cielo y la tierra: Religion y desarrollo en la sierra ecuatoriana.* Quito: CEPLAES-ABYA-YALA.
Annis, Sheldon. 1987. *God and Production in a Guatemalan Town.* Austin: University of Texas Press.

Antrosio, Jason. 2002. Inverting Development Discourse in Colombia: Transforming Andean Hearths. *American Anthropologist* 104 (4): 1110–22.

Appadurai, Arjun. 1990. Disjuncture and Difference in the Global Cultural Economy. In *Global Culture: Nationalism, Globalization and Modernity*, ed. M. Featherstone, 295–310. London: Sage Publications.

Arizpe, Lourdes. 1996. Chiapas: The Basic Problems. *Identities* 3 (1–2): 219–233.

Atupaña, Jose. 2001. Asumimos el reto de construir una organización independiente, laica y participativa. *Instituto Científico de Culturas Indigenas* 3 (32).

Becker, Marc. 1999 Comunas and Indigenous Protest in Cayambe, Ecuador. *The Americas* 55 (4): 531–59.

———. 2004. Indigenous Communists and Urban Intellectuals in Cayambe, Ecuador (1926–1944). *International Review of Social History* 49:41–64.

Benevides, Maria-Victoria, and Rosa-Maria Fischer-Ferreira. 1991. Popular Responses and Urban Violence: Lynching in Brazil. In *Vigilantism and the State in Modern Latin America: Essays on Extralegal Violence*, ed. M. K. Huggins, 33–45. New York: Praeger Publishers.

Berlin, Isaiah. 1991. *The Crooked Timber of Humanity: Chapters in the History of Ideas*. New York: Alfred A. Knopf.

Berry, Wendell. 1990. *What Are People For?* New York: North Point Press.

Bohannan, Laura. 1958a. Political Aspects of Tiv Social Organization. In *Tribes Without Rulers*, ed. J. Middleton and D. Tait. New York: Routledge and Kegan Paul.

Bohannan, Paul. 1958b. Extra-Processural Events in Tiv Political Institutions. *American Anthropologist* 60 (1): 1–12.

Bourque, Nicole L. 1997. Making Space: Social Change, Identity and the Creation of Boundaries in the Central Ecuadorian Andes. *Bulletin of Latin American Research* 16:153–167.

Breton, Victor. 2003. Desarrollo rural y etnicidad en las tierras altas de Ecuador. In *Estado, etnicidad y movimientos sociales en America Latina: Ecuador en Crisis*, ed. V. Breton and F. Garcia, 217–53. Barcelona: Icaria.

Briggs, Charles L. 1984. Learning How to Ask: Native Metacommunicative Competence and Incompetence of Fieldworkers. *Language in Society* 13 (1): 1–28.

Brown, Lawrence A., Jorge A. Brea, and Andrew R. Goetz. 1988. Policy Aspects of Development and Individual Mobility: Migration and Circulation from Ecuador's Rural Sierra. *Economic Geography* 64 (2): 147–170.

Brysk, Alison. 2000. *From Tribal Village to Global Village: Indian Rights and International Relations in Latin America*. Stanford: Stanford University Press.

Buitrón, Aníbal. 1947. Situación económica y social del indio Otavaleño. *America Indígena* 7:45–67.

Buitrón, Aníbal and Barbara Buitrón Salisbury. 1945. Indios, blancos, y mestizos en Otavalo, Ecuador. *Acta Americana* 3: 190–216. Burgos-Debray, Elisabeth

———. 1984. *I Rigoberta Menchu: An Indian Woman in Guatemala*. London: Verso.

Burns, E. Bradford. 1980. *The Poverty of Progress: Latin America in the Nineteenth Century*. Berkeley and Los Angeles: University of California Press.

Carrion, Fernando, and Rene Vallejo. 1994. La planificación de Quito: del Plan Director a la cuidad democratica. In *Quito: Transformaciones urbanas y arquitectonicas*, 15–19. Quito: Trama.

Casagrande, Joseph B, and Arthur R. Piper. 1969. La transformación estructural de una parroquia rural en las tierras altas del Ecuador. *America Indígena* 29:1039–64.

Cervone, Emma. 1999. Racismo y vida cotidiana: las tacticas de la defensa etnica. In *Ecuador racista: Imagenes e identidades*, ed. E. Cervone and F. Rivera, 137–56. Quito: Flacso Ecuador.

Chavez, Leo Ralph. 1982. Commercial Weaving and the Entrepreneurial Ethic: Otavalo Indian Views of Self and the World. PhD diss. Stanford University.

Chibnik, Michael. 2003. *Crafting Tradition: The Making and Marketing of Oaxacan Wood Carvings*. Austin: University of Texas Press.

Collier, George with Elizabeth Lowery Quaratiello. 1999. *Basta! Land and the Zapatista Rebellion in Chiapas*, revised edition. Oakland, CA.: Food First Books, Institute for Food and Development Policy.

Colloredo-Mansfeld, Rudi. 1994. Architectural Conspicuous Consumption and Economic Change in the Ecuadorian Andes. *American Anthropologist* 96 (4): 845–65.

———. 1999. *The Native Leisure Class: Consumption and Cultural Creativity in the Andes*. Chicago: University of Chicago Press.

———. 2002. Autonomy and Interdependence in Native Movements: Towards a Pragmatic Politics in the Ecuadorian Andes. *Identities: Global Studies in Culture and Power* 9:173–195.

Colvin, Jean. 2005. *Arte de Tigua: Una reflexión de la cultura indígena en Ecuador*. Quito: Abya-Yala.

Comaroff, John L, and Jean Comaroff. 1999. Introduction. In *Civil Society and the Political Imagination in Africa, Critical Perspectives*, ed. J. L. Comaroff and J. Comaroff, 1–43. Chicago: University of Chicago Press.

CONAIE. 1994. *Proyecto Politico de la CONAIE*. Quito: Consejo de Gobierno de la CONAIE.

Conklin, Beth A., and Laura R. Graham. 1995. The Shifting Middle Ground: Amazonian Indians and Eco-Politics. *American Anthropologist* 97 (4): 695–710.

Cook, Scott D. N. 1994. Autonomy, Interdependence and Moral Governance: Pluralism in a Rocking Boat. *American Behavioral Scientist* 38 (1): 153–71.

Cook, Scott, and Jong-Taick Joo. 1995. Ethnicity and Economy in Rural Mexico: a Critique of the Indigenista Approach. *Latin American Research Review* 30 (2): 33–59.

Coronil, Fernando. 1997. The Magical State: Nature, Money and Modernity in Venezuela. Chicago: University of Chicago Press.

de la Cadena, Marisol. 1995. "Women Are More Indian": Ethnicity and Gender in a Community Near Cuzco. In *Ethnicity, Markets, and Migration in the Andes: At the Crossroads of History and Anthropology*, ed. B. Larson, O. Harris, and E. Tandeter, 329–48. Durham, NC: Duke University Press.

———. 2000. *Indigenous Mestizos: The Politics of Race and Culture in Cuzco, Peru, 1919–1991*. Durham, NC: Duke University Press.

de la Torre, Carlos. 1999. Everyday Forms of Racism in Contemporary Ecuador: The Experiences of Middle-Class Indians. *Ethnic and Racial Studies* 22 (1): 92–112.

————. 2000. Racism in Education and the Construction of Citizenship in Ecuador. *Race and Class* 42 (2): 33–45.

Deere, Carmen Diana, and Magdalena Leon. 2001. Institutional Reform of Agriculture under Neoliberalism: The Impact of the Women's and Indigenous Movement. *Latin American Research Review* 36 (2): 31–63.

Demmers, Jolle, Alex E Fernandez Jilberto, and Barbara Hogenboom. 2001. *Miraculous Metamorphoses: The Neoliberalization of Latin American Populism.* New York: Zed Books.

Escobar, Arturo. 1992. Imagining a Post-Development Era? Critical Thought, Development and Social Movements. *Social Text* 31–32:20–56.

————. 1995. *Encountering Development: The Making and Unmaking of the Third World.* Princeton: Princeton University Press.

Evans-Pritchard, E. E. 1940. *The Nuer.* New York: Oxford University Press.

FIDA (Fondo Internacional de Desarrollo Agricola). 1989. Informe de la Misión Especial de Programación a la Republica del Ecuador. Rome: FIDA.

Field, Les. 1991. Ecuador's Pan-Indian Uprising. *NACLA Report on the Americas* 25, no. 3 (December): 39–46.

————. 1994. Who Are the Indians: Reconceptualizing Indigenous Identity, Resistance, and the Role of Social Science in Latin America. *Latin America Research Review* 29 (3): 237–48.

Fischer, Edward F, and Peter Benson. 2006. *Broccoli and Desire: Global Connections and Maya Struggles in Postwar Guatemala.* Stanford: Stanford University Press.

Fiske, John. 1993. *Power Plays, Power Works.* New York: Verso.

Ford, Richard T. 2001. Law's Territory (A History of Jurisdiction). In *The Legal Geographies Reader*, ed. N. Blomley, D. Delaney, and R. T. Ford, 200–217. Malden, MA: Blackwell Publishers.

Foster, George. 1965. Peasant Society and the Image of the Limited Good. *American Anthropologist* 67 (2): 292–315.

Fox, Jonathan. 2005. Lessons from Action Research Partnerships. *LASA Forum* 35 (4): 5–8.

Garcia Serrano, Fernando. 1999. Formas indigenas de administración de justicia: El caso de los pueblos y nacionalidades quichuas de la Sierra y la Amazonia. Presentation at the conference Conversatorio Sobre Genero y Sociedad, Quito, 1999.

————. 2003. Política, estado y diversidad cultural: A proposito del movimiento indígena Ecuatoriana. In *Estado, etnicidad y movimientos sociales en America Latina*, ed. V. Breton and F. Garcia, 193–216. Barcelona: Icaria and the University of Lleida.

Gellner, Ernest. 1983. *Nations and Nationalism.* Ithaca: Cornell University Press.

Ginsberg, Faye D. 1989. *Contested Lives: The Abortion Debate in an American Community.* Berkeley: University of California Press.

Glance, Natalie S., and Bernardo A. Huberman. 1994. The Dynamics of Social Dilemmas. *Scientific American* (March): 76–81.

Goldstein, Daniel M. 2004. *The Spectacular City: Violence and Performance in Urban Bolivia.* Durham, NC: Duke University Press.

Gose, Peter. 1994. *Deathly Waters and Hungry Mountains: Agrarian Ritual and Class Formation in an Andean Town*. Toronto: University of Toronto Press.

Graham, Laura. 2002. How Should an Indian Speak? Amazonian Indians and the Symbolic Practices of Language in the Global Public Sphere. In *Indigenous Movements, Self-Representation, and the State in Latin America*, ed. K. B. Warren and J. Jackson, 181–228. Austin: University of Texas Press.

Grandin, Greg. 1997. To End with All These Evils: Ethnic Transformation and Community Mobilization in Guatemala's Western Highlands, 1954–1980. *Latin American Perspectives* 24 (2): 7–34.

Granovetter, Mark. 1978. Threshold Models of Collective Behavior. *American Journal of Sociology* 83 (6): 1420–43.

Gray, John. 1996. *Isaiah Berlin*. Princeton: Princeton University Press.

Green, Duncan. 1995. *Silent Revolution: The Rise of Market Economies in Latin America*. London: The Latin American Bureau.

Gudeman, Stephen. 2001. *The Anthropology of Economy*. Malden, MA: Blackwell Publishers Inc.

Gudeman, Stephen, and Alberto Rivera. 1990. *Conversations in Colombia: The Domestic Economy in Life and Text*. Cambridge: Cambridge University Press.

Guerrero, Andres. 1989. Curagas y tenientes politicos: La ley de la costumbre y la ley del estado (Otavalo 1830–1875). *Revista Andina* 7 (2): 321–65.

Guerrero Cazar, Fernando, and Pablo Ospina Peralta. 2003. *El poder de la comunidad: Ajuste estructural y movimiento indígena en los Andes ecuatorianos*. Buenos Aires: Consejo Latinamericano de Ciencias Sociales (CLACSO).

Hale, Charles R. 1994. Between Che Guevara and the Pachamama: Mestizos, Indians, and Identity Politics in the Anti-Quincentenary Campaign. *Critique of Anthropology* 14 (1): 9–39.

———. 1996. Mestizaje, Hybridity, and the Cultural Politics of Difference in Post-Revolutionary Central America. *Journal of Latin American Anthropology* 2 (1): 34–61.

———. 1997. Cultural Politics of Identity in Latin America. *Annual Review of Anthropology* 26:567–90.

———. 2005. Neoliberal Multiculturalism: The Remaking of Cultural Rights and Racial Dominance in Central America. *PoLAR: Political and Legal Anthropology Review* 28 (1): 10–28.

Hamilton, Sarah. 1998. *The Two-Headed Household: Gender and Rural Development in the Ecuadorean Andes*. Pittsburgh: University of Pittsburgh Press.

Harvey, Neil. 2001. Globalization and Resistance in Post–Cold War Mexico: Difference, Citizenship and Biodiversity Conflicts in Chiapas. *Third World Quarterly* 22 (6): 1045–61.

Healy, Kevin, and Susan Paulson. 2000. Political Economies of Identity in Bolivia 1952–1998. *The Journal of Latin American Anthropology* 5 (2): 2–29.

Hentschel, Jesko, William F. Waters, and Anna Kathryn Vandever Webb. 1996. Rural Poverty in Ecuador—A Qualitative Assessment, WPS 1576. In Policy Research Working Paper, 1–37. Washington D.C.: The World Bank.

Herzfeld, Michael. 2005. Political Optics and the Occlusion of Intimate Knowledge. American Anthropologist 107 (3): 369–76.

Huggins, Martha K. 1991. Introduction: Vigilantism and the State—A Look South and North. In *Vigilantism and the State in Modern Latin America*, ed. M. K. Huggins, 1–18. New York: Praeger Publishers.

Hurtado, Osvaldo. 1980. *Political Power in Ecuador*. Trans. N. D. Mills. Albuquerque: University of New Mexico Press.

Isbell, Billie Jean. 1978. *To Defend Ourselves: Ecology and Ritual in an Andean Village*. Austin: Institute of Latin American Studies. The University of Texas at Austin.

Jackson, Jean E. 1995. Culture, Genuine and Spurious: The Politics of Indianness in the Vaupes, Colombia. *American Ethnologist* 22 (1): 3–27.

Jackson, Jean E., and Kay B. Warren. 2005. Indigenous Movements in Latin America 1992–2004: Controversies, Ironies and New Directions. *Annual Review of Anthropology* 34:549–73.

Jacobs, Jane. 1969. *The Economy of Cities*. New York: Random House.

Kearney, Michael. 1996. *Reconceptualizing the Peasantry*. Boulder, CO: Westview Press.

Kearney, Michael, and Stefano Varese. 1995. Latin America's Indigenous Peoples: Changing Identities and Forms of Resistance. In *Capital, Power, and Inequality in Latin America*, ed. S. Halebsky and R. L. Harris, 207–31. Boulder, CO: Westview Press.

Kleinman, Arthur. 2006. *What Really Matters: Living a Moral Life Amidst Uncertainty and Danger*. New York: Oxford University Press.

Korovkin, Tanya. 1997. Indigenous Peasant Struggles and the Capitalist Modernization of Agriculture: Chimborazo, 1964–1991. *Latin American Perspectives* 24 (3): 25–49.

———. 1998. Commodity Production and Ethnic Culture: Otavalo, Northern Ecuador. *Economic Development and Cultural Change* 47 (1): 125–54.

Lema, Mercedes, Vanessa Saltos, Jose Barrionuevo, Enrique Chimbo, and Fernando Garcia. 2000. *Proyecto de investigación, formas indígenas de administración de justice: Tres casos de estudio de la nacionalidad Quichua de la Sierra y Amazonia Ecuatoriana*. Quito: Facultad Latinoamericano de Ciencias Sociales.

Leon, Jorge. 1993. Versiones de los protagonistas: Los hechos historicos y el valor de los testimonios disidentes. In *Sismo etnico en el Ecuador*, 113–44. Quito: Abya-Yala-Centro de Investigacion de los Movimientos Sociales del Ecuador (CEDIME).

Lyons, Barry. 2006. *Remembering the Hacienda: Religion, Authority, and Social Change in Highland Ecuador*. Austin: University of Texas Press.

Macas, Luis. 2001. Forward. In *Ethnopolitics in Ecuador: Indigenous Rights and the Strengthening of Democracy*,Melina Selverston-Scher, i–xix. Miami: North-South Center Press at the University of Miami.

Macas, Luis, Linda Belote, and Jim Belote. 2003. Indigenous Destiny in Indigenous Hands. In *Millennial Ecuador: Critical Essays on Cultural Transformations and Social Dynamics*, ed. N. Whitten Jr., 216–41. Iowa City: University of Iowa Press.

Mannheim, Bruce, and Dennis Tedlock. 1995. Introduction. In *The Dialogic Emergence of Culture*, ed. D. Tedlock and B. Mannheim, 1–32. Champaign-Urbana: University of Illinois Press.

Martinez Valle, Luciano. 2003. Los nuevos modelos de intervención sobre la sociedad rural: De la sostenibilidad al capital social. In *Estado, etnicidad y movimientos sociales en America Latina: Ecuador en crisis*, ed. V. Breton and F. Garcia, 129–57. Barcelona: Icaria.

Mattiace, Shannon. 1997 ¡Zapata vive! The EZLN, Indian Politics, and the Autonomy Movement in Mexico. *Journal of Latin American Anthropology* 3 (1): 32–71.

Mauss, Marcel. 1990. *The Gift: The Form and Reason for Exchange in Archaic Societies*. Trans. W. D. Hall. New York: W. W. Norton.

Mayer, Enrique. 1991. Peru in Deep Trouble: Mario Vargas Llosa's "Inquest in the Andes" Reexamined. *Cultural Anthropology* 6:466–504.

Medina, Laurie K. 1998. History, Culture, and Place-Making: "Native" Status and Maya Identity in Belize. Journal of Latin American Anthropology 4 (1): 134–65.

Meisch, Lynn A. 1994. We Will Not Dance on the Tomb of Our Grandparents: 500 Years of Resistance in Ecuador. *The Latin American Anthropology Review* 4 (2): 55–74.

———. 1997. *The Prevention of Intractable Inter-Ethnic Violence in Contemporary Ecuador*. Stanford: Stanford Center on Conflict and Negotiation Working Paper Series.

———. 2002. *Andean Entrepreneurs: Otavalo Merchants and Musicians in the Global Arena*. Austin: University of Texas Press.

Miller, Daniel. 1995. Consumption Studies as the Transformation of Anthropology. In *Acknowledging Consumption*, ed. D. Miller, 264–95. New York: Routledge.

Muratorio, Blanca. 1980. Protestantism and Capitalism Revisited, in the Rural Highlands of Ecuador. *Journal of Peasant Studies* 8 (1): 37–60

Nagengast, Carole, and Michael Kearney. 1990. Mixtec Ethnicity: Social Identity, Political Consciousness, and Political Activism. *Latin American Research Review* 25 (2): 61–91.

Nash, June C. 1994. The Reassertion of Indigenous Identity: Mayan Responses to State Intervention in Chiapas. *Latin American Research Review* 30 (3): 7–41.

———. 1997. The Fiesta of the Word: The Zapatista Uprising and Radical Democracy in Mexico. *American Anthropologist* 99 (2): 261–74.

———. 2001. *Mayan Visions: The Quest for Autonomy in an Age of Globalization*. New York: Routledge.

Ng'weno, Bettina. 2007. *Turf Wars: Territory and Citizenship in the Contemporary State*. Stanford: Stanford University Press.

Niezen, Ronald. 2003. *The Origins of Indigenism: Human Rights and the Politics of Identity*. Berkeley and Los Angeles: University of California Press.

Nugent, David. 1997. *Modernity at the Edge of Empire: State, Individual and Nation in the Northern Peruvian Andes*. Stanford: Stanford University Press.

Ong, Aihwa. 2006. Neoliberalism as Exception: Mutations in Citizenship and Sovereignty. Durham, NC: Duke University Press.

Orlove, Benjamin S. 1994. The Dead Policemen Speak: Power, Fear, and Narrative in the 1931 Molloccahua Killings (Cusco). In *Unruly Order: Violence, Power, and Cultural Identity in the High Provinces of Southern Peru*, ed. D. Poole, 63–96. Boulder, CO: Westview Press.

———. 1998. Down to Earth: Race and Substance in the Andes. *Bulletin of Latin American Research* 17 (2): 207–22.

Orta, Andrew. 2001. Remembering the Ayllu, Remaking the Nation: Indigenous Scholarship and Activism in the Bolivian Andes. *The Journal of Latin American Anthropology* 6 (1): 198–201.

———. 2004. *Catechizing Culture: Missionaries, Aymara, and the "New Evangelization."* New York: Columbia University Press.

Ortiz Crespo, Alfonso, and Rosemarie Teran Najas. 1993. Las reducciones de indios en la zona interandina de la real audiencia de Quito. In *Pueblos de indios: Otro urbanismo de la region andina*, ed. R. Gutierrez, 205–61. Quito: Ediciones Abya Yala.

Pallares, Amalia. 2002. *From Peasant Struggles to Indian Resistance: The Ecuadorian Andes in the Late Twentieth Century*. Norman: University of Oklahoma Press.

Paz, Maria Fernanda. 1996. Searching for Root Causes: A Historical Background Sketch of the Protagonists of the Zapatista Uprising. *Identities* 3 (1–2): 235–52.

Phillips, Susan A. 1999. *Wallbangin': Graffiti and Gangs in L.A.* Chicago: University of Chicago Press.

Pitt-Rivers, Julian. 1965. Who Are the Indians? *Encounter* 25 (3): 41–49.

Poole, Deborah. 1994a. Introduction: Anthropological Perspectives on Violence and Culture—A View from the Peruvian High Provinces. In *Unruly Order: Violence, Power, and Cultural Identity in the High Provinces of Southern Peru*, ed. D. Poole, 1–30. Boulder, CO: Westview Press.

———. 1994b. Peasant Culture and Political Violence in the Peruvian Andes: Sendero Luminoso and the State. In *Unruly Order: Violence, Power, and Cultural Identity in the High Provinces of Southern Peru*, ed. D. Poole, 247–81. Boulder, CO: Westview Press.

———. 1994c. Performance, Domination, and Identity in the Tierras Bravas of Chumbivilcas. In *Unruly Order: Violence, Power, and Cultural Identity in the High Provinces of Southern Peru*, ed. D. Poole, 97–132. Boulder, CO: Westview Press.

Popkin, Samuel. 1979. *The Rational Peasant*. Berkeley and Los Angeles: University of California Press.

Powelson, Michael. 1996. The Use and Abuse of Ethnicity in the Rebellions in Chiapas. *Blueprint for Social Justice* 49 (5): 1–7.

Preston, David A., Gerado A. Taveras, and Rosemary A. Preston. 1981. Emigración rural y desarrollo agricola en la sierra Ecuatoriana. *Revista Geográfica* 93 (Enero-Junio): 7–35.

Putnam, Robert. 1993. *Making Democracy Work: Civic Traditions in Modern Italy*. Princeton: Princeton University Press.

Quimbo, Jose. 1992. Derecho indígena. In *Pueblos indios, estado y derecho*, vol. 36, ed. C. Editorial, 205–12. Quito: Corporación Editora Nacional.

Radcliffe, Sarah A. 1997. The Geographies of Indigenous Self-representation in Ecuador: Hybridity, Gender and Resistance. *European Review of Latin American and Caribbean Studies* 63:9–27.

Rahier, Jean. 2003. Racist Stereotypes and the Embodiment of Blackness: Some Narratives of Female Sexuality in Quito. In *Millennial Ecuador: Critical Essays on Cultural Transformations and Social Dynamics*, ed. N. E. Whitten, 296–324. Iowa City: University of Iowa Press.

Rappaport, Joanne. 2005. Intercultural Utopias: Public Intellectuals, Cultural Experimentation, and Ethnic Pluralism in Colombia. Durham, NC: Duke University Press.

Reddy, Movindri. 2001. Ethnic Conflict and Violence: South Africa, Punjab and Sri Lanka. In *Ethnicity and Governance in the Third World*, ed. J. Mukum Mbaku, P. Ogaba Agbese, and M. S. Kimeni, 295–326. Burlington, VT: Ashgate.

Rheingold, Howard. 2002. *Smart Mobs: The Next Social Revolution*. New York: Basic Books.

Robson, Terry. 2000. *The State and Community Action*. London: Pluto Press.

Rohter, Larry. 1998. Nobel Winner Accused of Stretching Truth. *New York Times*, December 15.

Rose, Nikolas. 1999. *Powers of Freedom: Reframing Political Thought*. New York: Cambridge University Press.

Rus, Jan. 1995. Local Adaptation to Global Change. *European Review of Latin American and Caribbean Studies* 58 (June): 71–98.

Sachs, Jeffrey. 2005. *The End of Poverty: How We Can Make It Happen In Our Lifetime*. New York: Penguin.

Sahlins, Marshall. 1961. The Segmentary Lineage: An Organization of Predatory Expansion. *American Anthropologist* 63 (2): 322–45.

Salomon, Frank. 1981. Weavers of Otavalo. In *Cultural Transformations and Ethnicity in Modern Ecuador*, ed. N. E. Whitten, 420 49. Urbana: University of Illinois Press.

————. 2002. Patrimonial Khipu in a Modern Peruvian Village: An Introduction to the Quipocamayos of Tupicocha. In *Narrative Threads: Accounting and Recounting in Andean Khipu*, ed J. Quilter and G. Urton, 293–319. Austin: University of Texas Press.

Salomon, Frank, and George L. Urioste. 1991. *The Huarochiri Manuscript: A Testament of Ancient and Colonial Andean Religion*. Austin: University of Texas Press.

Sawyer, Suzana. 2004. *Crude Chronicles: Indigenous Politics, Multinational Oil, and Neoliberalism*. Durham, NC: Duke University Press.

Schild, Veronica. 1998. New Subjects of Rights? Women's Movements and the Construction of Citizenship in the "New Democracies." In *Cultures of Politics, Politics of Cultures: Re-Visioning Latin American Social Movements*, ed. S. E. Alvarez, E. Dagnino, and A. Escobar, 93–117. Boulder, CO: Westview Press.

Scott, James C. 1998. *Seeing Like a State*. New Haven: Yale University Press.

Seligmann, Linda J. 2004. *Peruvian Street Lives: Culture, Power, and Economy among Market Women of Cuzco*. Urbana and Chicago: University of Illinois Press.

Selverston, Melina. 1994. The Politics of Culture: Indigenous Peoples and the State in Ecuador. In *Indigenous Peoples and Democracy in Latin America*, ed. D. L. V. Cott, 131–52. New York: St. Martins Press.

Selverston-Scher, Melina. 2001. *Ethnopolitics in Ecuador: Indigenous Rights and the Strengthening of Democracy*. Miami: North-South Center Press.

Serrano, Vladimir. 1993. *Economia de solidaridad y cosmovisión indígena*. Quito: Ediciones Abya Yala.

Shils, Edward. 2003. The Virtue of Civil Society. In *The Civil Society Reader*, ed. V. A. Hodgkinson and M. W. Foley, 292–305. Hanover, NH: Tufts University and University Press of New England.

Shweder, Richard A. 2000. Moral Maps, "First World" Conceits, and the New Evangelists". In *Culture Matters: How Values Shape Human Progress*, ed. L. Harrison and S. Huntington, 158–76. New York: Basic Books.

———. 2003. *Why Do Men Barbecue: Recipes for Cultural Psychology*. Cambridge, MA: Harvard University Press.

Simons, Anna. 1995. *Networks of Dissolution: Somalia Undone*. Boulder, CO: Westview Press.

———. 1997. Democratization and Ethnic Conflict: The Kin Connection. *Nations and Nationalism* 3 (2): 273–89.

Smith, Barbara H. 1997. *Belief and Resistance*. Cambridge, MA: Harvard University Press.

Smith, Carol A. 1995. Race-Class-Gender Ideology in Guatemala: Modern and Anti-Modern Forms. *Comparative Studies in Society and History* 37:723–49.

Starn, Orin. 1991. Missing the Revolution: Anthropologists and the War in Peru. *Cultural Anthropology* 6:63–91.

———. 1992. "I Dreamed of Foxes and Hawks": Reflections on Peasant Protest, New Social Movements, and the Rondas Campesinas of Northern Peru. In *The Making of Social Movements in Latin America*, ed. A. Escobar and S. Alvarez, 89–111. Boulder, CO: Westview.

———. 1994. Rethinking the Politics of Anthropology: The Case of the Andes. *Current Anthropology* 35 (1): 13–38.

———. 1999. Nightwatch: The Politics of Protest in the Andes. Durham, NC: Duke University Press.

Stephen, Lynn. 1991. Culture as a Resource: Four Cases of Self-Managed Indigenous Craft Production in Latin America. *Economic Development and Cultural Change* 40 (1): 101–30.

———. 1997. Redefined Nationalism in Building a Movement for Indigenous Autonomy in Southern Mexico. *Journal of Latin American Anthropology* 3 (1): 72–101.

Stoll, David. 1999. *Rigoberta Menchu and the Story of All Poor Guatemalans*. Boulder, CO: Westview Press.

Striffler, Steve. 2002. *In the Shadows of State and Capital: The United Fruit Company, Popular Struggle and Agrarian Reform Restructuring in Ecuador, 1900–1995*. Durham, NC: Duke University Press.

Stutzman, Ronald. 1981. El Mestizaje: An All-Inclusive Ideology of Exclusion. In *Cultural Transformations and Ethnicity in Modern Ecuador*, ed. Norman E. Whitten, 45–94. Urbana: University of Illinois Press.

Taussig, Michael. 1996. *The Magic of the State*. New York: Routledge.

Thompson, E. P. 1993. *Customs in Common: Studies in Traditional Popular Culture*. New York: The New Press.

Tilly, Charles. 1998. *Durable Inequality*. Berkeley and Los Angeles: University of California Press.

Turner, Victor. 1957. *Schism and Continuity in an African Society: A Study of Ndembu Village Life*. Manchester: Manchester University Press.

Urton, Gary. 2002. An Overview of Spanish Colonial Commentary on Andean Knotted-String Records. In *Narrative Threads: Accounting and Recounting in Andean Khipu*, ed. J. Quilter and G. Urton, 3–25. Austin: University of Texas Press.

Van Cott, Donna Lee. 2000. The Friendly Liquidation of the Past: The Politics of Diversity in Latin America. Pittsburgh: University of Pittsburgh Press.

———. 2001. Explaining Ethnic Autonomy Regimes in Latin America. *Studies in Comparative International Development* 35 (4): 30–58.

van den Berghe, Pierre. 1993. Tourism and the Ethnic Division of Labor. *Annals of Tourism Research* 19:234–49.

Veltmeyer, Henry. 1997. New Social Movements in Latin America: The Dynamics of Class and Identity. *The Journal of Peasant Studies* 25 (1): 139–69.

Villavicencio Rivadeneira, Gladys. 1973. *Relaciones interetnicas en Otavalo ¿Una nacionalidad india en formación?* ediciones especiales 65. Mexico City: Instituto Indigenista Interamericano.

Wachtel, Nathan. 1973. *Sociedad e ideologia*. Lima: Instituto de Estudios Peruanos.

Walter, Lynn. 1981. Social Strategies and the Fiesta Complex in an Otavaleño Community. *American Ethnologist* 8 (1): 172 85.

Warren, Kay B. 1998a. *Indigenous Movements and Their Critics: Pan Mayanism and Ethnic Resurgence in Guatemala*. Princeton: Princeton University Press.

———. 1998b. Indigenous Movements as a Challenge to the Unified Social Movement Paradigm for Guatemala. In *Cultures of Politics, Politics of Cultures: Re-Visioning Latin American Social Movements*, ed. S. E. Alvarez, E. Dagnino, and A. Escobar, 165–95. Boulder, CO: Westview Press.

Warren, Kay B., and Jean E. Jackson. 2002. Introduction: Studying Indigenous Activism in Latin America. In *Indigenous Movements, Self-Representation, and the State in Latin America*, ed. K. B. Warren and J. B. Jackson, 1–46. Austin: University of Texas Press.

Watanabe, John. 1992. *Maya Saints and Souls in a Changing World*. Austin: University of Texas Press.

Waters, William F. 1997. The Road of Many Returns: Rural Bases of the Informal Urban Economy in Ecuador. *Latin American Perspectives* 24 (3): 50–64.

Weber, Max. 1992. *The Protestant Work Ethic and the Spirit of Capitalism*. New York: Routledge.

Weismantel, Mary. 1988. *Food, Gender, and Poverty in the Ecuadorian Andes*. Philadelphia: University of Pennsylvania Press.

———. 2001. *Cholas and Pishtacos: Stories of Race and Sex in the Andes*. Chicago: University of Chicago Press.

———. 2006. The Ayllu, Real and Imagined: The Romance of Community in the Andes. In *The Seductions of Community: Emancipations, Oppressions, Quandaries*, ed. G. Creed. Santa Fe: School of American Research Press.

Whitten, Dorothea S. 2003. Actors and Artists from Amazonia and the Andes. In *Millennial Ecuador: Critical Essays on Cultural Transformations and Social Dynamics*, ed. N. E. Whitten, 242–74. Iowa City: University of Iowa Press.

Whitten, Norman E., Jr. 1985. *Sicuanga Runa: The Other Side of Development in Amazonian Ecuador.* Urbana: University of Illinois Press.

———. 2004. Ecuador in the New Millennium: 25 Years of Democracy. *The Journal of Latin American Anthropology* 9 (2): 429–60.

Whitten Norman E., Jr., Dorothea Scott Whitten, and Alfonso Chango. 1997. Return of the Yumbo: The Indigenous Caminata from Amazonia to Andean Quito. *American Ethnologist* 24 (2): 355–91.

Whyte, William. 1976. Conflict and Cooperation in Andean Communities. American Ethnologist 2 (2): 373–92.

Wibbelsman, Michelle. 2005. Otavaleños at the Crossroads: Physical and Metaphysical Coordinates of an Indigenous World. *Journal of Latin American Anthropology* 10 (1): 151–85.

Wilkie, James W., Enrique C. Ochoa, and David E. Lorey. 1990. *Statistical Abstract of Latin America*, vol. 20. Los Angeles: UCLA Latin American Center Publications, University of California.

Wolf, Eric R. 1969. *Peasant Wars of the Twentieth Century*. New York: Harper.

———. 1990. Distinguished Lecture: Facing Power—Old Insights, New Questions. *American Anthropologist* 92:586–96.

———. 1999. *Envisioning Power: Ideologies of Dominance and Crisis*. Berkeley and Los Angeles: University of California Press.

Yashar, Deborah. 2005. *Contesting Citizenship in Latin America: The Rise of Indigenous Movements and the Postliberal Challenge*. New York: Cambridge University Press.

Yúdice, George. 1998. The Globalization of Culture and the New Civil Society. In *Cultures of Politics, Politics of Cultures: Re-Visioning Latin American Social Movements*, ed. S. E. Alvarez, E. Dagnino, and A. Escobar, 353–79. Boulder, CO: Westview Press.

Zamosc, Leon. 1994. Agrarian Protest and the Indian Movement in the Ecuadorian Highlands. *Latin American Research Review* 29 (3): 37–68.

———. 1995. *Estadistica de las areas de predominio etnico de la sierra ecuatoriana*. Quito: Abya-Yala.

Index